AF308859

THE RETRENCHMENT RULE

WHEN IT'S TOO LATE TO SAVE MORE FOR RETIREMENT

Gordon B. Pye

This book shows the risk of various strategies in making withdrawals from retirement assets. The author has attempted to accurately provide the assumptions that produce these risks and the basis for making these assumptions. Readers, however, will have to evaluate whether these assumptions provide a reasonable basis for making decisions in particular situations. In individual cases it may be desirable to modify the assumptions, or consider the opinion of others with professional expertise.

ISBN: 0615646611
ISBN-13: 978-0615646619
Library of Congress Control Number: 2012940312

GBPPress, New York, New York

To the late Lynn Hopewell who 15 years ago envisioned the importance of Monte Carlo techniques for personal financial planning

Contents

Preface

Many retirees are anxious about how much they can spend from their retirement assets each year and avoid later running out of funds. I know the feeling as I have been there myself. Many years ago, I unexpectedly faced early retirement.

There were some investments, a pension, and future Social Security. But how much could I spend each year? Could I keep on living as I had been, or did I need to undertake some serious retrenchment?

Unlike most in such a predicament, I should have known the answer. Earlier, I had been a financial economist as a tenured professor at the University of California, Berkeley. In fact, at that time I published a paper in the *American Economic Review* with an academic solution to such a problem. The title was: "Lifetime Portfolio Selection in Continuous Time for a Multiplicative Class of Utility Functions."

My experience, however, had not just been academic. I also had practical experience as a business economist. For 10 years I headed up the economics area of a New York bank.

None of this experience, however, seemed of much help. I had no clue as to whether I needed to undertake some serious retrenchment, or whether I could continue living as I had been. But if I didn't know the answer, presumably I wasn't the only one. Finding an answer was clearly a worthy topic for some serious research.

If I had known how long it would take I likely would not have started. And as usual, most of the effort ended up on the cutting room floor. Nevertheless, I believe that I have now come up with the answer I was looking for many years ago.

The answer is the Retrenchment Rule, which is the subject of this book. The answers it provides are easy to understand and implement. And the rule is flexible enough to deal with changing conditions in the future. Even if some of its assumptions are somewhat faulty, retirees will not go too far astray.

Every year the decisions made by the rule are rebased to what has actually happened up until that time, and on an updated view of the future.

The introductory chapter has some examples that show how the decisions made by the rule compare with some possible alternatives. These examples are based on the returns that were actually realized in the past on U. S. stocks and fixed income issues. Subsequent chapters validate the rule and investigate its implications based on simulated investment returns. These are drawings from probability distributions for the returns each year that could have produced returns like those that have actually been observed.

To simplify, the early chapters assume that the probability distributions of the annual returns on either stocks or fixed income issues do not vary over time. Later chapters assume that the expected returns on these investments each year depend on their prior valuations and that these valuations vary over time. The effect of variation in the volatility of returns over time is also investigated as is the effect of an error in the expected return assumed for a given valuation.

The early chapters also make some other simplifying assumptions that are later relaxed. For instance, retirees are at first assumed to be in good health at the beginning of retirement. Also, at first the effect of income taxes is ignored. And at first no emergencies occur which may significantly increase the expense required to maintain a given standard of living. The effect of changing all of these assumptions is investigated in later chapters.

Those trained in economics are accustomed to determining the optimal withdrawals from an investment by maximizing a utility function for these withdrawals. For use in practice, however, this approach begs the question as to the appropriate utility function to use for implementation. This book assumes that the Retrenchment Rule has sufficient intuitive appeal to be attractive. To enhance this intuition the last chapter shows that the rule is consistent with utility maximization when investment returns and the length of life are known beforehand.

This book is written so as to be accessible to a wide range of readers concerned about their own retirement or advising others on these issues. Readers with professional training in business or engineering will welcome the quantitative measures used to present many of the results. Sufficient technical backup is provided in appendices to allow readers who are so inclined to verify results or develop their own modifications.

Acknowledgements

Fifteen years ago, Lynn Hopewell, who earlier had been an editor of the *Journal of Financial Planning,* set forth in that journal his vision for the profession. His article, "Decision Making Under Conditions of Uncertainty: A Wakeup Call for the Financial Planning Profession," foresaw a major change in how financial planners would present the results of plans to their clients. Instead of certain outcomes the results would be in terms of the probability of different outcomes. These probabilities would be generated using Monte Carlo techniques. He pointed out that these techniques had become relatively easy to implement due to the Monte Carlo add-in programs available for spreadsheets.

One of his examples was determining the size of the investment to be accumulated before retirement. This was to provide a given stream of constant real withdrawals for a given number of years. Planners had been determining the size of this investment with a standard present value calculation. To do so they assumed a given return on the investment and a given rate of inflation.

Hopewell instead assumed that the return on the investment and the rate of inflation were each drawings from probability distributions. He then used a Monte Carlo enabled spreadsheet to make thousands of runs for the size of the required investment. These runs depended on the drawings each time for the return on the investment and the rate of inflation. Based on these runs the software showed the probability that an investment of a given size would successfully provide the required stream of withdrawals. Individuals could then determine how much they needed to accumulate depending on how confident they wanted to be of being able to make the required withdrawals over their retirement.

Reading his paper, the Monte Carlo enabled spreadsheet clearly rang a bell for me. This was indeed a powerful tool to use for retirement planning. The model he was using for retirement planning, however, needed improvement. As he intended, the model demonstrated the use of such a spreadsheet, but the model needed to be more realistic.

Retirees would surely not continue to make the same withdrawal each year when there was a significant risk of running out of funds. They would reduce their withdrawal until the risk of running out of funds became tolerable. The possible need for such reductions needed to be included in the model.

One way of limiting the risk of running out of funds would be to put a limit on the amount that could be withdrawn each year. This limit would depend on the value of the investment that year and the number of withdrawals that remained to complete the plan. For instance, a withdrawal might be limited to the largest constant real withdrawal that could be made each year over the remainder of the plan. This was when the investment earned each year its expected real return.

There was also another major problem with the model. He assumed the same rate of return on the investment each year over retirement, and the same rate of inflation. This was a major problem because poor returns or high inflation would have a more adverse effect on the results if they occurred early in retirement rather than later on. To make the model more realistic the real return on the investment each year should be a drawing from a probability distribution. And historical data on annual real investment returns could then be used to estimate a realistic probability distribution to use in the simulations.

Fortunately, it turned out to be possible to set up a Monte Carlo enabled spreadsheet with both of these improvements. The real return on investment each year was a random drawing. And the withdrawal in a future year was reduced when the risk of not being able to sustain the prior real withdrawal was too high. In this model future withdrawals might have to be reduced. But retirees would never experience a catastrophic loss of funds later in retirement. And if the initial horizon was set equal to their maximum possible length of life they would never run out of funds.

I published a paper showing the sustainability of a series of possible initial withdrawals under these conditions. Subsequently, I received a call from Hopewell. He wanted to provide some encouragement, and also tell me he had set up a website. This was a website to encourage the use of Monte Carlo techniques in financial planning. And he said that my paper was highlighted on the site.

Hopewell said he thought that such studies of the sustainability of investment withdrawals were interesting and useful. But he also thought that using conventional planning software at that time with certain inputs would continue to be needed for some planning questions. For instance, he said one question he frequently gets is: "Do I have enough for a beach house?" Hopewell thought that the conventional techniques would be needed to answer a question like that. Perhaps, however, Monte Carlo techniques are even more versatile than he envisioned at that time. Chapter 8 of this book contains an analysis that attempts to answer such a question.

After the paper was published I also heard from Ahmet Tezel. I had known him at Berkeley when he was a doctoral student and we wrote a paper together. Among other things he pointed out that Monte Carlo techniques could be incorporated into Excel spreadsheets without special add-in software. The procedure he told me about is provided in Appendix 3-1 of this book. This procedure is not efficient. It does, however, provide an easy way for readers to get a general sense of using Monte Carlo techniques without the add-in software.

The first Eureka moment for me during this project was Hopewell's suggestion of using Monte Carlo add-in programs for spreadsheets. The second Eureka moment came several years later. This was when I realized that the key question in spending retirement assets was not achieving sustainable withdrawals, but when to retrench.

Earlier, when simulating investment withdrawals over retirement, I had been reducing the withdrawals when it appeared necessary to avoid later running out of funds. It subsequently dawned on me, however, that a similar consideration should be applied to determining the initial withdrawal. The initial withdrawal should be the one required to provide the prior or desired standard of living subject to a limit.

That limit should be the largest withdrawal that could be made without increasing too much the risk of low withdrawals later in retirement. Moreover, this limit should be based on the discount rate that gives the best results in a series of simulated withdrawals. This discount rate might not be the expected return on the investment as I had been assuming. Using the discount rate that gives the best results in a series of simulations over a hypothetical retirement became the Retrenchment Rule.

I wrote a new paper using this approach. At the time, Maureen Peck was the Managing Editor of the *Journal of Financial Planning,* and Bruce Most was the Senior Editor. The topic of when to retrench was unconventional, but they agreed to publish it. And they made a number of very helpful suggestions for improving the exposition. One was to include a scenario at the beginning of the paper. This was to provide an example of someone facing retrenchment and how the Retrenchment Rule provided an answer.

When Monte Carlo techniques are used for financial planning the results must be put into charts and tables to be useful. The design and presentation of these charts and tables becomes a key part of the analysis. It is a pleasure to acknowledge the contribution of the design team for this project at CreateSpace in getting this material for the book into print.

During this project I have increasingly been impressed by the value of the interaction between theory and practice. At the same time, the difficulty of achieving this interaction has also increasingly become apparent. Much fertile ground exists between theory and practice in Financial Economics. I am convinced that rewards exist for those who are willing to till it.

Gordon B. Pye

Summer 2012

1

Introduction

Few retirees have saved enough to feel highly confident that they can sustain their standard of living over their retirement. And the poor investment returns since the 1990s have heightened the concerns of many. But the key is whether these retirees need to take action immediately. Are prospects sufficiently bleak that painful retrenchment is necessary at this time to reduce their standard of living?

The Retrenchment Rule answers this question. The threat is the possibility of insufficient funds in old age. But current retrenchment requires accepting immediate pain. The Retrenchment Rule weighs whether this immediate pain is justified given that the future funds provided may turn out to never be needed.

This book shows that retrenchment may lower the standard of living earlier in retirement without improving the standard of living later in retirement sufficiently to cover the cost of the earlier retrenchment. The Retrenchment Rule identifies such cases in which retrenchment can be deferred. It recommends retrenchment in those cases when future risks are reduced sufficiently to justify the pain of a current reduction in standard of living.

William Bengen (1994) showed that an initial annual withdrawal of 4 percent from an investment can be sustained over a long retirement. This is when the withdrawals are adjusted each year for inflation, and the portfolio is appropriately diversified. But there are some major problems with planning a retirement based on making and sustaining a 4 percent initial withdrawal.

One problem is that many individuals have to begin retirement without having saved nearly enough to cover essential expenses with a 4 percent withdrawal. Living on the funds provided by a withdrawal this small will require painful retrenchment. But is accepting this pain really justified?

A recent paper Pye (2008) argues that it is not. The Retrenchment Rule shows that significantly more than 4 percent can be withdrawn initially to avoid painful retrenchment. This is without significantly increasing the risk that more retrenchment will be required later in retirement than would have been necessary anyway. Some retrenchment may be necessary immediately, but there is a better way of reducing much of the risk of insufficient funds late in retirement. For those in good health this is to annuitize a large portion of the portfolio and seek part-time employment.

Another problem is large unexpected expenses. The 4 percent rule says to keep on withdrawing the initial amount each year adjusted for inflation. But this is impossible if an emergency occurs. Suppose water incursion requires major home repairs, or a child requires major financial aid. What should the response be to such a shock?

Perhaps significant retrenchment is required, but maybe not. Perhaps investment returns in the past have been sufficiently favorable that the current standard of living does not need to be reduced. The Retrenchment Rule takes such a shock into account along with the then current value of the portfolio. Using these inputs it determines whether retrenchment is required in making subsequent investment withdrawals.

Another critical need for the rule is after a period of extremely poor investment returns such as following the 1990s. Studies have shown that a 4 percent withdrawal is sustainable over a long retirement. But much financial wisdom has been called into question by the poor investment returns in the period following the 1990s. Tests on historical data show that the Retrenchment Rule should be used even by those who have saved enough to cover their expenses by a 4 percent withdrawal. This is even if they do not have any large unexpected expenses, but do experience a period of poor investment returns like those that have occurred in the past.

1.1 Testing on Historical Returns

Almost all of this book tests the Retrenchment Rule using simulated investment returns. These are drawings from probability distributions that appear to give a good representation of the investment returns that have been observed in the past, and can be expected in the future. The historical returns that have been observed are presumed to be specific realizations of the general process used to make the simulations.

Testing the Retrenchment Rule on the historical returns provides a simple illustration of the results to be obtained. And for anyone a series of observed returns has credibility. The problem is that it is difficult to draw credible general conclusions based on the small number of historical observations available.

To test the rule on historical returns it is assumed that a withdrawal is made from an investment portfolio at the beginning of each year. Also, at the beginning of each year the portfolio is allocated to have 75 percent in the S&P 500 and 25 percent in intermediate U. S. government issues. Over the ensuing year these issues earn the real returns that are reported for a given calendar year in the *SBBI Yearbook* (2010). Any transaction costs or taxes are ignored.

As the first test suppose that retirement begins in 1991. This is for individuals who were age 65 at that time and in good health. Suppose also that they have to withdraw 7.5 percent of their portfolio to cover living expenses for the coming year to avoid painful retrenchment.

At the beginning of 1991 as is typically the case there was reason to be apprehensive about the outlook for stocks. In the 1980s there had been a strong bull market. For the calendar years 1982 through 1989 the S&P 500 on average had annual real returns of 15 percent. In 1990 there was only a moderate correction following that bull market with a negative real return of 9 percent. At the time there was certainly no reason to believe that 1991 was a particularly good year to begin retirement.

For those in good health at age 65 the Retrenchment Rule allows a 7.5 percent withdrawal to avoid painful retrenchment. Suppose in 1991 that these retirees did withdraw 7.5 percent to sustain their existing standard of living, and avoid painful retrenchment. Based on the returns that were actually earned in the following years the rule would have advised continuing to sustain that standard of living. Following the rule these retirees would have continued making the same withdrawal each year in real terms that they did in 1991.

For those who survived this withdrawal could have continued until 2010, when this is being written, and the survivors would be age 84. In 2009, however, following the severe bear market of 2008 the rule was close to requiring some retrenchment. And it is, of course, unknown whether retrenchment will be required in 2011 or subsequently.

Nevertheless, it seems safe to conclude that 1991 was a very good year to retire. And that these retirees would be very thankful that they had followed the Retrenchment Rule. By following the rule they avoided unnecessary painful retrenchment in 1991. And they avoided retrenchment that would have been necessary in 2009 if they had increased their spending later in the 1990s. This is as the value of their portfolio rose in the bull market of those years.

The year 1991 was a very good time to retire, but there was no way of knowing that at the time. On the other hand, the year 1966 turned out to be the worst year to retire of all the years since 1926 recorded in the *SBBI Yearbook*. But there was, of course, no way of knowing that at the time either.

Suppose that the same test is repeated starting in 1966 with retirees at age 65 making a 7.5 percent withdrawal. In this case some retrenchment was required in the following year as there was a moderate bear market in 1966. In this case, the Retrenchment Rule would have advised that only 6.4 percent could be withdrawn from 1967 through 1969. And in 1970 and 1971 further retrenchment turned out to be necessary. Over 1971 through 1973 the withdrawal allowed by the rule was down to 5.1 percent.

Then, the severe bear market of 1973-74 hit with the S&P 500 declining a cumulative 49 percent over those two years. This is adjusted for dividends and inflation. As a result, each year from 1975 through 1978 the rule advised that only 2.8 percent could be withdrawn. And further retrenchment was required in 1979 and 1980. By 1982 the withdrawal advised by the Retrenchment Rule had declined to 2.1 percent. But that was the low point. No further retrenchment was required no matter how much longer any of these retirees survived. And in addition to this withdrawal these retirees presumably also had Social Security and perhaps other sources of funds such as equity in their home to help cover expenses.

So ends the worst scenario for retirees using the Retrenchment Rule. This is assuming that their retirement might have started under these same conditions in any of the years recorded in the *SBBI Yearbook*. But what if these retirees started in 2000 or 1929? Those were also very bad years to start retirement, but not as bad as 1966.

If they started in 2000 ten years later in 2010 they would have been withdrawing 3.0 percent. This compares with the 2.8 percent they were withdrawing in 1976, which was ten years after starting in 1966. And ten years after starting in 1929 they would have been withdrawing 3.7 percent in 1939. This was after enduring the worst bear market for stocks in the *SBBI Yearbook* over 1929-31, and a comparable severe bear market in 1937 to that in 2008. The reason that starting in 1929 was less severe was the high real returns on the 25 percent of intermediate governments in the portfolio. These high real returns were due to the extreme deflation that occurred during the Great Depression.

1.2 Alternatives to the Retrenchment Rule

But what were the alternatives to using the Retrenchment Rule for those starting in 1966? The commonly recommended sustainable annual withdrawal rate is 4 percent. Suppose instead of withdrawing 7.5 percent to avoid painful retrenchment that these retirees had undertaken the drastic retrenchment required and had withdrawn only 4 percent. Such retrenchment may not look that difficult on paper. But in practice wrenching adjustments are necessary whose results may be highly uncertain. Some examples of the types of adjustments that may be necessary are provided later in Section 1.4.

Suppose after retrenching sufficiently to live on a 4 percent withdrawal that these retirees continued to sustain that lower standard of living. Each year they continued to withdraw the same amount in real terms as they did in 1966. It turns out when doing so, however, that their portfolio would have run out of funds 30 years later in 1996. At that time they would have been 95 so most would not have survived that long.

Most, however, would have at least survived for from 15 to 30 years and they too would have been affected. They would have experienced rising anxiety as their portfolio eroded and their original 4 percent withdrawal became a rising percentage of their portfolio. For instance, in 1986 when they would have been age 85 their portfolio would have been equal to 28 percent of its initial value in real terms. And their initial 4 percent withdrawal would have risen to 14 percent of their portfolio in 1986, as 4/28=.14.

Retrenching enough to live on a 4 percent withdrawal turned out not to be a viable strategy starting in 1966. But there is another alternative that would have been viable, and presumably preferable. Suppose they retrenched and withdrew only 4 percent in 1966 and then followed the Retrenchment Rule. That is certainly a possible strategy although the initial 4 percent withdrawal is not consistent with using the rule.

In this latter case they would have been able to sustain the 4 percent withdrawal up through the severe bear market of 1973-74. But in 1975 the Retrenchment Rule would have required that they reduce their withdrawal from 4.0 to 3.6 percent. And further retrenchment would have been required in 1979 and 1980. By 1982 their withdrawal would have declined to 2.7 percent. The 2.7 percent withdrawal could thereafter have been sustained for as long as any of these retirees might have survived.

1.3 Benefits versus Costs

The bottom portion of Chart 1-1 compares the withdrawals just described to those obtained by withdrawing 7.5 percent in 1966 as allowed by the Retrenchment Rule. This comparison shows that those who withdrew 4 percent in 1966 and then used the Retrenchment Rule were able to withdraw somewhat more starting in 1975 than those who withdrew 7.5 percent in 1966. But this benefit came at the cost of undertaking a drastic retrenchment in 1966 sufficient to live on a 4 percent instead of a 7.5 percent withdrawal at that time.

Those who withdrew 7.5 percent in 1966 eventually had to retrench somewhat more. But they had 10 years over which to plan and make these adjustments. A hasty major retrenchment is likely to result in many mistakes as there is insufficient time to weigh the pros and cons of different possible adjustments. Also, with good health, and perhaps some pent-up enthusiasm for activities such as travel, increments of spending early in retirement are likely to provide more satisfaction than equal increments later on.

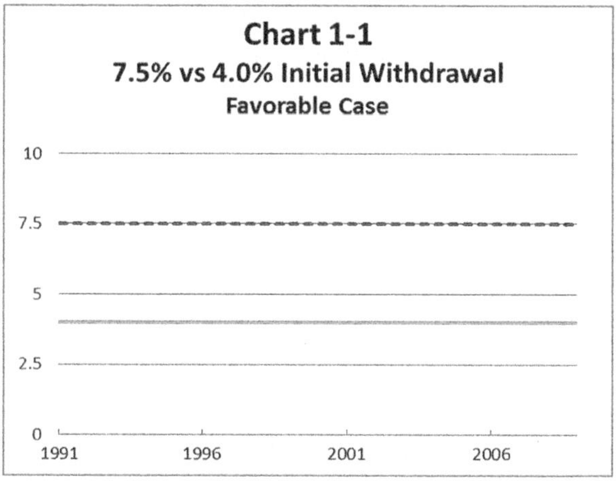

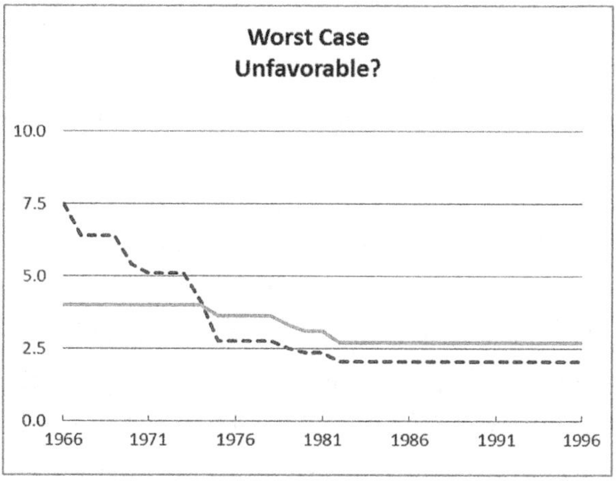

Chart 1-1. Annual withdrawals obtained as a percentage of a given initial investment when using the Retrenchment Rule. The initial withdrawal is 7.5% for the dashed lines and 4.0% for the solid lines. Withdrawals start at the beginning of 1991 in the top chart and at the beginning of 1966 in the bottom chart. At the beginning of each year the investment is allocated to have 75% in the S&P 500 and 25% in intermediate term U. S. government issues. The real returns are those given for calendar years by the *SBBI Yearbook*. Withdrawals at the beginning of each year are those given by the Retrenchment Rule. Use of the rule assumes an RDR of 0.08, and an initial age of 65 with a limit on the maximum age each year of 110.

The series of returns starting in 1966 used for the test at the bottom of the chart are the least favorable for withdrawals of any of those since 1926. Thus, on this basis these withdrawals can be viewed as the downside risk of withdrawing 7.5 percent to avoid painful retrenchment. This downside risk is the cost of somewhat lower withdrawals later in retirement as shown in the chart. But this cost is limited if retirees do not survive very long. And in any case this cost is offset by significant benefits earlier in retirement.[1]

After comparing the costs and benefits some retirees may see a net cost at the bottom of the chart while others may see a net benefit or be indifferent. Even those who see a net cost, however, will see a strong net benefit over all of retirement when the returns turn out to be much more favorable. Such a possibility is shown at the top of the chart for the returns that start in 1991. In addition to these much more favorable cases, there are many other cases in which starting with 7.5 percent is nevertheless clearly better, even if not much more favorable. For instance, in 70 percent of the cases overall, the withdrawals for starting with 7.5 percent are always above 4 percent.

Thus, those who see little or no downside risk in terms of a net cost at the bottom of the chart will surely want to withdraw 7.5 percent initially to avoid painful retrenchment. For them withdrawing 7.5 percent is a win/win decision. Even those who do see some downside risk, however, should also be persuaded to withdraw 7.5 percent initially. This is because the downside risk for the case at the bottom of the chart is easily more than compensated for by the upside benefits of the 7.5 percent withdrawal in other cases like that at the top of the chart.

These tests of the Retrenchment Rule on actual historical returns indicate the possible benefits and costs of using the rule. But what needs to be done is to validate the Retrenchment Rule in general terms. To do so it is necessary to consider all of the myriad possible future trajectories for investment returns and weigh them by their relative likelihood. This can be done by testing the Retrenchment Rule using many thousands of possible simulated series of returns on a computer.[2] Such an analysis is carried out in this book. It shows that the Retrenchment Rule is a simple and reasonable way of dealing with a very difficult question: When should retirees retrench?

1.4 Painful Retrenchment

It is very important to keep in mind that the Retrenchment Rule determines when painful retrenchment can be avoided. Less painful cuts should be made when withdrawals are unsustainable. This is even when the less essential spending can be covered by the largest withdrawal allowed by the rule.

The reason is that withdrawing to cover the non-essentials is reducing the value of the investment. A lower value for the investment increases the possibility that more drastic retrenchment will be necessary in the future for more essential expenses. Moreover, the Retrenchment Rule is likely to require that the non-essential spending be cut in the near future anyway. Thus, by cutting non-essentials when a withdrawal has poor sustainability there is much to gain and little to lose.

On the other hand, suppose that there are sufficient funds to cover expenses with a reasonably sustainable withdrawal. In this case spending on existing non-essentials is permitted if these items are providing sufficient satisfaction. There is now a significant benefit to covering the non-essentials because it is now likely this spending can be sustained. And when a withdrawal is reasonably sustainable covering the non-essentials causes only a slight rise in the retrenchment risk for the more essential spending. A later chapter develops some guidelines as to when withdrawals can be made to cover existing less essential expenses.

At this point what is important is understanding the sort of painful retrenchment that should be avoided by using the rule. A good way to develop this understanding is to consider a scenario in which a retiree is faced with such decisions. Such a scenario follows in which Louise Logan has found it necessary to begin retirement without sufficient funds. This is to cover her essential expenses with a reasonably sustainable withdrawal.

Louise Logan was planning to save enough to provide her preretirement standard of living on a reasonably sustainable basis. But since the 1990s her investment returns have been extremely poor. Even with additional savings her portfolio has not increased in real value since the 1990s.

Due to the shortfall she had planned to keep on working, but that is no longer possible. She has been affected by a round of cost cutting layoffs and forced to retire. And at age 65 there is little prospect of finding something else.

She starts Social Security, which will provide $20,000 for the coming year. She also cuts any non-essential spending. But even after these cuts she expects that she will need $60,000 in the coming year to cover her remaining expenses.

Her portfolio has a current value of $600,000. At the commonly recommended 4 percent "sustainable" rate that will provide $24,000 for the coming year. But with her Social Security that provides only $44,000 to cover her expected expenses of $60,000.

Moreover, her expenses could be even higher. She is not providing for any possible emergencies in the $60,000 estimate. And she has included only an expected normal level for a number of vital needs that must be covered, and whose expense varies considerably from year to year. These items include medical or dental expense not covered by insurance and repairs to her home and various other items.

Closing a gap of this size will clearly require radical changes in her life. In particular, she has little choice but to move to a less expensive home. The gain from the downsizing can be added to her portfolio. And there will be lower annual expenses for property taxes and other items.

Louise, however, is comfortably situated, having lived where she is for many years. It is painful for her to even think about moving to an unfamiliar and less attractive neighborhood. There are many uncertainties involved in such a move including the extent of the savings she will be able to realize.

In any case, given the size of her shortfall she doubts that such a move by itself will be sufficient. Other painful cuts will be necessary. In particular, she will no longer be able to afford the summer rental she has enjoyed for many years. And it is likely she will also have to sharply curtail if not eliminate her frequent trips to visit her daughter, just when she has more time.

Such painful initial retrenchment will be necessary if Louise limits her initial annual withdrawal to 4 percent. The Retrenchment Rule advises, however, that painful retrenchment of this sort is not warranted when such retrenchment is necessary to reduce investment withdrawals to a reasonably sustainable level. In such cases some retrenchment may be necessary to make the withdrawal more sustainable, but nowhere near as much as to reduce the withdrawal to a reasonably sustainable amount, such as 4 percent.

The reasonably conservative version of the Retrenchment Rule recommended in this book advises that an annual withdrawal of up to about 7.5 percent can be made from an investment under these conditions to avoid painful retrenchment. This is for retirees who are in good health and about age 65. And it assumes that the portfolio will be appropriately invested.

A 7.5 percent withdrawal from her $600,000 portfolio is $45,000. With the $20,000 of Social Security this provides a limit on her expected spending in the coming year to avoid painful retrenchment of $65,000. If she is using the Retrenchment Rule none of the cuts just described need to be made at this time.

It is important to note, however, that the $65,000 is not her budget for the coming year. It is the limit on her expected spending for the coming year to avoid painful retrenchment. Given this limit she does not need to undertake at this time any of the painful cuts just described. She should, however, continue to eliminate the non-essential spending as planned. The pain of eliminating these non-essentials is not sufficient to outweigh the benefit these reductions may provide in avoiding cuts in more essential spending later on.

Except for her planned cuts of non-essentials in the coming year Louise keeps on doing what she has been doing. What she actually spends, however, will in general differ from the $60,000 she expects. Her spending on vital needs will generally differ from the normal level that she expected. And the increase in cost of her other activities due to inflation will in general also differ from what she expected. Whatever she actually does spend will show up in the value of her portfolio at the end of the coming year. It will be taken into account in deciding whether she needs to retrench for the following year. Whatever she has earned on her investments over the coming year will also be in the value of her portfolio and considered in her next retrenchment decision.

Suppose at the end of the coming year that she is still in good health. The Retrenchment Rule allows her to now withdraw a slightly larger percentage of her investment as the longest she might possibly live is now one year less. But practically speaking this difference is very small and she can still withdraw about 7.5 percent for the following year. But there is virtually sure to have been a change in the real value of her portfolio as the total real return she has earned is unlikely to equal what she withdrew to cover her expenses.

Some painful retrenchment may well be required for the following year even if none was required for the coming year. Over the year, however, she has had some time to think about the cuts she should make if the need should arise. Some such tentative planning should help ease the pain if any retrenchment should turn out to be necessary. This is in comparison to the large immediate cuts that would have been necessary if she had tried to live initially on a reasonably sustainable withdrawal.

1.5 A Roadmap

The results of using the Retrenchment Rule have been described for some specific cases. And these results have been compared to those for some possible alternatives. Chapter 2 formulates the Retrenchment Rule and describes more fully how it is implemented.

Future investment withdrawals of the same real value are worth less the further in the future they are expected to occur. One reason is that it becomes increasingly less likely that retirees will survive that long. Another is that many have pent-up plans for activities after they retire such as travel, but these desires become satisfied. Also, later on withdrawals of the same real value are likely to provide less satisfaction as lifestyles slow and mobility declines even for those who remain in as good health as can be expected.

To reflect this decreasing value the Retrenchment Rule discounts future withdrawals by a constant rate of interest for each year in the future until they will be made. The value of this discount rate is selected by simulating the use of the rule with different rates over a hypothetical retirement period. This is to see which rate gives the best performance. The discount rate selected is called the Retrenchment Discount Rate, or RDR.

To make these simulations the return on the investment each year is a drawing from a probability distribution. Chapter 3 discusses the specification of this distribution and shows how to make the simulations using a spreadsheet. An example using Excel is provided in an appendix. Based on the results of these simulations Chapter 4 significantly narrows the reasonable choices for the RDR. It is shown that virtually all retirees will want to withdraw significantly more than a reasonably sustainable amount to avoid painful retrenchment.

The Retrenchment Rule allows withdrawals when there is significant risk of much lower withdrawals later in retirement. But if earlier retrenchment is not the way to reduce this risk, how should it be reduced? Chapter 5 shows that a cost effective way to reduce the risk of low withdrawals for those in good health is to annuitize a large portion of the investment and seek part-time employment. Examples of the simulations using Excel to obtain these results are provided in an appendix. Similar examples of the simulations for later results are also provided in later chapters.

Chapter 5 also shows that allocating a portion of the portfolio to fixed income issues is not an effective way to reduce risk later in retirement unless the initial withdrawal is reasonably sustainable. When the initial withdrawal is reasonably sustainable a smaller portion of the portfolio can be annuitized. Alternatively, when the withdrawal is sufficiently sustainable it may be preferable to allocate this smaller portion to fixed income issues for greater flexibility.

Retirees have the possibility of effectively annuitizing a limited portion of their investments by deferring the start of their Social Security. The last part of Chapter 5 shows that the rates for this implicit annuitizing are attractive. It also shows how deferring Social Security for those in good health improves the sustainability of their standard of living at the cost of some reduction in the future value of their investments.

Some retirees have effectively already annuitized a portion of their investment by having a pension included in their retirement assets. Chapter 6 includes a pension in the analysis. It shows how a pension should be taken into account in deciding if further annuitization is desirable and how the portfolio should be allocated. It also shows that pensions of varying size, or annuitization, do not significantly affect the choice of the RDR.

The retirement assets of some consist largely of just a pension with nominal benefits and Social Security. They need to use the Retrenchment Rule to determine the savings from earlier benefits necessary to make up for later erosion in the real value of their pension benefits from inflation. Retirees in these circumstances without any stocks may be uncomfortable investing in stocks and strongly prefer investing in fixed income issues. This chapter shows how investing in fixed incomes instead of stocks affects the results and the RDR that retirees should use.

Suppose when they retire that individuals will use the Retrenchment Rule and appropriately allocate their portfolios. Chapter 7 considers how much they need to save to achieve a given standard of living with a given degree of sustainability. To do so uncertainty is first assumed to exist only with respect to future investment returns.

It is shown that saving enough to cover expenses with the annual withdrawal of 4 percent that is generally considered to be sustainable is at best at the upper end of the reasonably sustainable range. Additional savings are desirable to further improve sustainability. Whether additional savings are optimal, however, requires assessing whether the added sustainability is worth the reduced preretirement standard of living required.

Besides uncertainty about future investment returns retirees also face uncertainty about the expenses that will have to be covered to sustain their desired standard of living. Emergencies may arise that require large extra withdrawals. Examples of such emergencies are major home repairs, or the need to provide major assistance to a child.

To evaluate the additional savings needed to cover possible emergencies it is assumed that there is a very small chance of a major emergency each year. This additional uncertainty reduces the upper end of the reasonably sustainable range from 4 percent to close to 3 percent. Although possible emergencies increase the need for savings it is shown that they have only a small effect on the choice of an RDR.

Besides the need to cover emergencies, additional savings could also be necessary to cover elevated health care costs later in retirement. To meet such needs the Retrenchment Rule in effect provides a reserve for later assisted care by assuming an unusually long maximum lifespan for those in good health. When their health takes a turn for the worse the lifespan assumed in using the rule is reduced making additional funds available for assistance.

If full time nursing care becomes necessary, however, the funds provided by the Retrenchment Rule will likely be insufficient for those in the middle income range. Use of the rule will have to be discontinued and the necessary funds withdrawn to pay for the care. Simulations show the probable length of time such care can be provided depending on the portfolio remaining when the care becomes necessary.

These results are then compared to data that show the probable length of time for nursing home stays of varying length. The comparison indicates that those saving enough to cover their living expenses with reasonably sustainable investment withdrawals will also very likely have sufficient funds to cover any nursing home care they may require. For single retirees the need for either additional savings or for insurance to cover this contingency appears doubtful.

Chapter 7 also considers the need for increased savings to retire early. Increased savings are needed to get comparably sustainable withdrawals over the longer period, and to cover the absence of Social Security early in the period. Those in the middle income range may need savings that are 50 percent or more larger to retire at age 55 instead of 65.

When an unsustainable withdrawal is necessary to cover living expenses it is generally assumed that retirees do not withdraw more than is required to cover their existing standard of living. The reason is that it is assumed that the satisfaction from the increase will be more than offset by the possible pain of increased retrenchment in the future. This increased retrenchment is due to the reduced value of the investment due to the extra withdrawal. When the withdrawal required to cover the existing standard of living is sufficiently sustainable, however, voluntary extra withdrawals can be considered.

Chapter 8 considers the possibility of large voluntary extra withdrawals in such cases. Examples are purchasing a property for recreational use at the beginning of retirement, or making a large donation to a non-profit organization. Another is covering continuing non essential expenses that provide significant satisfaction, but are not sufficiently vital to be painful to eliminate.

Purchasing a property equal to 20 percent of the portfolio is shown to be affordable when the initial withdrawal is reasonably sustainable. A donation of the same amount is affordable, however, only if the withdrawal is significantly more sustainable. The difference is that the property can be sold if retrenchment becomes necessary. It is also shown that existing continuing expense can be covered that is not painful to eliminate. This is when the withdrawal is reasonably sustainable, but not when it is unsustainable.

So far it has been assumed that individuals are beginning retirement at age 65 in good health with a limit on their life expectancy of age 110. It has also been assumed that investment valuations are normal at the beginning of retirement and each year thereafter. The volatility of the returns each year has been assumed to be the same. And taxes have been ignored. Relaxing these assumptions is investigated in the next five chapters.

Chapter 9 assumes that retirees have a shorter horizon either because they are in poor health or because they have become older. Chapter 9 shows that a shorter horizon for either reason has little effect on the choice of an RDR. Thus, there is little reason to change the RDR over retirement due to the shortening horizon.

Those who start in poor health should not annuitize. They can, however, reduce their risk of low withdrawals by allocating a portion of their portfolio to fixed income issues. Also, they have less risk of low withdrawals late in their retirement because of their shorter horizon. As a result those who start retirement in poor health have a similar risk of low withdrawals late in their retirement as do those who start in good health. Chapter 9 also looks at how the length of the horizon affects portfolio allocation.

The budget interval in this book is generally considered to be one year. The last part of Chapter 9 considers the effect on the withdrawals of using a shorter budget interval. A shorter interval provides some modest improvement. But the improvement does not appear to be sufficient to warrant the additional disruptions and effort involved in more frequent budgeting.

Earlier simulations assume normal investment valuations each year. But measures of valuation show significant variation over time. Estimating the relation between valuations and expected investment returns, however, is very difficult. This is because changes in valuation account for only a very small portion of changes in subsequent realized investment return.

Chapter 10 makes best guesses as to the distribution of the returns on stocks and fixed income issues that depend on current valuations in subsequent years. But suppose the distributions are viewed in the long run when the influence of the current valuations has faded. These distributions in the long run are specified so as to be the same as those for the earlier simulations.

Chapter 11 shows how these valuation dependent distributions affect the results of the earlier simulations. As an approximation cyclical variation in valuations and expected returns can be ignored in selecting and using the RDR. Thus, valuations have little effect on the largest withdrawals that can be made to avoid painful retrenchment.

Cyclical variation in valuations and expected returns also has little effect on savings requirements for a sustainable withdrawal when starting retirement when valuations are normal. Starting with significantly abnormal valuations, however, has a significant effect on savings requirements. Savings requirements were more than 50 percent higher for funding a given sustainable withdrawal in early 2000 or 2010 when valuations were high than in 1982 when valuations were low. This is assuming the best guesses about the relationships made in Chapter 10 are reasonably valid.

Chapter 11 also tests the effect of changing the allocation of the portfolio in response to changes in the relative valuation of stocks and fixed income issues. Such a strategy significantly increases portfolio values later in retirement. It provides little reduction in the risk of low withdrawals, however, compared to a large fixed allocation to fixed incomes when starting from normal valuations. When starting when stock valuations are high relative to those for fixed incomes as in the late 1990s, however, some risk reduction occurs. Since changes in valuation account for only a very small portion of changes in realized returns, however, such shifts in allocation frequently turn out to be incorrect after the fact. This is even though the shifts improve performance on average viewed from beforehand.

Chapter 12 considers the effect of structural change in the return on investment. A structural change occurs when there is a change in the expected return for a normal valuation. Unlike cyclical change such structural change does affect the choice of the RDR. Moderate changes in the normally expected return change the RDR in the same direction by the same number of percentage points. The possibility that the normally expected return may be less than estimated, however, does not make it advisable to further reduce as a precaution an RDR chosen on the basis of a reasonably conservative estimate.

Chapter 12 also looks at the effect of significant random variation from year to year in the standard deviation of the annual return on stocks. This change increases the chances of very low returns when the standard deviation of the returns remains the same before the random drawing for the standard deviation each year. The increased chances of low returns increase the risk of low withdrawals somewhat reducing sustainability. There is no change in the choice of the RDR, however, since the withdrawals for different discount rates are affected in the same way.

Many middle income retirees have accumulated a significant portion of their investments as a result of tax free contributions to pension accounts where they have worked. These retirees face large future tax payments after age 70½ when required minimum distributions (RMD) begin from these accounts. As a result, their withdrawals to pay income tax may be large and vary significantly over time. Chapter 13 therefore applies the Retrenchment Rule to the after tax withdrawals that directly affect the standard of living.

Federal income tax payments are assumed similar to those for the rules in the U. S. in 2009. The possibility of higher tax rates in the future is also tested. Simulations show that the federal income tax causes a large increase in savings requirements when a large portion of the initial investment is in a traditional IRA or similar such account.

Other tests show that converting a portion of a traditional IRA into a Roth IRA does not provide any help. Also, the income tax reduces the increased chances of higher withdrawals provided by part-time earnings and annuitization. But due to progressivity in the tax schedule the tax has much less of an effect on the reduced risk of low withdrawals provided by these measures.

The Retrenchment Rule is intuitively appealing, but is it the best way to make withdrawals? In economics the best withdrawals are determined by maximizing a utility function for the withdrawals subject to constraints. When the investment returns and length of life are known Chapter 14 shows that the Retrenchment Rule provides the optimal withdrawals for two different forms of the utility function. Although these conditions are artificial the optimality of the rule in these cases enhances its credibility.

Notes

1. The withdrawals starting in 1966 are the worst of those starting in any year from 1926 to 2008. This is for the withdrawals that start either from 7.5 or 4.0 percent. Another question, however, is how do the streams of withdrawals compare to each other when starting in different years? In this respect, some may judge that the stream starting from 7.5 percent looks worse in one of the several years before 1966. For instance, suppose the withdrawals start in 1960. In this case, the withdrawals starting at 4.0 percent are sustained over the entire period. This

is instead of falling to 2.7 percent in 1982 as occurs when starting in 1966. In contrast, the withdrawals starting at 7.5 percent in 1960 continue to fall to 2.1 percent in 1982 as they do when starting in 1966. The withdrawals starting with 7.5 percent in 1960, however, do have a significant increased benefit. This is the much higher withdrawals provided earlier in retirement. These withdrawals are 7.0 percent or better till 1967, 6.7 percent till 1970, and 5.4 percent till 1974. Nevertheless, the much better protection after 1974 provided by starting with 4.0 percent in 1960 may make this stream look more attractive to some relative to starting with 7.5 percent. This is when starting in 1960 rather than 1966. Given that the stream starting at 7.5 percent is preferred in an overwhelming majority of other cases, however, this difference causes little change in the overall conclusion. Using the Retrenchment Rule starting with a 7.5 percent withdrawal appears to be the best strategy.

2. Suppose thousands of independent tests are made with simulated returns each year for withdrawals like those made with the historic returns. And suppose these simulated returns are drawings from the distributions for the annual real returns on the S&P 500 and intermediate U. S. government issues that are assumed later in Chapter 5. For a constant annual withdrawal of 4 percent starting at age 65 the chances of running out of funds by age 95 are over .10. Thus, running out of funds starting in 1966 with the historic returns should not be considered as especially unusual. Also, low withdrawals when using the Retrenchment Rule under these conditions should not be considered as especially unusual. When withdrawing 7.5 percent initially at age 65 the chances of a 2 percent or less withdrawal at age 95 are about .20, and somewhat less than half that when initially withdrawing 4 percent.

References

Bengen, William P. 1994. "Determining Withdrawal Rates Using Historical Data." *Journal of Financial Planning* 7, 1 (January): 14-24.

Morningstar. *2010 Ibbotson SBBI Classic Yearbook*. Chicago, Illinois.

Pye, Gordon B. 2008. "When Should Retirees Retrench? Later Than You Think." *Journal of Financial Planning* 21, 9 (September): 50-59.

2

The Retrenchment Rule

It is assumed that retirees would like to provide their existing standard of living for as long as they live. The first step is to estimate in real terms the stream of withdrawals from their investments required to do so. This is for the longest that they might possibly live.

The further in the future these withdrawals occur, however, the less critical they become. The most important reason is that the further in the future the withdrawals occur the less likely retirees will still be alive to need them. But there are other reasons as well.

One is that many have pent-up plans for activities after they retire such as travel. But such desires become satisfied, and such activities are likely to no longer provide as much satisfaction later on as they do initially. And later on withdrawals of the same real value may in general provide less satisfaction as life-styles slow and mobility declines. This is even for those who remain in as good health as can be expected as they grow older.

To reflect their declining value future withdrawals are discounted by a constant rate of interest for each year in the future until they occur. This discounting gives the present value of a future withdrawal based on the discount rate that has been used. Adding up these discounted values for each of the withdrawals gives the present value of the stream. This is the present value of the future withdrawals in real terms needed to provide the existing standard of living.

The present value of the funds available to make these withdrawals is the current value of the investment portfolio. Suppose the present value of the stream of withdrawals required to provide the existing standard of living is less than the value of the portfolio. Then retrenchment is not required. Retirees can keep on doing what they have been doing. As valued by the discount rate that has been used there are sufficient funds to provide the existing standard of living in the future.

On the other hand, suppose that the present value of the stream to provide the existing standard of living exceeds the value of the portfolio. Then retrenchment is required. Expenses for voluntary activities must be reduced sufficiently that the present value of the stream of withdrawals required is equal to the value of the portfolio.

But how is the interest rate used for the discounting determined? The discount rate is determined by simulating the use of a series of possible discount rates over a hypothetical retirement period. The discount rate that gives the best performance is selected. The rate selected is called the Retrenchment Discount Rate, or RDR.

When the discount rate is too large there is too high a risk of low withdrawals late in retirement. When the discount rate is too small too much retrenchment occurs early in retirement. This is more retrenchment than can be justified by the reduced risk of low withdrawals that the added retrenchment provides later in retirement.

The simulations show the withdrawals provided by the discount rates between these two extremes. The discount rate among these that gives the best balance is selected as the RDR. It is the interest rate used to calculate the present value of the stream of future withdrawals required to provide a given standard of living.

2.1 Expected Future Withdrawals

The first step in using the Retrenchment Rule at any time is an estimate. Suppose a given retiree keeps on doing in the future what he or she has been doing. The stream of future investment withdrawals is estimated that will be required to do so.

To make such an estimate it is helpful to divide living expenses into two categories. One is the expense of activities that occur each year and that are expected to continue in the coming year and thereafter. The other category is non-recurring expense. An example of the latter is the cost of major medical or dental care not covered by insurance. Other examples are the cost of home repairs, or the cost of repairing a car or various household items.

Estimating recurring expense for the coming year is relatively straight forward. Determine the expenditure on these activities in the year just completed. Then adjust this cost for any expected net change in the cost for the coming year.

This is to provide for these same needs with goods and services of comparable quality.

Estimating an expected normal amount of expense for non-recurring items is, of course, more difficult. Some of these items may not have occurred in the past, and others that have occurred may not occur again. Many non-recurring items are for vital needs for which there may be little discretion as to the amount of expense. When there is discretion, as when replacing some durable goods, choices are made consistent with the existing standard of living.

Both expected recurring expense and expected normal non-recurring expense stay the same in real terms in future years in most cases. In some cases, however, there may be some non-recurring expense of known value in future years. For instance, suppose there are deferred payments on a contract. Such known non-recurring expenses are not included in the projected normal non-recurring expense, but included separately in full in real terms in the applicable years.

After projecting future expected expenses the next step is to project the future expected funding available each year from sources other than making withdrawals from the portfolio. Deducting the expected value of such funding in real terms from the expenses gives the expected withdrawals required from the portfolio to cover the existing standard of living.

Suppose the only other funding is Social Security, and there are not any known non-recurring expenses. In this case, the expected withdrawal each year will be the same in real terms and equal to the expected expenses in the coming year less Social Security. On the other hand, suppose that there is funding in addition to Social Security such as part-time earnings, pension benefits, or rental income from a property. The expected value of these funds each year in real terms is deducted from the expected expenses in real terms along with Social Security to get the expected withdrawals for those years.

The remaining issue in projecting the stream of expected withdrawals is the longest the retiree might possibly live. For someone in good health at age 65 the chances that they will reach age 100 are about .05 for men and .08 for women. For someone in good health at any age, however, there is virtually no chance that they will reach an age of 110.

As someone approaches an age of 110 the chances of mortality in the coming year approaches 1.0. Although a few do reach 110 the chances of this possibility are so small that they can be disregarded for planning purposes. But if virtually no one reaches an age of 110 is it reasonable to plan on an age this high?

It is reasonable because planning on a limit of age 110 for those in good health at any time has a benefit. Suppose health earlier takes a turn for the worse as is virtually sure to happen. The retirees may then need to increase their spending to cover assisted care or for various other medical problems. Having earlier assumed a very long lifespan effectively provides a reserve for such contingencies. Reducing the limit on age increases the withdrawal allowed by the rule and provides more funds.

Suppose plans are being made for retirees who are not in good health. Then judgment is required based on medical opinion as to the longest they might possibly live. An age should be selected that is comparable to the limit of 110 for those who are in good health. Plans for those who are not in good health when they retire are discussed further in Chapter 9.

2.2 Simulating a Stream of Withdrawals

The procedure has been described for estimating the future stream of withdrawals that will be required to provide an existing standard of living. The Retrenchment Rule calculates the present value of this stream by discounting each of the withdrawals by a given rate of interest for each year in the future until they are made. If this present value is less than the value of the portfolio at that time retirees can keep on doing what they have been doing. Otherwise, retrenchment is required until the present value of the reduced stream of projected withdrawals is equal to the value of the portfolio.

To obtain the interest rate to use for the discounting the withdrawals are simulated that will be obtained using the rule over a hypothetical retirement period. This is for a series of different discount rates. The discount rate that gives the best performance is selected and used as the interest rate for calculating the present values. This section gives an example of one run of such a set of simulations for one possible discount rate. The following section describes how the results for a full set of simulations are run and compiled on a computer. This is so a choice can be made as to the best discount rate to use for the RDR.

To illustrate one run of the simulations for one possible discount rate suppose that retirees have just reached age 65 in good health. As discussed earlier it is assumed that the limit on their life expectancy is age 110. This means that they must plan on making 45 annual withdrawals. This includes one at the beginning of each year starting at age 65 and ending with age 109.

Suppose that the only source of funding for these retirees besides their investment portfolio is Social Security. Suppose also that there are not any known non-recurring expenses in the future. Their expected withdrawals in the future are therefore a constant stream each year in real terms for as long as they might possibly live.

Suppose that these retirees require an 8 percent withdrawal to avoid painful retrenchment, and are using the Retrenchment Rule. Suppose that the discount rate being simulated is equal to .06. These retirees will have to retrench. A stream of 45 withdrawals equal to 8 percent of their portfolio discounted at an interest rate of .06 has a present value that exceeds the value of their portfolio.

That this is true can be verified by making a conventional present value calculation using a handheld calculator. It is assumed that the withdrawals are made at the beginning of a year so make sure that the calculator is set for this mode. Suppose that the value of the investment is 100 so that the required withdrawal is 8. Input n=45, i=6.0, PMT=8, and FV=0. Calculate the present value of this stream getting 131.1, which exceeds the value of the investment of 100.

Suppose now that the withdrawals are reduced so that their present value declines. When the withdrawals have declined from 8 to 6.1 their present value has fallen to 100. As this is the value of the portfolio this withdrawal is allowed. It is the largest withdrawal allowed by the Retrenchment Rule with a discount rate of .06.

Note that this largest allowed withdrawal can be calculated directly by making an annuity calculation. It is the largest fixed annuity that can be obtained each year from the investment for the longest that the retiree might live. This is when the investment earns a return equal to the assumed discount rate of .06. A larger stream of withdrawals than this annuity will have a present value that exceeds the value of the investment and will require retrenchment.

For making the simulations it is assumed that 6.1 is withdrawn at the beginning of the year and spent over the year. Another withdrawal is not made until the beginning of the following year. Suppose the real return on the portfolio over the coming year is .03. The value of the portfolio at the beginning of the following year before a withdrawal is made is then (100-6.1)(1.03), or 96.72. This is in real terms because the return of .03 is in real terms. The 96.72 is 96.72 percent of the initial investment because the initial investment is equal to 100.

The Retrenchment Rule is now applied just as it was initially to get the next withdrawal. All of the inputs have changed, however, except that the discount rate is still .06. To calculate the largest allowed withdrawal input n=44, PV=96.72, i=6.0, and FV=0. Calculate PMT getting 5.9 as the largest withdrawal allowed by the Retrenchment Rule. As 6.1 must be withdrawn to sustain the prior standard of living some retrenchment is required.

Suppose that a severe bear market occurs over the coming year and that the real return is −.25 instead of .03. In this case the value of the investment at the beginning of the following year is (100-6.1)(.75), or 70.42. Calculating PMT in this case the largest allowed withdrawal is 4.3. Now a major retrenchment is required. The withdrawal must be reduced from 6.1 to 4.3.

Suppose only 4.0 had been withdrawn initially instead of 6.1. In this case a major retrenchment is required initially, but no retrenchment is necessary at the beginning of the following year. The value of the investment is now (100-4.0)(.75), or 72.00. But this is only slightly higher than the 70.42 obtained with the 6.1 withdrawal.

Thus, suppose a severe bear market occurs in the coming year. It then makes little difference if the Retrenchment Rule is used with a .06 discount rate or there is a 4 percent withdrawal. For either withdrawal a major retrenchment is soon required, and the value of the investment at the beginning of the following year is just about the same. The advantage of the higher withdrawal is the very strong chance that a much better return will be earned over the coming year. In this event major retrenchment may never be necessary. And even if it is necessary it may be deferred for a long time. If only 4 percent is withdrawn initially a major retrenchment occurs for sure immediately.

Suppose that the real return over the coming year is .09 instead of .03 or −.25. In this case the value of the investment is (100-6.1)(1.09), or 102.35.

Retrenchment is therefore not required. This is because the present value of a stream of 44 withdrawals of 6.1 discounted at an interest rate of .06 is equal to 99.47, which is less than the value of the investment of 102.35.

The value of the portfolio if the return were .09 would allow a somewhat larger withdrawal than 6.1. It is assumed, however, that retirees are content to sustain their existing standard of living. They do not spend more because an increase in spending will increase any retrenchment that may be required in the future. The pain from that increased retrenchment is viewed as sufficient to more than offset any satisfaction they might obtain from the increase in standard of living. An exception might occur only if assets become so large that there is virtually no possible need for future retrenchment.

Whatever the withdrawal it is deducted from the value of the portfolio. A new drawing from the probability distribution is made, and a new value for the investment determined for the following year. Another retrenchment decision is then made in the same way.

This process continues each year until the last retrenchment decision is made at age 109. For the base case simulations it is assumed that retirees remain in as good health as can be expected as they grow older. Thus, at any age they continue to have a limit on their life expectancy of age 110. If they ever reach age 109, however, there is only one more year. No one ever becomes a super centenarian in these simulations.

In reality, of course, virtually everyone is going to have a turn for the worse in health at a much earlier age. Simulations that depart from the base case can consider questions about what happens in such cases. An example is how much might be available to cover assisted care at various ages from the investment portfolio. The answer to this question is considered in some detail in Chapter 7.

Note in the simulations to choose a discount rate that the actual withdrawal for the coming year is the same as the expected withdrawal. Generally when the Retrenchment Rule is used in practice the actual withdrawal in a coming year differs from what was expected. And the value of the portfolio at the end of the year on which the next retrenchment decision is based depends on the actual withdrawal. Chapter 7 considers cases in which an emergency can occur over the coming year requiring a large extra withdrawal in addition to the withdrawal that was expected. This extra withdrawal is considered in the simulations.

2.3 Multiple Streams and Discount Rates

Suppose many thousands of runs are made on a computer for the simulation just described. This is for a discount rate of .06 and the largest allowed initial withdrawal for that discount rate of 6.1. The real return each year on the investment for these runs is an independent random drawing from a specified probability distribution. These runs will have a myriad of different streams of withdrawals depending on the returns obtained each year from the random drawings for the returns.

The computer compiles statistical measures of the withdrawals at selected ages. One measure is the average value of the withdrawals. These averages give the expected stream of withdrawals to be obtained under these conditions. The computer also compiles the proportion of withdrawals falling in different ranges at the selected ages. These proportions give the probability of sustaining the initial withdrawal to various ages, and the risk of low withdrawals.

When many thousands of these runs are repeated just about the same statistical measures are obtained at the selected ages. These measures can therefore be used to compare the performance of different discount rates.

Suppose next that the discount rate is .08 instead of .06. In this case the largest allowed initial withdrawal is the value of the annuity obtained when the investment earns a return of .08 instead of .06. The largest allowed initial withdrawal in this case rises from 6.1 to 7.6 percent. If the required withdrawal to avoid initial retrenchment is still 8 percent the initial withdrawal increases to 7.6 percent.

If the discount rate rises further from .08 to .10 the largest allowed initial withdrawal increases from 7.6 to 9.2 percent. But if only 8 percent is required to avoid retrenchment only 8 percent is withdrawn. The 8 percent requirement to avoid retrenchment, however, applies only to the initial withdrawal.

Suppose a bear market occurs over the first year. Then a withdrawal of 10 percent or more will be required to avoid retrenchment at the beginning of the next year. Suppose the Retrenchment Rule with a discount rate of .10 or .12 determines this withdrawal. The withdrawal at the beginning of the next year will then be the largest allowed by these discount rates.

Thus, to determine the best discount rate the results for higher discount rates should be evaluated assuming the initial withdrawal is the largest allowed for each discount rate. The initial withdrawal actually required to cover expenses in a given situation may be less than that allowed by a given discount rate. Nevertheless, a larger percentage withdrawal may be required in a subsequent year due to a decline in the value of the investment.

The possible use of higher discount rates needs to be considered for cases in which they may limit the size of future withdrawals. This is even if they do not limit the initial withdrawal in a given situation. Chapter 9 shows that the performance of different discount rates relative to each other is affected very little by the length of the horizon. Evaluating the discount rates relative to each other starting from the initial year is therefore also a valid test for evaluating different rates when starting from a future year.

2.4 Conclusions

To use the Retrenchment Rule the expected stream of withdrawals in real terms is estimated that would be needed to provide the existing standard of living as long as retirees might survive. The present value of this stream is calculated using as an interest rate a discount rate called the RDR. If this present value does not exceed the value of the investment retirees can keep on doing what they have been doing in the coming year. Otherwise, they must scale back their voluntary activities until the present value of the stream of expected withdrawals no longer exceeds the value of their investment.

The discount rate to use as the RDR is determined by simulating the use of the Retrenchment Rule over a hypothetical retirement period with a series of possible discount rates. The discount rate that gives the best performance is selected as the RDR. These tests are based on many thousands of runs for each discount rate with simulated investment returns each year. Performance is judged by comparing the streams of expected withdrawals for different discount rates and the risk of low withdrawals that each causes.

The initial withdrawal in the test for each discount rate is the largest it will allow. This is even if a smaller withdrawal is required to sustain the initial standard of living. The reason is the largest allowed withdrawal for that discount rate may be applicable in the future if the value of the investment declines. And the largest allowed withdrawal for different discount rates must be taken into account in comparing their performance.

3

Making the Simulations

The last chapter described the general process for choosing an RDR by making simulations. But there are some key inputs for making these simulations that have not yet been described. One is to specify the probability distribution for the random drawings that gives the returns on the investment each year. Another is setting up the relations for simulating the withdrawals on a spreadsheet.

The next chapter presents the results for a set of base case simulations using these inputs. These simulations show the lowest discount rate that virtually any retiree will choose as his or her RDR. This RDR gives the largest withdrawal that these retirees can make to avoid painful retrenchment.

This withdrawal is well above the 4 percent that is generally considered to be reasonably sustainable. To make this much larger withdrawal reasonably conservative the focus in this chapter is on specifying a probability distribution for the investment returns that is both realistic and reasonably conservative. Before considering the inputs in this chapter in more detail some readers may prefer to first skip to the next chapter and see the results obtained.

3.1 Probability Distribution of Returns

The investment for the base case simulations in the next chapter is assumed to be a well diversified portfolio of large capitalization stocks with returns like those on the S&P 500. After that, the following chapter shows the effect of annuitizing a portion of the portfolio, or allocating a portion to fixed income issues. These changes can reduce the risk of low withdrawals for a given discount rate. These changes, however, have little effect on the performance of one discount rate relative to another. They therefore have little effect on the choice of an RDR.

At the beginning of a year the possible real returns on a stock portfolio over that year have a probability distribution. And that distribution has a mean value, which is the expected return. But these probability distributions and expected returns are unknown and can never be observed. All that is known is the single drawing from that distribution that is observed at the end of the year, which is the realized return.

Presumably the expected real return at the beginning of a year depends on the valuation on the market of the stocks in the portfolio at the beginning of that year. A good measure of the valuation of the S&P 500 is its dividend yield. Another good measure is its P/E10 ratio as compiled by Robert Shiller, or its reciprocal, the E10/P ratio.[1] For this latter measure E10 is the trailing 10 year average earnings for the S&P 500 adjusted for inflation.

Presumably the expected real return on the S&P 500 over a year moves up and down with its dividend yield and E10/P ratio at the beginning of that year. Estimating this relationship, however, is very difficult. Only the realized real returns are observed each year and these realized returns are highly volatile. At best, observed changes in valuation at the beginning of a year account for only a very small portion of the observed changes in the realized returns over those years.

Despite the difficulty, in Chapter 10 a best guess is made for the relation between the dividend yield of the S&P 500 at the beginning of a year and its real return over the subsequent year. A relation is also estimated for the behavior of the dividend yield on the S&P 500 over time. These relationships are then used to simulate real returns on the S&P 500 that vary over time and depend on its valuation at the beginning of each year. These simulated returns are then used to simulate investment withdrawals that depend on valuations.

Abnormal valuations tend to persist for a number of years. Thus, abnormal expected returns associated with abnormal valuations also tend to persist for a number of years. As a result, valuations that are significantly abnormal at the beginning of retirement have a significant effect on the sustainability of investment withdrawals.

A change in valuations, however, changes the withdrawals obtained from different discount rates in much the same way. For this reason changes in valuation have only a small effect on the performance of one discount rate relative to another. And there is little change in the discount rate selected when the performance of a series of discount rates is simulated over a hypothetical retirement period.

As a result the same discount rate can be used over all of retirement even if cyclical changes are occurring in expected returns. And the RDR can be selected by assuming the expected return each year is the same and equal to that for a normal valuation at the beginning of a year. Moreover, this RDR can also be used if retirement starts at a time when valuations are abnormal.

To determine the sustainability of withdrawals that begin with abnormal valuations, however, the simulated returns developed in Chapter 10 that depend on valuations must be used. And the size of a sustainable withdrawal can be significantly affected by the valuation at the beginning of retirement. These differences are demonstrated by the results for simulated withdrawals obtained in Chapter 11.

Suppose, however, that the valuation at the beginning of retirement is close to normal. In this case the sustainability of a withdrawal is little affected by future cyclical variation in valuations and expected returns. The sustainability of a withdrawal can be approximated by assuming that the expected returns each year are the same and equal to the expected return when there is a normal valuation at the beginning of a year.

To simplify for the simulations in the next chapter the returns each year are drawings from the same probability distribution. And this probability distribution is the distribution of returns when the S&P 500 has a normal valuation at the beginning of a year. The next section of this chapter estimates an appropriate expected return to use for this distribution. The following section estimates an appropriate standard deviation for this distribution.

3.2 Estimating the Mean Return

An estimate is needed for the mean return on the S&P 500 over a year that starts when it has a normal valuation. There are several possibilities for obtaining such an estimate. One is to average the real returns each year for the S&P 500 over a period sufficiently long that the conditions at the beginning and end have little effect on the result. Another is to average the real returns over one or more complete market cycles each with a bull and bear phase. Yet another is to average the real returns over a reasonably long period that begins and ends with reasonably normal conditions.

Given the high volatility of the returns each year for the S&P 500, however, any of these averages is an unreliable indication of the required mean return. In fact, the volatility is sufficiently large that an average would be an unreliable estimate of the mean return even under ideal conditions. Ideal conditions would be if the average was for a long period over which the return on the S&P 500 was identically and independently distributed each year.

To provide some comfort for the results from the simulations an estimate for the mean return is desired that appears reasonably conservative. With this in mind averages are calculated using each of the methods just described. A mean return is then chosen that appears to be reasonably conservative given the averages obtained by all of the methods at the time of writing in 2010.

A well known source for the returns on large capitalization stocks is the series in the *SBBI Yearbook* starting in 1926. Since the late 1950s when the S&P 500 was introduced the returns for this series are those of the S&P 500. The average real return for each year of this series starting with 1926 and ending with 2009, which is the last available at the time of writing, is .087.

This average may be biased downwards because it ends with the generally poor returns following the 1990s. On the other hand, it may be biased upwards because it starts at the beginning of the strong bull market over 1926 to 1928. If this bull market is eliminated and the average starts in 1929 instead of 1926 the average declines to .078. A more general problem with this average is whether including returns from so far in the past is representative of more recent experience.

Consider next an average over the most recent complete market cycle containing both a long bear and bull phase. The last long bull market can be dated as running from 1982 through 1999. That bull market was preceded by a bear market that might be dated as starting in 1973. A better starting date for that bear market, however, is 1966 as the returns over 1966 through 1972 were also below average. The average real return on the S&P 500 each year from 1966 through 1999 is .084, which is somewhat less than the average of .087 just obtained for 1926 through 2009.

Finally, consider an average over a recent long period that starts and ends when the S&P 500 has a reasonably normal valuation. And suppose this valuation is indicated by the dividend yield on the S&P 500 prior to a year. A convenient period that meets these conditions is the 50 years running from 1960 through 2009.

The average dividend yield prior to each of these 50 years is .032. The dividend yield prior to 2009 was also .032. And the dividend yield prior to 1960 was .031. Moreover, 1960 is a reasonable year to start because earlier years in the 1950s had higher dividend yields than the assumed normal of .032. In fact, the dividend yields in the early 1950s were about twice as high.

The average real return on the S&P 500 for the 50 years from 1960 to 2009 was .067. The other averages calculated earlier ranged from .078 to .087. In view of these earlier averages and to be reasonably conservative suppose .067 is rounded up to .07. It will be assumed that the mean real return on the S&P 500 for a year beginning with a normal valuation is .07. And this is assumed to be the expected return each year for the simulated withdrawals in the next chapter.

3.3 Volatility

Reasonable variation in the volatility of the annual real returns for the S&P 500 has less effect on the withdrawals than reasonable variation in the mean return. For the period from 1960 through 2009 the sample standard deviation of the annual real returns on the SP 500 is .17. Moreover, the sample standard deviation is either .17 or .18 starting from any year in the period that begins in 1938 and ends in 1987. These 50 alternative sample standard deviations are for periods that end in 2009.

Stock price volatility was abnormally high in the late 1920s and ensuing Great Depression. It was also abnormally high for the period starting in the late 1990s through the financial crisis of 2008 and 2009. Consistent with these periods of higher volatility the sample standard deviation is in the .19 to .21 range for periods starting from 1926 to 1937, or for periods starting since 1988. Again these calculations are all for periods that end in 2009.

The periods of higher volatility at the beginning and end of the span from 1926 to 2009 appear related to the high valuations of the late 1920s and the late 1990s. The objective is to estimate the distribution of real returns of the S&P 500 for years starting with a normal valuation. The estimate will therefore be based on the sample standard deviations of .17 and .18 that begin in the intervening 50 years.

The higher of these is .18. To be conservative it will therefore be assumed that the standard deviation of the real returns of the S&P 500 for a year beginning with a normal valuation is .18. For the simulations in the next chapter it is assumed that the real return each year has a mean of .07 and a standard deviation of .18. It is also assumed that these returns are normally distributed.

Frequently it is assumed that stock returns are lognormally distributed. The lognormal assumption has important advantages in applications such as valuing stock options, and for some theoretical studies. For simulating withdrawals over a long retirement period with an annual planning cycle, however, using the lognormal is questionable.

For this purpose the lognormal distribution is not conservative. Lognormally distributed returns have a smaller risk of large negative returns than normally distributed returns with the same mean and standard deviation. Moreover, the chances of large negative returns are likely larger than those given by a normal distribution with a constant standard deviation.

This is because in reality the volatility of the annual returns is likely to vary significantly over time. Such random variation causes an increase in the risk of large negative returns, and the risk of severe bear markets. This is for a given expected standard deviation.

The effect of random variation in the standard deviation is considered in Chapter 12. Random variation in the standard deviation of the returns has a similar effect as random variation in the expected return. Either type of random variation reduces the sustainability of investment withdrawals. The withdrawals obtained from different discount rates, however, are affected in much the same way by the random variation. It therefore has little effect on the performance of one discount rate relative to another, and on the choice of an RDR.

The RDR selected with an assumed distribution of returns may differ from the one that would be selected using the true distribution. Note, however, that retirees using the rule will nevertheless not go too far astray making retrenchment decisions using the RDR based on a reasonable assumption about the distribution. This is because each year in practice the retrenchment decision is based on the actual value of the investment, which is based on the true distribution of the returns.

3.4 Computations

The simulations are carried out using spreadsheet software such as Excel. An example of an Excel spreadsheet set up to do this is given in the appendix to this chapter. This spreadsheet illustrates how results for the base case simulations given in the next chapter can be obtained for a given discount rate. The conditions for the base case have been discussed earlier and are as follows.

Retirees have just reached age 65 in good health with a limit on their life expectancy of age 110. They are assumed to remain in as good health as can be expected as they grow older so that the limit on their life expectancy remains at age 110. The funding for their living expenses each year is provided only by Social Security and an investment withdrawal at the beginning of the year. There are not any known non-recurring future expenses.

The discount rate is given and for this example is equal to .06. The expected expenses in the initial year to avoid painful retrenchment exceed what is allowed by a discount rate of .06. The initial withdrawal is therefore the largest allowed under these conditions by a discount rate of .06. Real returns on the investment each year are independent drawings from a normal probability distribution with a mean of .07 and a standard deviation of .18. It is assumed that the initial value of the investment is 100 so that future withdrawals are obtained as a percentage of the initial value of the investment.

The spreadsheet is set up to calculate the average withdrawal for 10,000 replications at ages 75, 85, and 95. The proportions of the withdrawals at these ages falling in the ranges from 0 to 1.0, 1.0 to 3.0, 3.0 to 5.0, and 5.0 to 7.0 are also calculated. Further details are given in the appendix along with the spreadsheet.

The spreadsheet is helpful in understanding how the results are obtained. It can also be used to verify the results for a discount rate of .06 at ages 75, 85, and 95 given in the next chapter. Using this spreadsheet as an illustration it is also relatively easy to set up and obtain results for various modifications that may be of interest. It is not necessary to go through and set up such spreadsheets, however, to make use of the results reported in the next chapter and subsequently.

With such a spreadsheet the results in the next chapter can be obtained using only standard Excel software. To obtain 10,000 replications in this way for each case, however, can be time consuming. The simulations can be made more quickly when @Risk or Crystal Ball software is added to Excel. Alternatively, special Macros can be developed for making the simulations using Excel.

The author originally obtained the results for the simulations using Excel augmented with @Risk software. He is indebted to Ahmet Tezel for pointing out that the results can alternatively be obtained using just Excel. This is the procedure in the spreadsheet given in the appendix.

3.5 Conclusions

The next chapter selects the discount rate to use as the RDR assuming the investment is allocated to stocks with real returns like those on the S&P 500. Presumably the expected real return on the S&P 500 over a year depends on its valuation at the beginning of that year as given, for instance, by its dividend yield. And the expected annual real returns move up and down over time with the dividend yield.

Chapter 11 shows, however, that the selection of the RDR is little affected by cyclical changes in the expected annual real return. This is because such changes affect the withdrawals provided by different discount rates in much the same way and therefore have little effect on the performance of one discount rate relative to another. As an approximation it is therefore possible to assume that the RDR does not change over time and that the RDR can be selected by assuming that the returns each year are drawings from the same distribution. This is the distribution when the valuation at the beginning of a year is at a normal level.

To estimate the expected annual real return for a normal valuation various historical averages were examined over appropriate periods for the real returns on the S&P 500. An estimate of .07 was selected at the lower end of these to provide a conservative basis for selecting the RDR in the next chapter.

To estimate the standard deviation of the annual real returns various historical sample standard deviations were examined. This was over historical periods when the returns did not appear to be unduly influenced by high valuations. An estimate of .18 was selected at the upper end of these for the simulations in the next chapter. The effect of random variation over time in the standard deviation of returns is discussed later in Chapter 12.

Thus, in the next chapter the RDR is selected assuming that the real return on the investment each year is a drawing from a normal distribution with a mean of .07 and a standard deviation of .18. A description has also been provided of how annual investment withdrawals are simulated using these returns.

Note

1. This series is given by the Information Site for *Irrational Exuberance* given at http://www.econ.yale.edu/~shiller.

Appendix 3-1

Simulations Using Excel

The spreadsheet shown in Table 3-1 gives the required results for the conditions just specified. The 45 withdrawals for each run of a simulation are calculated by the relations in rows 6 through 50 as shown on the first page. The withdrawals at ages 75, 85, and 95 for 10,000 of these runs are compiled in rows 55 through 10,054 as shown on the second page. The averages and relative frequencies of the 10,000 withdrawals at each age are calculated by the relations in rows 10,056 through 10,061.

The numbers of the rows from 1 to 45 for the 45 withdrawals are given in column A. The first of these withdrawals is made at the beginning of age 65 and the last at the beginning of age 109. The value of these withdrawals is calculated in column B as the smaller of the prior withdrawal or the limit for that row calculated in column D. For this simulation it is assumed that the first withdrawal is equal to its limit given by D6, but in general it could be some given smaller amount.

Column C gives the value of the investment at the beginning of the year. This is before the withdrawal occurs. In the first year this is the given value of 100. In other years it is the prior corresponding value of the investment reduced for the prior withdrawal and adjusted for the return on the investment over the prior year given in column E.

Column D calculates the limit on the withdrawal for the beginning of a year using the Excel function PMT(v, w, x, y, z). This gives the fixed annuity that can be obtained at the beginning of each of w years from an investment of amount x earning a return equal to v. The return v is the discount rate in B2. The number of years of remaining withdrawals w is the total at the beginning given in D2 less the number of the row given in column A plus 1. The amount of the investment x is the negative of the value shown in column C for that row. The negative is used because of the convention that an annuity has a positive value when the value of the investment is input as a negative number.

The argument y is any desired residual value, but in this case that is zero. The argument z is set equal to 1 as this is the convention when the withdrawals are made at the beginning of a year.

The entries in column E are the return on the investment over the year for each row. These are random drawings from a normal distribution with a mean of .07 and a standard deviation of .18. In particular NormInv(Rand(), .07, .18) is the value that has a cumulative probability of Rand() for a normal distribution with a mean of .07 and a standard deviation of .18. Rand() is an independent random drawing for each row made by the software with an equal chance of any value from 0 to 1. As specified these are the required random drawings from a normal distribution with a mean of .07 and a standard deviation of .18.

To run the simulation highlight the area from the blank cell A54 on the upper left to the cell D10,054 on the lower right. From the menu select Data/What-If Analysis/Data Table/Column input cell. Enter [ ] where [ ] designates any blank cell in the spreadsheet and click OK. After what may be a long wait depending on the speed of the computer the value of each run appears in the rows of the table from 55 to 10,154. The averages and the proportions for the frequencies for the simulation with the discount rate are calculated by the relations shown respectively in row 10,056 and rows 10,058/61. A new simulation is made by pressing F9. Setting up far fewer replications can more easily demonstrate the process.

Table 3-1

Simulating Withdrawals Using Excel

	A	B	C	D	E
1					
2	Discount Rate	.06	Total Withdrawals	45	
3					
4	Year	Withdrawal	Investment Value	Withdrawal Limit	Investment Return
5					
6	1	=D6	100	=PMT($B$2,$D$2-A6+1,-C6,0,1)	=NormInv(Rand(),.07,.18)
7	2	=Min(B6,D7)	=(C6-B6)*(1+E6)	=PMT($B$2,$D$2-A7+1,-C7,0,1)	=NormInv(Rand(),.07,.18)
8	3	=Min(B7,D8)	=(C7-B7)*(1+E7)	=PMT($B$2,$D$2-A8+1,-C8,0,1)	=NormInv(Rand(),.07,.18)
- -	- -	- -	- -	- -	- -
16	11	=Min(B15,D16)	=(C15-B15)*(1+E15)	=PMT($B$2,$D$2-A16+1,-C16,0,1)	=NormInv(Rand(),.07,.18)
- -	- -	- -	- -	- -	- -
26	21	=Min(B25,D26)	=(C25-B25)*(1+E25)	=PMT($B$2,$D$2-A26+1,-C26,0,1)	=NormInv(Rand(),.07,.18)
- -	- -	- -	- -	- -	- -
36	31	=Min(B35,D36)	=(C35-B35)*(1+E35)	=PMT($B$2,$D$2-A36+1,-C36,0,1)	=NormInv(Rand(),.07,.18)
- -	- -	- -	- -	- -	- -
50	45	=Min(B49,D50)	=(C49-B49)*(1+E49)	=PMT($B$2,$D$2-A50+1,-C50,0,1)	=NormInv(Rand(),.07,18)

Table 3-1

Simulating Withdrawals Using Excel Continued

	A	B	C	D
51				
52	Replication	Age 75	Age 85	Age 95
53				
54		=B16	=B26	=B36
55	1			
56	2			
- -	- -			
10,054	10,000			
10,055				
10,056	Averages	=Average(B55:B10054)	=Average(C55:C10054)	=Average(D55:D10054)
10,057				
10,058	Prob(5.0<With.<7.0)	See Sample Calculation	- -	- -
10,059	Prob(3.0<With.<5.0)	- -	- -	- -
10,060	Prob(1.0<With.<3.0)	- -	- -	- -
10,061	Prob(0.0<With.<1.0)	- -	- -	- -
10,062				
10,063	Sample Calculation	=(Countif(B55:B10054,		
		"<7.0")-Countif(B55:B10054,		
		"<5.0"))/Count(B55:B10054)		

4

Choosing the Retrenchment Discount Rate

The Retrenchment Rule requires a discount rate. The rate to use is determined by simulating the use of a series of possible rates and selecting the one that gives the best performance. The last two chapters described the procedure for making these simulations, and specified a base case for the probability distribution of the returns each year.

This chapter presents the results of the simulations for the base case, and narrows the choices for the discount rate. Virtually all retirees will want to use a discount rate of at least .08 for the base case conditions. This means that they can withdraw up to about 7.5 percent annually early in retirement to avoid painful retrenchment.

The first step in establishing this proposition is examining the streams of expected withdrawals provided by a series of possible discount rates. The expected withdrawals for a discount rate of .08 are clearly preferred to those for lower discount rates. Lower discount rates might be chosen only if they sufficiently reduce the risk of low withdrawals. It is shown, however, that any such reduction in risk is insufficient to compensate for the lower expected withdrawals.

A discount rate of .10 gives higher expected withdrawals early in retirement than .08, but more risk of low withdrawals later on. Some may be willing to accept this added risk to further reduce earlier painful retrenchment. It is shown, however, that few if any will choose a discount rate of .12 or higher. In any case, choosing .08 is sufficiently high to withdraw significantly more than a reasonably sustainable amount to avoid painful retrenchment.

It is important to keep in mind that the withdrawals allowed by the Retrenchment Rule are those required to avoid painful retrenchment. Examples of painful retrenchment were provided in Chapter 1 in the scenario about Louise Logan. Suppose an unsustainable withdrawal is required to avoid painful retrenchment and allowed by the rule. In such cases any non-essential spending that might also be allowed by the rule should be cut. Such cuts are discussed further at the end of this chapter and in Chapter 8.

Chapter 9 shows that the selection of the RDR is little affected by a shorter horizon. Chapter 11 shows that the selection of the RDR is also little affected by abnormally high or low expected annual real returns due to cyclical variation in stock valuations. Also, Chapter 12 shows that selection of the RDR is little affected by random variation in the volatility each year of the annual returns. Since the RDR is not dependent on these factors it is reasonable to assume that the RDR remains the same over all of retirement. On the other hand Chapter 12 shows that the RDR does increase or decrease with increases or decreases in the annual expected return for a normal stock valuation.

4.1 Expected Withdrawals

Consider a range of discount rates from .04 up to .12. Chapter 2 argued that the initial withdrawal for each discount rate in the simulations to select the RDR should be the largest allowed for that rate. It also showed that the largest allowed withdrawal for a given discount rate is given by an annuity calculation.

The initial withdrawal is the largest fixed annuity that can be obtained from the value of the investment for the longest that the retiree might possibly live. This is when the investment earns a return equal to the discount rate. As it is assumed that the maximum possible age is 110 for those in good health this annuity continues for 45 years for someone at age 65.

Table 4-1 shows the initial withdrawals at age 65 for the possible discount rates. For instance, for a discount rate of .06 the initial withdrawal is 6.1 percent as calculated earlier in Chapter 2. Subsequent withdrawals for each discount rate are the averages obtained from the simulations for 10,000 replications.

Note in Table 4-1 that the expected withdrawals increase at every age when the discount rate rises from .04 to .06, and from .06 to .08. Moreover, for a discount rate of .08 the expected withdrawals are higher than the commonly recommended sustainable initial withdrawal of 4 percent up until age 95. And over the first 15 years the expected withdrawals are significantly higher than 4 percent.

When the discount rate increases above .08 the expected withdrawals increase earlier in retirement, but decline later on. Some retirees might be willing to accept the lower expected withdrawals later on to get the higher expected withdrawals earlier in retirement. Making such a choice depends on their willingness to accept future costs so as to achieve earlier benefits.

Table 4-1

Expected Withdrawals for Selected Discount Rates
Stock Returns for Normal Valuation Each Year

Discount Rate	Expected Withdrawals*							
	65	70	75	80	85	90	95	100
.04	4.6	3.9	3.7	3.5	3.5	3.4	3.4	3.3
.06	6.1	5.0	4.5	4.3	4.1	4.0	3.9	3.8
.08	7.6	6.0	5.2	4.8	4.4	4.2	4.0	3.9
.10	9.2	6.9	5.8	5.0	4.5	4.1	3.8	3.5
.12	10.8	7.6	6.0	4.9	4.2	3.6	3.2	2.8

*Expected withdrawals are as a percentage of the value of the investment at age 65, and are in real terms.

Choosing a discount rate of .08 over a lower one, however, does not require such a tradeoff. In this case, retirees need only prefer a higher stream of declining expected withdrawals to a lower stream at every age. Presumably retirees will prefer the higher stream unless the higher expected withdrawals have a higher risk of low withdrawals. This latter possibility will be investigated shortly.

Suppose retirees require an initial withdrawal of 7.6 percent or higher to avoid painful retrenchment. By choosing a discount rate of .08 they can avoid the additional initial retrenchment required by a lower discount rate. The table shows, however, that significant additional retrenchment is expected to be necessary in the future when withdrawing 7.6 percent initially.

Over the next 10 years the expected withdrawal declines from 7.6 to 5.2 percent. But 10 years is a long time. Instead of needing to quickly make some major decisions about retrenchment there is likely to be a number of years to decide how to cut so as to retain as much satisfaction as possible. Until the cuts are necessary retirees also continue to enjoy their earlier activities.

Suppose they survive for a long time. For ages 80 to 90 the expected withdrawals decline from 4.8 to 4.2 percent; for ages 90 to 100 the decline is from 4.2 to 3.9 percent. Thus, the expected rate of retrenchment slows appreciably later on when cuts will be more difficult to make.

To be sure, those choosing a discount rate of .08 and requiring an initial withdrawal of 7.6 percent must expect that significant retrenchment will be required over the next 10 years. But what is the alternative? Suppose these same retirees choose a discount rate of .06 instead of .08.

In the latter case they must retrench further initially so as to be able to live on a 6.1 percent withdrawal. And over the next 10 years further retrenchment is expected as the expected withdrawal declines from 6.1 to 4.5 percent. Thus, by choosing .06 more retrenchment is required overall from 7.6 to 4.5 instead of 5.2 percent. And about half must occur immediately instead of over the next 10 years. Presumably retirees will prefer retrenching later and less rather than sooner and more. And if retirees choose a discount rate of .04, or just withdraw 4 percent initially, the results are worse than selecting a discount rate of .06.

Clearly, there is a very strong argument for retirees using the Retrenchment Rule with an RDR of at least .08. A lower discount rate might be advisable only if it sufficiently reduces the risk of low withdrawals. The next section shows that it does not.

4.2 Risk of Low Withdrawals

The only way for a discount rate less than .08 to be desirable is if it sufficiently reduces the risk of low withdrawals. This is sufficient to more than compensate for the lower stream of expected withdrawals that it provides in Table 4-1. To investigate this possibility Table 4-2 shows the probability of the withdrawals for different discount rates at selected ages.

In particular, Table 4-2 shows the probabilities at ages 65, 75, 85, and 95 for discount rates of .04, .06, and .08. Probabilities are given for withdrawals of 0, 2, 4, 6, and 8 percent as shown at the top of the table. These values represent ranges for the withdrawals from one percentage point below to one above the stated number.

For example, the probabilities given for a withdrawal of 4 cover withdrawals that are in a range of from 3 to 5 percent. At age 65 for a discount rate of .04 the withdrawal is certain and equal to 4.6 percent. In the table for this case the Withdrawal Probability for 4 is therefore given as 1.00. By age 75 for a discount rate of .04, however, there is a probability of .24 that the withdrawal has declined to a range of from 1 to 3 percent. Thus, in the table the probability for 2 percent is shown as .24, and the probability for 4 percent as .76.

Table 4-2

Withdrawal Probabilities for Selected Discount Rates
Stock Returns for Normal Valuation Each Year

Age	Discount Rate	Withdrawal Probability*				
		8	6	4	2	0
65	.08	1.00	0	0	0	0
	.06	0	1.00	0	0	0
	.04	0	0	1.00	0	0
75	.08	.23	.32	.32	.13	0
	.06	0	.43	.41	.16	0
	.04	0	0	.76	.24	0
85	.08	.17	.23	.30	.27	.03
	.06	0	.35	.36	.27	.02
	.04	0	0	.67	.31	.02
95	.08	.15	.19	.27	.31	.08
	.06	0	.32	.33	.30	.05
	.04	0	0	.64	.33	.03

*Probability that withdrawal is in a range from one above to one below 8, 6, 4, or 2, or from 0 to 1. Withdrawals are in real terms, and as a percentage of the investment at age 65.

There are two very important points to note in Table 4-2. One is the relatively high chance that the withdrawal is in the range of 2 at ages 85 and 95. The other is that reducing the discount rate does not appreciably lower these chances.

Note that the probability for a withdrawal in the range of 2 at ages 85 and 95 is from .27 to .33. Louise Logan in the scenario in Chapter 1 started retirement at age 65 with an investment portfolio of $600,000. For her a withdrawal in the range of 2 is an amount in real terms to cover annual expenses of from $6,000 to $18,000. Including her annual Social Security of $20,000 this would mean a reasonable chance that she will be required to live on from $26,000 to $38,000 a year if she survives to age 85 or longer.

Clearly it is necessary to deal with this risk. The first inclination is to deal with it by retrenching initially. The Retrenchment Rule shows, however, that this inclination is incorrect. Retrenching enough even to live on a 4.6 percent withdrawal initially by using a discount rate of .04 provides little reduction in the risk.

In fact, the table shows that lowering the discount rate below .08 can increase the risk of a withdrawal being in the range of 2. At age 95 lowering the discount rate from .08 to .06 does provide some help. The probability of a 2 percent withdrawal declines slightly from .31 to .30, and the probability of 0 percent from .08 to .05. That, however, is still a large amount of risk.

Moreover, to get even this small benefit from choosing .06 it is necessary to survive to age 95. And it is necessary to give up the benefits of a discount rate of .08 earlier in retirement, and also later on when returns have been more favorable. Note by choosing .08 that the chances of continuing to withdraw 7 percent or more at ages 65, 75, 85, and 95 are 1.00, .23, .17, and .15. When choosing a discount rate of .06 there is no chance of these higher withdrawals.

Thus, presumably almost everyone will choose an RDR of at least .08. A discount rate of .06 offers a small chance of higher withdrawals late in retirement when investment returns have been unfavorable. But this benefit appears too small to compensate for the lower withdrawals that a discount rate of .06 provides otherwise. In general, lower discount rates than .08 require more retrenchment than is desirable to avoid future retrenchment.

Table 4-2 shows that initial retrenchment is not effective in reducing the risk of low withdrawals. This is retrenchment in excess of that required by an RDR of

.08. Nevertheless, retirees do need to do something to reduce their risk of low withdrawals later in retirement. What should they do?

One possibility is to include fixed income issues in their portfolio. Fixed incomes, however, turn out not to help. What is helpful is investing a large portion of their portfolio in a lifetime annuity, and seeking part-time employment. These possibilities are considered in the next chapter.

4.3 Stronger Discounting

Virtually all retirees will want to use a discount rate of at least .08 under the conditions of these simulations. But what is the largest discount rate that any retiree might choose? This section argues that some may choose a discount rate of .10, but few if any will choose a discount rate as high as .12.

To choose .10 they must decide whether accepting additional risk of low withdrawals later in retirement is worth earlier avoiding additional retrenchment. If they use .08 as the discount rate they can avoid making such a decision. But using .08 means that some retirees who are more willing to heavily discount the future may be retrenching more than is optimal for them early in retirement.

Table 4-1 shows that choosing .10 instead of .08 provides a significant increase in the expected withdrawals over the first 10 years. The cost of these increases is some reduction in the expected withdrawals starting at age 90. The chances of surviving long enough to experience any of these reductions, however, is somewhat less than even. Nevertheless, these reductions are from expected withdrawals that have already declined significantly with a .08 discount rate. They are also coming at an age when retrenching may be more difficult.

Based on these considerations some retirees may prefer the stream for a discount rate of .08 to that for .10. Others may prefer the stream for .10 to that for .08. Still others may be indifferent between the two streams.

In contrast, the cost of choosing a discount rate of .12 over .10 is more significant. The declines start at age 80 and by age 90 have become fairly appreciable. And retirees are more likely than not to survive long enough to experience at least some of these declines. Few if any retirees appear likely to choose .12 over .10 and none will do so decisively.

Table 4-3 compares the risk of low withdrawals for discount rates of .10 and .12 to those for .06 and .08. The probabilities for .06 and .08 are the same as those shown in Table 4-2. Consider the chances of withdrawals in the range of 2 or 0 percent at age 95. These increase from .31 and .08 to .34 and .14 respectively when the discount rate increases from .08 to .10. Some might be willing to tolerate this increased risk to get the increased expected withdrawals early in retirement for .10. But few if any seem likely to accept the further increase to .38 and .23 required by a discount rate of .12.

Tests of the sustainability of investment withdrawals including tests in some financial planning software frequently assume that the initial withdrawal continues until the portfolio runs out of funds. But this is effectively assuming that retirees are using the Retrenchment Rule with an infinite RDR. Since even a discount rate of .12 seems too high such an assumption is highly unreasonable. To see that allowing an initial withdrawal to continue until the portfolio runs out of funds is implicitly assuming an infinite RDR consider the following argument.

Increasing the RDR reflects decreasing concern about having enough to make withdrawals in the future. An increasing portion of the investment is therefore available to cover the prior withdrawal. When the RDR becomes as large as possible, or infinite, there is no concern about having enough for future withdrawals. All of the investment is available to cover the prior withdrawal. But this is just what happens when the initial withdrawal continues until the portfolio runs out of funds. Thus, if retirees continue to make their initial withdrawal until their portfolio runs out of funds they are using the Retrenchment Rule. But this is an extreme version of the rule with an infinite RDR.

Testing the sustainability of initial withdrawals using an RDR that is too high gives misleading results. Withdrawals early in retirement will appear sustainable even when they are not. Using an infinite RDR, for instance, withdrawals will always appear sustainable early in retirement. But even retirees who are not using the Retrenchment Rule will reduce their withdrawals if they believe too much risk is developing that they will run out of funds. Such precautionary retrenchment needs to be reflected in simulated withdrawals as it reduces sustainability.

Table 4-3

Withdrawal Probabilities for Selected Discount Rates
Stock Returns for Normal Valuation Each Year

Age	Discount Rate	Withdrawal Probability*					
		10	8	6	4	2	0
75	.12	.16	.18	.26	.28	.12	0
	.10	.12	.20	.27	.29	.12	0
	.08	0	.23	.32	.32	.13	0
	.06	0	0	.43	.41	.16	0
85	.12	.08	.09	.14	.26	.36	.07
	.10	.08	.12	.18	.27	.30	.05
	.08	0	.17	.23	.30	.27	.03
	.06	0	0	.35	.36	.27	.02
95	.12	.06	.06	.09	.18	.38	.23
	.10	.06	.09	.14	.23	.34	.14
	.08	0	.15	.19	.27	.31	.08
	.06	0	0	.32	.33	.30	.05

*Probability that withdrawal is in a range from one above to one below 10, 8, 6, 4, 2, or 0 to 1. Withdrawals are in real terms, and as a percentage of the investment at age 65.

4.4 Cutting Non-Essentials

Earlier analysis argued that virtually all retirees will want to use a discount rate of at least .08 and withdraw at least 7.6 percent to avoid painful retrenchment. But suppose a 7.6 percent withdrawal is necessary to cover existing expenses, but not all of these expenses are essential. The non-essential expenses are providing satisfaction, but are not really sufficiently vital to be painful to eliminate.

In such a case the non essential expenses should be eliminated even when they can be covered by a 7.6 percent withdrawal. The reason is that withdrawing to cover the non-essentials is reducing the value of the investment. A lower value for the investment increases the possibility that more drastic retrenchment will be required in the future for essential expenses. Moreover, the Retrenchment Rule is likely to require that the non essential expenses be eliminated anyway in the near future. Thus, by failing to cut the non-essentials there is little to gain and much to lose.

On the other hand, suppose that their withdrawal required to cover expenses is reasonably sustainable instead of being as large as allowed. This causes a significant shift in the costs and benefits of eliminating non-essentials. There is now a significant benefit to covering the non-essentials because it is now likely that this spending can be sustained. Also, there is little cost to covering the non-essentials because doing so causes only a slight rise in the sustainability risk for the essential spending.

When expenses can be covered by a reasonably sustainable withdrawal there is an argument for covering existing expenses that are not painful to eliminate. This is assuming they are providing a reasonable degree of satisfaction even if they cannot be deemed as essential. Chapter 8 shows how the Retrenchment Rule can be used to determine when this is true.

4.5 Conclusions

Under the base case conditions virtually all retirees will prefer a discount rate of .08 to lower discount rates. A discount rate of .08 gives higher expected withdrawals over all of retirement and only a slightly higher risk of very low withdrawals late in retirement. With an RDR of .08 retirees in good health at age 65 can withdraw at least 7.5 percent for the coming year to avoid painful retrenchment.

Some retirees may prefer a discount rate of .10 to .08. This is to further reduce earlier painful retrenchment at the cost of increased risk of low withdrawals later in retirement. It appears, however, that few if any will choose a discount rate as high as .12 for their RDR. A discount rate this high causes too large an increase in the risk of low withdrawals late in retirement.

Unless the withdrawal is reasonably sustainable cuts that are difficult to make, but are not really sufficiently vital to be painful, should be made. This is because these cuts in non-essential expenses will likely soon have to be made anyway. And the increase in the withdrawal to cover these non-essentials is increasing the risk of further cuts to essential expenses later in retirement.

5

Reducing Retrenchment Risk

The last chapter showed that withdrawing significantly more than a reasonably sustainable amount is justified to avoid painful retrenchment. Additional retrenchment does not reduce the future risk of low withdrawals enough to warrant the earlier reduction in standard of living. But how should the risk of future low withdrawals be reduced when further retrenchment is not cost effective at doing so?

For those in good health this chapter advises doing so by annuitizing a large portion of the portfolio and seeking part-time employment. The situation of those who are not in good health is considered in Chapter 9. Even if only minimal part-time earnings are achieved this strategy significantly reduces the risk. If finding part-time work is more successful almost all of the risk of very low withdrawals can be eliminated.

When only minimal part-time earnings are achieved there are some costs to the annuitizing. There is some reduction in the chances of sustaining the initial withdrawal. And there is some reduction in the estate. If the search for part-time work is more successful, however, there is no reduction in the chances of sustaining the initial withdrawal. And there is an increase in the value of the estate despite the annuitizing.

There is a cost to looking for part-time work and undertaking the work itself. And there could be a reduction in the chances of sustaining the initial withdrawal, and a loss to the estate if the search is not successful. Those who have not saved enough for retirement, however, must expect to pay a penalty. The penalty for this strategy appears less onerous than the costs of the alternatives.

The first step in this chapter is to show the benefit of part-time earnings. The next step is to show the effect of annuitizing a portion of the investment. Another possible way to reduce the risk of low withdrawals is to allocate a portion of the investment to fixed income issues.

This chapter shows that allocating to fixed incomes is inferior to annuitizing when the initial withdrawal is unsustainable. Fixed incomes and annuitizing are more competitive, however, when the initial withdrawal is reasonably sustainable. For reasonably sustainable initial withdrawals allocating to fixed incomes may be preferable due to the greater flexibility.

A simple way to undertake a limited amount of annuitizing is to defer the start of Social Security. The last section of this chapter shows that the rate on the annuity effectively obtained by such deferral can be attractive. Simulations that include the deferral of Social Security show meaningful reduction in the risk of low withdrawals. The improvement in the withdrawals appears to be sufficient to outweigh the lower future investment values caused by deferring the start of Social Security.

Some individuals begin retirement with their retirement assets largely in the form of a pension. Others may be largely dependent on their investments, but also have a pension. In this latter case retirees are already partially annuitized. The next chapter considers how to deal with these situations.

5.1 Part-Time Earnings

In the scenario in Chapter 1 illustrating painful retrenchment, Louise Logan wanted to keep on working. But she was forced to retire by a cost cutting program where she worked. And at her age she was unable to find something else that was suitable.

This is a common problem for those who have not saved enough for retirement. They plan to keep on working, but that turns out to be impossible. For those at a normal retirement age or somewhat younger full time work may be difficult to find, even if economic conditions are reasonably good. Finding part-time work on a seasonal or casual basis is much easier. These part-time earnings can provide a meaningful improvement in the prospects for the standard of living over retirement. This improvement will now be demonstrated by including some possible earnings in the simulations for the future investment withdrawals.

The simulations so far have assumed a constant future stream of expected withdrawals is required to cover the existing standard of living. The components of this constant real stream are equal to the expected expenses to cover the existing standard of living for the coming year less the annual Social Security benefit. The Retrenchment Rule requires retrenchment when the present value of this stream using the RDR as the rate of interest exceeds the value of the investment.

When there are part-time earnings these must be deducted from the expected expenses along with the Social Security to get the expected withdrawal as discussed in Chapter 2. The earnings, however, continue for only a relatively short time after which just the Social Security is deducted from the expected expenses. To get the present value of the future expected withdrawals an additional step is now required.

The expected earnings are projected into the future for an expected number of years. The present value of this stream is calculated using the RDR as the rate of interest. This present value is deducted from the present value of the expected withdrawals calculated before. This remainder is then compared to the value of the investment to determine whether retrenchment is required. Doing so is equivalent to adding the present value of the earnings to the value of the investment and determining whether the investment value after this increase is sufficient to provide the stream of expected withdrawals without the earnings.

When included in the simulations the receipt of additional funds in the future could affect the discount rate selected for the RDR. The simulations that have just been made should be rerun including the possible earnings to see if this changes the RDR that is selected. When this is done, however, the additional funds do not significantly affect the choice. An RDR of .08 is therefore used again for the tests.

Two other modifications are also required in the simulations. In the years in which the earnings are expected to be received they are added to the value of the portfolio at the beginning of the year. Also the withdrawals that are obtained in the simulations should now be viewed as those from the investment and the earnings. Including the earnings in the spreadsheet for simulating the withdrawals is discussed in Appendix 5-2 of this chapter.

To see how such earnings might affect the results two possibilities are considered. One is a minimal level that might be achieved for part-time earnings, and the other is a maximal level. The minimal level assumes earnings equal to 2 percent of the initial investment in real terms each year for five years.

The maximal level is 4 percent for 10 years. For Louise in the scenario of Chapter 1 these annual earnings would be $12,000 for five years or $24,000 for 10 years.

Earlier it was assumed that Louise was age 65 and had started Social Security. If Louise had just reached age 65 at the beginning of 2010 her full retirement age for Social Security would be age 66. Upon reaching the full retirement age earnings have no effect on Social Security benefits. For the prior year in 2010, however, the benefits would be reduced $1 for every $2 of earnings above $14,160.[1]

For the 2 percent earnings assumption the earnings would have no effect on her benefits for the first year in 2010, or subsequently. There would, however, be a significant reduction in her benefits for the first year for the 4 percent earnings assumption. Under the Social Security rules, however, this reduction is compensated for by an increase in her annual benefits when she reaches her full retirement age. Any net loss therefore appears small, and will be ignored.[2]

Table 5-1 shows the effect of the earnings on the future withdrawals when the initial withdrawal is 7.5 percent and the RDR is .08. Results are provided at ages 75, 85, and 95 for the expected value of the withdrawal, the probabilities that the withdrawal is in different ranges, and the median value of the investment. All values are in real terms as a percentage of the value of the investment at age 65.

The top row at each age shows the results without any part-time earnings. These are the same as the results reported in the tables in the last chapter for a discount rate of .08. As earlier there is a substantial risk of very low withdrawals especially at ages 85 and 95.

The minimal effort with respect to part-time earnings provides a meaningful reduction in this risk. The maximal effort provides a significant reduction. With the minimal effort the chances that the withdrawal is 3 percent or less at ages 75, 85, and 95 drop respectively from .13, .30, and .39 to .09, .25, and .34. For the maximal effort the decline is to .01, .13, and .22.

Besides reducing the risk of very low withdrawals the part-time earnings also significantly increase the chances of higher withdrawals. For the minimal effort the chances that the withdrawals will be above 7 percent increase at ages 75, 85, and 95 respectively from .23, .17, and .15 to .33, .25, and .22. For the maximal effort the increase is to .61, .46, and .41.

Note with the maximal effort that there is now a better than .40 chance of sustaining the initial standard of living over all of retirement. This is up from chances of less than .20 of doing so without the extra earnings. And it is in addition to reducing the chances from .39 to .22 that 3 percent or less can be withdrawn at age 95. These benefits should certainly be sufficient to get the attention of those who have to withdraw as much as 7.5 percent to avoid retrenchment. By generating some part-time earnings they can substantially improve their prospects.

Table 5-1

Effect of Part-Time Earnings for 7.5% Withdrawal Age 65

Stock Returns for Normal Valuation Each Year RDR .08

Age	Earn	Earn Years	Expected Withdrawal	Withdrawal Probability*					Median Portfolio
				8	6	4	2	0	
75	0	0	5.23	.23	.32	.32	.13	0	85
	2	5	5.65	.33	.32	.26	.09	0	94
	4	10	6.60	.61	.24	.14	.01	0	126
85	0	0	4.41	.17	.23	.30	.27	.03	77
	2	5	4.81	.25	.23	.27	.23	.02	88
	4	10	5.75	.46	.20	.21	.12	.01	121
95	0	0	3.98	.15	.19	.27	.31	.08	72
	2	5	4.37	.22	.20	.24	.28	.06	84
	4	10	5.26	.41	.17	.20	.19	.03	123

*Probability that withdrawal is in a range from one above to one below 8, 6, 4, or 2, or from 0 to 1. Withdrawals and median portfolio values are in real terms, and as a percentage of the investment at age 65.

Table 5-1 also shows significant improvement in what happens on average. This is shown by the change in the expected withdrawals. Without any extra earnings the initial withdrawal of 7.5 percent is expected to decline at ages 75,

85, and 95 to respectively 5.2, 4.4, and 4.0 percent. With the minimal effort these lower expected withdrawals rise to 5.7, 4.8, and 4.4 percent. With the maximal effort the rise is to 6.6, 5.8, and 5.3 percent. For Louise in the earlier scenario the maximal effort reduces the expected retrenchment over the first 20 years to $500 per year, and $300 per year thereafter.

Finally, the table also shows significant benefits in increasing the future median value of the portfolio available for an estate. Increasing their estate may not be a significant concern for those facing major retrenchment. Nevertheless, it is worth noting that these increases can offset much or all of the declines caused by the annuitizing considered in the next section. Also, these investment values may be needed later, not just for an estate, but to cover emergencies as discussed in Chapter7.

5.2 Annuitizing

John Ameriks, Robert Veres, and Mark Warshawsky (2001) showed that annuitizing a portion of an investment improves the sustainability of a 4.5 percent initial withdrawal. It will now be shown that there are significant benefits to annuitizing for those who require much higher initial withdrawals. When combined with part-time earnings annuitizing makes it possible to reduce much of the risk of very low withdrawals later in retirement.

Suppose only a minimal level of part-time earnings is achieved. Nevertheless, if 50 percent of the initial portfolio is annuitized the risk of very low withdrawals can be reduced to that obtained with the maximal level of part-time earnings without annuitizing. If the maximal level of part-time earnings is achieved almost all of the risk of very low withdrawals can be eliminated.

The most familiar and widely available lifetime annuities are those with fixed nominal benefits over the lifetime of the beneficiary. The rates on these annuities depend primarily on the probability of survival for the beneficiary and the yield on long-term Treasury issues at the time of purchase. Rates are available on the Web for such annuities depending on the age and gender of the beneficiary, and the level of Treasury yields at the time.[3]

The withdrawals in the last chapter were assumed to begin at a time of reasonably normal conditions in financial markets. As this is written in 2010 a recent time with normal conditions is mid 2007. This was before the start of the major recession late in 2007 and the credit crisis of 2008.

At mid 2007 inflation was about 2.5 percent and the yield on a 20 year Treasury about 5.25 percent. The annuity rate quoted for a 65 year old woman at that time was about 7.5 percent. This rate gives as a percentage of the purchase price the nominal benefit payable at the beginning of each year starting soon after the annuity is purchased. Corresponding to the scenario for the 65 year old Louise Logan in Chapter 1 a 7.5 percent rate will be used to simulate the benefits of an annuity in the simulations.

Due to shorter life expectancy the rate for a 65 year old man is about 50 basis points higher. Very early in 2010 inflation was less than at mid 2007 and the yield on a 20 year Treasury about 75 basis points less. The annuity rate for a 65 year old woman at that time had declined to about 7.0 percent. As a contrast, the effect of this lower annuity rate and lower initial inflation on the results of the simulations will also be indicated.

To simulate buying an annuity it is assumed that 25 or 50 percent of the investment is sold. The proceeds are then used to buy an annuity with a rate of 7.5 percent. This results in the receipt at the beginning of each year of a corresponding fixed nominal benefit.

These benefits are incorporated into the Retrenchment Rule and the simulations in a similar way to the earnings just considered. The difference is that the annuity benefits are in nominal terms and have to be adjusted for inflation. The method used to take inflation into account is discussed in Appendix 5-1 of this chapter. Appendix 5-3 discusses how nominal annuity benefits are included in the spreadsheet for simulating the withdrawals.

Suppose that 25 or 50 percent of the investment is annuitized initially, and that either the minimal or maximal levels of part-time earnings are achieved. Table 5-2 shows the effect of the annuitizing on the results given in Table 5-1.[4] To facilitate comparison the results from Table 5-1 are shown in the rows for Stocks/Annuity equal to 100/0. Results without either the earnings or the annuitizing are given in Table 5-1.

Table 5-2

Effect of Annuitizing and Part-Time Earnings for 7.5% Withdrawal

Base Case Stock Returns and Inflation*, Annuity 7.5%, RDR .08

Age	Earn	Earn Years	Stocks/ Annuity	Expected Withdrawal	Withdrawal Probability**					Median Portfolio
					8	6	4	2	0	
75	2	5	100/0	5.65	.33	.32	.26	.09	0	94
			75/25	5.74	.29	.38	.29	.04	0	76
			50/50	5.77	.20	.52	.27	.01	0	58
	4	10	100/0	6.60	.61	.24	.14	.01	0	126
			50/50	6.88	.64	.30	.06	0	0	86
85	2	5	100/0	4.81	.25	.23	.27	.23	.02	88
			75/25	4.96	.20	.30	.33	.18	0	72
			50/50	5.08	.14	.38	.37	.11	0	58
	4	10	100/0	5.75	.46	.20	.21	.12	.01	121
			50/50	6.11	.46	.28	.22	.04	0	89
95	2	5	100/0	4.57	.22	.20	.24	.28	.06	84
			75/25	4.51	.18	.24	.29	.28	.01	70
			50/50	4.67	.12	.32	.35	.21	0	60
	4	10	100/0	5.26	.41	.17	.20	.19	.03	123
			50/50	5.65	.40	.23	.25	.12	0	92

*Inflation simulated as specified in Appendix 5-1 with initial inflation of .025. Annual stock returns for normal valuation except adjusted for unexpected inflation each year as specified in Appendix 5-1.

**Same as Table 5-1.

Annuitizing a large portion of the investment could change the results of the simulations sufficiently for different discount rates to change the choice of the RDR. Running simulations like those in the last chapter for different discount rates, however, shows little change with the earnings and annuitization. With the earnings and annuitization for a given discount rate the future expected withdrawals are higher and there is significantly less risk of low withdrawals. Relative to each other, however, the results for different discount rates look very much the same as before. The argument for choosing an RDR of .08 when half of the portfolio is annuitized is just about the same as when none of it is annuitized. In fact, the next chapter shows that the argument for using an RDR of .08 remains about the same even if retirees begin retirement with just a pension.

Suppose that 50 percent of the investment is annuitized initially and the minimal level of earnings is achieved. The chances that the withdrawals are less than 3 percent at ages 75, 85, and 95 are then reduced respectively from .09, .25, and .34 to .01, 11, and .21. After the annuitizing the risk of very low withdrawals has become just about the same as when the maximal level of earnings is achieved without any annuitizing. And the expected withdrawals are also increased at all ages.

Suppose that 50 percent of the investment is annuitized when the maximal level of earnings is achieved. In this case, the chances that the withdrawals are less than 3 percent are reduced respectively from .01, .13, and .22 to .00, .04, and .12. There is less reduction in risk than when only the minimal level of earnings is achieved. But with the maximal earnings there is less risk to reduce, and almost all of the risk of very low withdrawals has been eliminated. There is also a significant increase in the expected withdrawals at all ages.

Louise Logan in the scenario in Chapter 1 started retirement at age 65 with an investment portfolio of $600,000. For her a 3 percent withdrawal is $18,000 in real terms to cover annual expenses. Including her annual Social Security of $20,000 this is a total of $38,000.

Suppose she follows the Retrenchment Rule with an RDR of .08 and doesn't work part-time or annuitize. Table 5-1 shows that her chances of having to live on less than $38,000 at ages 75, 85, and 95 are respectively .13, .30, and .39. If she annuitizes half of her initial portfolio and only achieves minimal earnings these chances drop to .01, .11 and .21. If she achieves the maximal earnings these chances decline further to .00, .04, and .12. Almost all of her risk of having to live on less than $38,000 a year has been eliminated.

These results from Table 5.2 assume an annuity rate of 7.5 percent and initial inflation of 2.5 percent. Suppose now as in early 2010 that both the annuity rate and inflation are lower. In particular suppose that the annuity rate is 7.0 percent and initial inflation is 1.5 percent. In this case for the minimal earnings the risk is the same at ages 75 and 85, and increases by only .01 at age 95. For the maximal earnings there is a .01 increase in the risk at both ages 85 and 95.

Why does annuitizing increase the future expected value of the withdrawals and reduce the risk of low withdrawals? The future real value of the annuity benefits is at risk to future inflation. But the volatility of future inflation is far less than the volatility of the future real returns on stocks. The annuity benefits provide a lower expected real return than stocks. But the lower volatility of the real return on the annuity is sufficient to more than compensate for this disadvantage when the annuity replaces some of the stocks in the portfolio.

Replacing stocks with fixed income issues also reduces volatility at the cost of a lower expected real return. For survivors, however, a lifetime annuity effectively has a higher expected real return due to the mortality of others in the pool. Thus, buying a lifetime annuity gives better results later in retirement than investing in fixed income issues. A later section of this chapter shows the results when the portfolio is allocated to fixed income issues instead of purchasing an annuity. First, however, the costs of annuitizing need to be considered.

5.3 Costs of Annuitizing

The annuitizing clearly provides significant benefits in reducing the risk of low withdrawals and increasing the expected value of the future withdrawals. There are, however, some costs to these benefits. If only the minimal earnings are achieved the annuitizing causes some reduction in the chances that the initial withdrawal can be sustained in the future. Also, the annuitizing reduces the median value of the future portfolio. If the maximal earnings are achieved, however, the median portfolio after both the earnings and annuitizing is higher than it would be otherwise.

Without the annuitizing the chances that the withdrawals will be above 7 percent at ages 75, 85, and 95 are respectively .33, .25, and .22. With 50 percent annuitizing and the minimal earnings these chances decline to .20, .14, and .12. Thus, for the minimal earnings the annuitizing reduces the chances of both higher and lower withdrawals. This is reasonable because annuitizing has the positive effect of reducing volatility, but also the negative effect of reducing the expected return on the investment.

Now suppose that the maximal level of earnings is achieved with 50 percent annuitizing. Note in this case that the annuitizing has little effect on the chances that the withdrawals will be above 7 percent in the future. With the maximal earnings the effect of the annuitizing is largely just to reduce the risk of low withdrawals.

Whatever level of earnings is achieved the annuitizing causes a significant reduction in the median portfolio value available for an estate. Suppose only the minimal level of earnings is achieved. With 50 percent annuitizing the median portfolio at ages 75, 85, and 95 then declines respectively from 94, 88, and 84 to 58, 58, and 60. For the maximal level of earnings the decline is from 126, 121, and 123 to 86, 89, and 92.

These reductions are significant costs for the annuitizing. But they seem acceptable to reduce the risk of low withdrawals. But retirees will also want to consider how the part-time earnings and annuitizing together affect how much will be available for their estate.

When the earnings and annuitizing are considered together the median portfolio values still decrease when only the minimal earnings are achieved. When the maximal earnings are achieved, however, the median portfolio values increase. For the minimum earnings the median values at ages 75, 85, and 95 decline respectively from 85, 77, and 72 to 58, 58, and 60. For the maximal earnings, however, there is an increase to 86, 89, and 92. Thus, retirees need not feel that overall such a strategy to improve their withdrawals is necessarily causing a cost to their heirs. If they succeed in achieving a good level of part-time earnings their bequest may increase.

5.4 Fixed Income Issues

The annual real returns on fixed income issues have significantly less volatility than those for stocks. This benefit, of course, comes at the cost of their much lower expected return. Chapter 3 calculated the average and sample standard deviation for the annual real returns on the S&P 500 over 1960-2009. Over the same period the average and standard deviation of the annual real returns for intermediate government issues are less than half those for the S&P 500. In particular, for intermediate governments the average and standard deviation are respectively .03 and .07 versus .07 and .17 for the S&P 500. For long-term governments the average increases somewhat from .03 to .035 and the standard deviation increases from .07 to .12.

Will the positive effect on the withdrawals of the lower volatility more than compensate for the negative effect of the lower mean return? The only way to tell is to run the simulations with a portion of the portfolio allocated to fixed incomes and compare the results. These simulations will also show whether allocating part of the portfolio to fixed incomes gives better or worse results than annuitizing.

To run these simulations it is assumed that the portfolio is rebalanced to a given allocation at the beginning of each year. Any transaction fees or taxes that might be payable to do so are ignored. Some variation in the allocation as conditions change might give somewhat better results. The results with a fixed allocation are sufficiently inferior to annuitizing, however, to show that varying the allocation is not going to make fixed incomes preferable.

The fixed incomes used in the simulations are the intermediate government issues mentioned earlier. In particular, these are the issues whose returns are reported in the *SBBI Yearbook* (2010). Using instead the returns on long-term government or corporate issues reported there give slightly worse results.

At times since 1960 the real returns on stocks and fixed income issues have tended to increase and decrease together. In particular, fixed incomes like stocks had a bear market in the major inflation of the 1970s. They both also had a bull market in the recovery from that inflation in the 1980s. Over these periods the abnormal returns on stocks and fixed income issues tended to reinforce each other instead of being offsetting.

On the other hand, fixed income issues experienced a bull market over both of the major bear markets for stocks in the 2000s. In these cases, fixed income issues were of more help in limiting the negative effects of the declines in stocks. With the contrasting experience over these different episodes since 1960 there may be little correlation either positive or negative on average for the entire period. And this turns out to be the case.

Suppose the real returns on the S&P 500 each year are regressed on those for intermediate governments over 1960-2009. The relation is only mildly positive, and does not differ from zero with statistical significance. It will therefore be assumed that the returns on the S&P 500 and intermediate governments each year in the simulations are independent drawings.[5]

Chapter 3 noted that the expected real return on the S&P 500 over a year should in theory move up and down with its valuation at the beginning of the year. It also assumed that the valuation for the S&P 500 is given by its dividend yield. Despite this cyclical variation, however, investment withdrawals can be simulated by drawings from the same distribution each year as an approximation under the following conditions.

These conditions are that the withdrawals start when the valuation is normal and that the distribution of returns each year is the distribution of returns for a year starting with a normal valuation. Chapter 3 assumed that this distribution could be estimated by the annual real returns over the period 1960-2009. The basis for this assumption was that this period started and ended with years that had a normal valuation at the beginning of the year.

For fixed income issues the valuation at the beginning of a year is given by the level of real interest rates. And real interest rates are indicated by the yields available on TIPS. As TIPS have been available only since 1997, however, a proxy must be used to include earlier years in comparisons. As a proxy it is assumed that the valuation of fixed income issues at the beginning of a year is given by the real return obtained by rolling over a series of short-term T Bills over the prior year. These returns are given in the *SBBI Yearbook*.

As for the S&P 500 the distribution of real returns on intermediates over a year is needed when the prior valuation for intermediates is at a normal level at the beginning of that year. The same period of 1960-2009 can be used for this estimate as for the S&P 500. This is because the prior valuation of the intermediates for the first and last year of this period is approximately normal just as for the S&P 500.

Based on the average and sample standard deviation over 1960-2009 it will be assumed that the annual real return for intermediate governments is normally distributed with a mean of .03 and a standard deviation of .07. As earlier the annual real returns on the S&P 500 are assumed to be normally distributed with a mean of .07, and a standard deviation of .18. Appendix 5-4 shows how allocating a portion of the investment to fixed income issues is included in the spreadsheet.

Table 5-3 is the same as Table 5-2 except instead of annuitizing 25 or 50 percent of the initial portfolio 25 or 50 percent is allocated to fixed income issues at the beginning of each year. Comparison of the two tables shows that the fixed incomes perform somewhat better early in retirement. But at age 95 annuitizing is far superior. In fact, at age 95 the results are better if the entire portfolio is allocated just to stocks instead of including any fixed income issues.

Note with the minimum earnings that a 25 percent allocation to fixed incomes reduces the chances that the withdrawal is less than 3 percent only from .34 to .33 at age 95. And this very slight benefit is clearly not worth the costs that accompany it. These are the reduced value of the expected withdrawal and the reduced median value of the portfolio.

If 50 instead of 25 percent is allocated to fixed incomes the chances of the low withdrawals increase from .34 to .39 instead of showing even a slight decline. And the declines in the expected withdrawal and median portfolio value are far worse. In contrast, when half of the portfolio is annuitized initially the risk of low withdrawals declines from .34 to .21. And the expected value of the withdrawal increases instead of declining significantly. Moreover, the median portfolio value declines only about as much as when the allocation to fixed incomes is only 25 percent.

Table 5-3

Effect of Fixed Incomes and Part-Time Earnings for 7.5% Withdrawal
Investment Returns for Normal Valuation Each Year* RDR .08

Age	Earn Years	Earn	Stocks/ IntGovts	Expected Withdrawal	Withdrawal Probability** 8	6	4	2	0	Median Portfolio
75	2	5	100/0	5.65	.33	.32	.26	.09	0	94
			75/25	5.87	.33	.38	.25	.04	0	88
			50/50	5.94	.28	.47	.24	.01	0	48
	4	10	100/0	6.60	.61	.24	.14	.01	0	126
			50/50	7.04	.72	.24	.04	0	0	111
85	2	5	100/0	4.81	.25	.23	.27	.23	.02	88
			75/25	4.92	.22	.26	.32	.20	0	72
			50/50	4.73	.15	.26	.42	.17	0	27
	4	10	100/0	5.75	.46	.20	.21	.12	.01	121
			50/50	6.01	.44	.27	.25	.04	0	84
95	2	5	100/0	4.57	.22	.20	.24	.28	.06	84
			75/25	4.34	.19	.20	.28	.30	.03	57
			50/50	3.90	.10	.16	.35	.38	.01	14
	4	10	100/0	5.26	.41	.17	.20	.19	.03	123
			50/50	5.18	.33	.19	.30	.18	0	56

*Returns on fixed income issues are based on those for intermediate government issues as reported in the *SBBI Yearbook* for the same period as for stocks. Real return for intermediates each year is independently and normally distributed with a mean of .03 and a standard deviation of .07. Stock returns are the same as for Table 5-1.
**Same as Table 5-1.

When the maximum earnings are achieved allocating 50 percent to fixed incomes reduces the chances that the withdrawal is less than 3 percent at age 95 from .22 to .18. But there is also a small decline in the expected withdrawal. In contrast, if half the portfolio is annuitized initially the chances of the low withdrawal decline from .22 to .12. And there is a significant increase in the expected withdrawal. Moreover, the median portfolio is 92 percent of its initial value, whereas for the allocation to fixed incomes it is only 56 percent.

At age 75 either the fixed incomes or the annuitizing eliminates any chance that the withdrawals will be less than 3 percent. Otherwise, at age 75 the fixed incomes show somewhat better performance as they increase the expected withdrawals somewhat more and cause less of a decline in portfolio value.

The primary objective, however, is to reduce the risk of low withdrawals later in retirement. Annuitizing a large portion of the portfolio initially does this, but allocating to fixed incomes does not. Fixed incomes, however, are attractive for those who are not in good health at the beginning of retirement and are only concerned about the shorter run favorable effects of fixed incomes. This issue is discussed in Chapter 9.

The simulations so far, however, have assumed that the initial withdrawal is at the upper end of those allowed by the Retrenchment Rule, and therefore unsustainable. The question remains as to the relative performance of annuitizing and fixed income issues when the initial withdrawal is reasonably sustainable. That question is considered in the next section.

5.5 Sustainable Withdrawals

Suppose retirees have saved enough to require only a 4 percent withdrawal to cover expenses instead of 7.5 percent. Table 5-4 compares the effect of allocating 25 percent of the portfolio to intermediate governments to annuitizing 25 percent when the initial withdrawal is 4 percent. For this reasonably sustainable initial withdrawal these two strategies are much more competitive with each other than when the initial withdrawal is unsustainable.

Both strategies increase the expected withdrawals somewhat at all ages. And they both provide some reduction in the risk of low withdrawals at all ages. The cost of this improvement in the withdrawals is some reduction in the median value of the portfolio available for an estate. The annuitizing causes somewhat more of a reduction in the portfolio early in retirement, but less later on.

Table 5-4

Fixed Incomes vs Annuitizing for 4% Withdrawal Age 65

Base Case Investment Returns and Inflation,* Annuity 7.5%, RDR .08

Age	Stocks/IntGovts/ Annuities	Expected Withdrawal	Withdrawal Probability**					Median Portfolio
			4	3	2	1	0	
75	100/0/0	3.83	.88	.08	.03	.01	0	116
	75/25/0	3.93	.95	.04	.01	0	0	112
	75/0/25	3.92	.94	.05	.01	0	0	97
	50/50/0	3.98	.99	.01	0	0	0	104
85	100/0/0	3.59	.77	.10	.09	.04	0	139
	75/25/0	3.75	.84	.09	.06	.01	0	130
	75/0/25	3.74	.83	.09	.07	.01	0	124
	50/50/0	3.87	.90	.07	.03	0	0	111
95	100/0/0	3.42	.72	.09	.10	.08	.01	175
	75/25/0	3.59	.78	.08	.09	.05	0	153
	75/0/25	3.60	.77	.10	.09	.04	0	165
	50/50/0	3.71	.83	.08	.07	.02	0	119

*Same as Tables 5-2 and 5-3

**Probability that withdrawal is in a range from 0.5 below or above 4, 3, 2, 1, or from 0 to .5.

Mortality may occur later on when annuitizing is more favorable for the estate. Nevertheless, the size of the improvement for annuitizing does not seem sufficient to outweigh the earlier advantage for fixed incomes and their greater flexibility. For a reasonably sustainable initial withdrawal allocating about a quarter of the portfolio to fixed incomes seems to be the better strategy. As the initial withdrawal becomes less sustainable, however, annuitizing clearly becomes the better choice. And the portion of the portfolio that is annuitized should be increased to 50 percent.

A puzzle that has interested academic researchers is why so few retirees voluntarily buy lifetime annuities when they appear to be a better choice for retirees than fixed income issues. Thomas Davidoff, Jeffrey Brown, and Peter Diamond (2005) provide a discussion of this question and references to earlier work. The results in Tables 5-2 & 5-3 further demonstrate the attractiveness of annuities for those who have not saved enough to sustainably cover their existing standard of living. On the other hand, Table 5-4 shows that annuities may be somewhat less attractive than fixed incomes for those who have saved enough to achieve a sustainable standard of living.

Suppose the allocation to intermediates is increased further from 25 to 50 percent. In this case there is a further improvement in the withdrawals at all ages. There is, however, also a significant decline in the median value of the investment at ages 85 and 95. These median values decline respectively from 130 and 153 to 111 and 119. Some retirees may feel that the further improvement in the withdrawals is not sufficient to compensate for this decline in the portfolio values given the low level of risk that already exits. Moreover, higher investment values may be needed to help cover extra withdrawals for emergencies or assisted care as well as for an estate as discussed in Chapter 7.

Chapter 9 shows, however, that an increased allocation to fixed incomes may be desirable later in retirement as the horizon becomes shorter if the withdrawal continues to be sustainable. Chapter 11 shows that a temporary increase in the allocation to fixed incomes may sometimes also be advisable. This is when valuations indicate that the expected return on stocks appears to be abnormally low relative to that on fixed income issues.

5.6 Annuitizing by Deferring Social Security

Earlier in this chapter, retirees annuitized by purchasing an immediate lifetime annuity from an insurance company. But retirees have another way in which they can annuitize a limited portion of their investments. If they simply delay the start of their Social Security they have in effect purchased a lifetime annuity. And unlike the earlier annuity this one has benefits that are indexed for inflation.

To see why delaying the start of Social Security can be viewed as equivalent to buying an annuity consider the following example. In the scenario in Chapter 1 Louise Logan had started her Social Security at age 65 and was scheduled to receive $20,000 of benefits each year in real terms. But suppose instead that she defers the start of her benefits for a year.

In particular, suppose that she turned 65 at the beginning of 2010 and started her Social Security at that time. Now suppose instead that she defers her benefits for a year and starts when she reaches her normal retirement age under the Social Security program of 66. In this case her benefit is increased by a factor of 100/93.33, or 7.14 percent.[6]

By deferring her benefits for a year she has to make an extra withdrawal of $20,000 from her investments over 2010 to cover expenses. But for this $20,000 she has obtained each year for the rest of her life a benefit equal to 7.14 percent of $20,000 that is indexed for inflation. In effect, by deferring the start of her Social Security by a year she has purchased a lifetime annuity for $20,000 with an annual benefit of 7.14 percent indexed for inflation.

Earlier in this chapter, retirees were assumed to purchase an annuity with a rate of 7.5 percent. But the benefit of this earlier annuity was fixed in nominal terms. After two years of 2.5 percent inflation the value of the earlier nominal benefit would be about the same in real terms as the one just obtained by deferring Social Security. Thus, implicitly buying an annuity as just described is clearly attractive.

Louise's opportunities for annuitizing by deferring Social Security, however, are not limited to waiting to start her benefits at her normal retirement age of 66. Suppose she defers the start of her benefits for another year until she is age 67. In this event under the Social Security rules her annual benefit at age 67 is increased by 8 percent of the benefit she would have received at age 66.

By waiting until she is 67 Louise has in effect implicitly purchased another annuity. And this one is even more attractive than the first because it has a rate of 8 instead of 7.14 percent.

Moreover, Louise need not stop at age 67. Under the Social Security rules in 2010 she has the possibility of implicitly purchasing three more annuities. She can do this by further delaying the start of her Social Security to ages 68, 69, and 70.

The rates for these additional annuities, however, successively decline to respectively 7.41, 6.90, and 6.45 percent. The rates decline because the increase in benefits each year continues to be 8 percent of the benefit at age 66. At the same time the cost of getting these increases is rising because the size of the benefit that must be replaced each year is rising. Nevertheless, even the rate for the last year of 6.45 percent continues to be attractive. After 6 years of 2.5 percent inflation a nominal rate of 7.5 percent would be about 6.45 percent in real terms.

Suppose based on the results in Table 5-2 that retirees are considering annuitizing a large portion of their investments. If they have not yet started Social Security they have an attractive alternative. They can replace part of their purchase of an annuity by using an equal amount of their investment to defer the start of their Social Security. Such a replacement should further improve the results shown in Table 5-2.

Those with a relatively small portfolio, however, may have their deferral limited by the size of their investment. Retirees will not want to defer their Social Security if doing so leaves them short of the investment balance they need to accommodate annual fluctuation in their living expenses, or to cover possible emergencies. If their portfolio is sufficiently small, retirees may not want to annuitize any of their investment or defer Social Security.

Suppose, for instance, that their currently available annual Social Security would be more than a quarter of the current value of their investment. Suppose that this Social Security is deferred for a year, and that the value of the investment would otherwise be the same. In this event the value of the investment will now be less than three times that of their Social Security. Having investments equal to at least three times their Social Security, however, may be the minimum that retirees feel is adequate to cover possible fluctuation in their annual living expenses or a possible emergency. If it leaves them short of the cushion of investments that they feel is necessary to manage their expenses retirees may not want to annuitize any of their investment or to defer Social Security.

Many retirees, on the other hand, have annual Social Security benefits that are only a small portion of the value of their investments. For instance, in the introductory scenario Louise Logan had annual Social Security of $20,000, which is 3.3 percent of her $600,000 portfolio. These retirees can annuitize a large portion of their investments and still have a large enough investment to manage their expenses. And they will want to undertake as much of the annuitizing as possible at the better rate available by deferring the start of their Social Security.

These latter retirees, however, do have other concerns about deferring their Social Security. They will want to know how the deferral of Social Security affects how much they are allowed to withdraw. And they will want to know how undertaking as much as possible of the annuitizing by deferring Social Security affects the results in Table 5-2.

In Table 5-2 the simulated withdrawal is coming from the investment, the earnings, and any annuity. Any Social Security is added to the withdrawal shown in the table from these sources. When Social Security is deferred the simulated withdrawal is coming from Social Security as well as these other sources. And the simulated withdrawal increases to reflect the Social Security.

In the simulations in this latter case, when Social Security begins it is added at the beginning of each year to the investment. And the present value of the future Social Security benefits before and after they begin is calculated each year using the RDR as the rate of interest. This present value is added to the value of the investment along with the present value of any future earnings or annuity benefits. This is to determine the largest withdrawal allowed by the Retrenchment Rule each year.

For Louise Logan her annual Social Security is a relatively small portion of her investments at the beginning of retirement, and there is very little chance that she will not be able to defer her Social Security to age 70. Nevertheless, there is a very slight chance of a very severe bear market before she reaches age 70. And a precaution needs to be taken in the simulations to start her Social Security if her investments do become unduly depleted before age 70.

This is done by testing at the beginning of each year whether the Social Security she would receive at that time exceeds a quarter of the value of her investment at that time. If this limit is exceeded she starts her benefits immediately. This is instead of deferring the start of her Social Security to age 70 as originally planned. The modification of the spreadsheet to include the deferral of Social Security is discussed in Appendix 5-5.

Table 5-5 assumes that the annual Social Security benefit would be 3 percent of the initial value of the investment if Social Security were to start at age 65. On the other hand, if Social security starts at age 70 the benefit increases to 4.24 percent of the initial value of the investment as discussed earlier. If a severe bear market requires an earlier start to Social Security the benefit at that time is also the one discussed earlier.

The initial withdrawal in Table 5-5 is 10.5 percent. This is comprised of the 7.5 percent withdrawal in Table 5-2 and the 3 percent of annual Social Security if the benefits begin at age 65. When Social Security begins at age 65 the results in Table 5-5 are those obtained by adding the Social Security to the results in Table 5-2. When Social Security begins at age 70 the results are from new simulations.

Suppose retirees are planning to defer the start of their Social Security to age 70. Doing so will require about 17 percent of their initial investment. Thus, only 33 percent of the initial investment is annuitized in Table 5-5 instead of the 50 percent in Table 5-2.

As expected, deferring the start of Social Security improves the withdrawals obtained from all of the assets including the Social Security. There are meaningful increases in the expected withdrawals and in the chances that the future withdrawals will equal at least 10 percent. And the risk of low withdrawals is also reduced.

Suppose, for instance, for the minimal earnings, that the start of Social security is deferred from age 65 to 70. The chances that the withdrawals at ages 75, 85, and 95 will be less than 6 percent are reduced respectively from .01, .11, and .21 to .00, .04, and .10. For the maximal earnings, the chances are reduced from .00, .04, and .12 to .00, .01, and .05.

Table 5-5

Social Security Deferral for 10.5% Combined Withdrawal Age 65

Base Case Returns and Inflation Soc. Sec. @ Age 65 3%

Annuity 7.5% RDR .08

Age	Earn/ Years	Stocks/ Annuity	Start* Soc. Sec.	Expected Withdrawal	Withdrawal Probability** 11	9	7	5	3	Median Portfolio
75	2/5	50/50	65	8.77	.20	.52	.27	.01	0	58
		67/33	70	8.98	.26	.51	.23	0	0	54
85		50/50	65	8.08	.14	.38	.37	.11	0	58
		67/33	70	8.40	.18	.40	.38	.04	0	53
95		50/50	65	7.67	.12	.32	.35	.21	0	60
		67/33	70	8.05	.16	.33	.41	.10	0	52
75	4/10	50/50	65	9.88	.64	.30	.06	0	0	86
		67/33	70	9.98	.68	.28	.04	0	0	83
85		50/50	65	9.11	.46	.28	.22	.04	0	89
		67/33	70	9.33	.51	.29	.19	.01	0	85
95		50/50	65	8.65	.40	.23	.25	.12	0	92
		67/33	70	8.99	.45	.25	.25	.05	0	88

*In all cases there is a combined initial withdrawal from the investment and other assets equal to 10.5% of the initial value of the investment. When Social Security starts at ages 65 or 70 it provides amounts at the beginning of each year starting at that age equal respectively to 3.00% or 4.24% of the initial value of the investment at age 65 in real terms. If the annual Social Security that would be received before age 70 exceeds .25 of the value of the investment at that time Social Security starts with that benefit at that earlier age.

**Probability that the combined withdrawal from the investment and other assets including Social Security is in a range from one above to one below 11, 9, 7, 5, or from 3 to 4. This is as a percentage of the value of the investment at age 65 in real terms.

The cost of the improvement in the withdrawals is a small reduction in the future median portfolio values. For instance, at age 85 for the minimal earnings, the decline is from 58 to 53 in real terms as a percent of initial value. For the maximal earnings, the decline is from 89 to 85 percent. Presumably, retirees will feel that the improvements in the withdrawals are sufficient to more than compensate for the losses in portfolio value.

Other restrictions on the desirability of deferring the start of Social Security are that individuals be in good health, and that the annuity rates available on the market not be much better than the rate assumed in Table 5-2. Under these conditions, and for those not overly dependent on Social Security, deferring the start of Social Security is an attractive way of undertaking some of the annuitizing that is desirable for those with unsustainable withdrawals. Those with reasonably sustainable withdrawals, and investing in fixed income issues, should also consider replacing some of their fixed income investments by deferring the start of Social Security.

5.6 Conclusions

Further retrenchment becomes ineffective for reducing the risk of low withdrawals later in retirement well before the initial withdrawal has become reasonably sustainable. A cost effective way of further reducing the risk of low withdrawals in such cases is to annuitize a large portion of the portfolio and seek part-time employment. Even if only minimal part-time earnings are achieved a significant reduction in the risk of low withdrawals is obtained. And significant earnings can eliminate almost all the risk of very low withdrawals.

There are costs to this strategy in terms of seeking and performing the part-time work. And if only minimal earnings are achieved the chances of sustaining the initial withdrawal are reduced by the annuity as is the size of the remaining investment available for an estate. On the other hand, if significant earnings are achieved the annuitizing has little effect on sustaining the initial withdrawal. And the size of the investment available for an estate is increased when the earnings and annuitizing are considered together. In any case, those who have not saved enough to cover their living expenses with a reasonably sustainable initial withdrawal should expect that they will have to pay a penalty.

When fixed income issues are substituted for the annuitizing they do not significantly reduce the risk of low withdrawals later in retirement. And other measures of performance deteriorate significantly compared to annuitizing. The fixed incomes, however, provide a similar reduction in risk early in retirement to annuitizing and otherwise perform relatively well at that time. But there is little risk to reduce early in retirement and the somewhat better performance of fixed incomes at that time is easily outweighed by their poor performance later in retirement compared to annuitizing.

When the initial withdrawal is reasonably sustainable, however, fixed incomes and annuitizing produce comparable reductions in risk later in retirement. And in general when the initial withdrawal is reasonably sustainable annuitizing and fixed income issues tend to be competitive. In this latter case fixed incomes may be preferred due to their greater flexibility.

A limited amount of annuitizing can effectively be achieved by deferring the start of Social Security. The rates on the annuities implicitly purchased in this way are attractive since the benefits are indexed for inflation. An additional limit may apply if annual Social Security is too large a portion of the value of the investment. Simulations show that most retirees will likely see the improvement in the withdrawals from deferring Social Security as sufficient to outweigh the cost in terms of lower median portfolio values.

Notes

1. This earnings limit is given at http://ssa.gov/OACT/COLA/rtea.html.
2. Examples of the increases at the full retirement age to compensate for earlier reductions due to exceeding the earnings limit are given at http://www.ssa.gov/retire2/whileworking3.htm.
3. One good source is http://brkdirect.com.
4. For the minimal earnings and 50 percent annuitization the Retrenchment Rule with an RDR of .08 limits the initial withdrawal to 7.3 percent. In all other cases an initial withdrawal of 7.5 percent is allowed.
5. An alternative to intermediate governments is intermediate TIPS. But since 2000 the annual real returns on both have been similar. They both had a bull market

over 2000-2002 as inflation slowed, and a moderate bear market over 2003-2006 as inflation increased. Over 2007-2010 they both had a moderate bull market as inflation slowed again. A difference is that TIPS had a sharp, but brief, bear market in late 2008. This appears to have been due to concern about a possible episode of deflation following the collapse of Lehman. Otherwise, the expected returns and volatility for both issues appear similar in the available data. Time series for various issues of TIPS are given at http://research.stlouisfed.org/fred2.

6. The increases for deferral are given at http://www.ssa.gov/pubs/10147.html.

References

Ameriks, John, Robert Veres, and Mark J. Warshawsky. 2001. "Making Retirement Income Last a Lifetime." *Journal of Financial Planning* 14, 12 (December): 62-76.

Davidoff, Thomas, Jeffrey R. Brown, and Peter A. Diamond. 2005. "Annuities and Individual Welfare." *American Economic Review* 95, (December): 1573-1590.

Pye, Gordon B. 2009. "When Should Retirees Retrench? Reducing the Need with Part-Time Work and Annuitization." *Journal of Financial Planning* 22, 1 (January): 48-55.

Appendix 5-1

Including Nominal Benefits

This chapter earlier described how to include in the Retrenchment Rule and the simulations future part-time earnings in real terms. Future benefits in nominal terms are treated in the same way except they must be put on a real basis. To do so future nominal benefits at any time are adjusted for inflation equal to the expected inflation rate in the long run. This is for each year in the future until the nominal benefits are received.

Also, as each run of the simulations unfolds a simulated rate of inflation is generated each year. This simulated inflation is used to determine the real value of a nominal benefit when it is received during that run. The simulated inflation also updates the total discount for the expected inflation being used to estimate the real value of benefits further in the future.

For the simulations the expected return on stocks each year is largely based on the average annual real return observed over 1960-2009. Over this same period the average annual inflation rate based on the CPI is about .041. Over the last 10 or 15 years of this period, however, inflation averaged only about .025.

Moreover, since the 1980s there are some structural changes that argue for a lower average inflation rate in the future. One is increased competition in domestic markets from increased globalization. Another is the lack of high profile industry wide wage settlements that tended to push up labor costs in the 1970s and earlier. And since the 1980s the Federal Reserve has been more vigilant in curbing inflationary pressures to avoid a new flare-up.

Nevertheless, as memory fades of the major inflation of the 1970s some complacency may develop in monetary policy. Also, rapid economic growth in China and India is now tending to put more upward pressure on the prices of oil and other basic commodities than in the past. A serious episode of inflation cannot be ruled out even if it is not on the scale of the 1970s. As this is being written in 2010 an expected rate of inflation in the long run of .03 seems reasonable, whatever the current rate of inflation might be.

Since the 1980s there have been other shifts in the behavior of inflation as well as a reduction in its average value. Annual rates of inflation have become less volatile, and also less predictable based on the rate for the prior year. These shifts tend to make nominal benefits more valuable as they tend to lessen the risk of sustained episodes of high inflation.

To be conservative in evaluating nominal benefits in the simulations, however, the volatility of inflation and its persistence has been based on averages over 1960-2009. Thus, in the simulations there is a possibility of an episode of high inflation. There is not as strong a likelihood of such an episode, however, as there would be if it were assumed that the expected rate of inflation in the long run is .041 instead of .03.

In particular, the annual rate of inflation in the simulations is the sum of a weighted average and a random drawing. The weighted average is .75 of inflation in the prior year and .25 of its expected normal value in the long run of .03. The random drawing is from a normal distribution with a zero mean and standard deviation of .02. With this relation whatever the current rate of inflation, inflation is tending to gradually revert to its expected normal value in the long run of .03.

The weights of .75 and .25 are those of the weighted average that best fits the observed annual inflation rates over 1960-2009. This is when the expected inflation rate in the long run is assumed to be the average inflation rate over 1960-2009 of .041. The standard deviation of the random drawing of .02 is the standard deviation of the error by which the estimated weighted average fits the observed inflation rates each year. This is over 1960-2009 and assumes that the inflation rate in the long run is the average over that period of .041.

As discussed earlier, in the simulations at any time future nominal benefits are put on a real basis by adjusting them for expected inflation of .03. Also, as a run of the simulations unfolds a simulated rate of inflation is determined each year using the relation just described. This simulated inflation is used to put nominal benefits on a real basis when they are received.

The major inflation of the 1970s coincided with a major bear market for stocks. Such a mutual occurrence tends to reinforce the negative effect of either on the withdrawals. In contrast, the major bear markets of 2000/2002 or 2008 did not appear to be significantly related to inflation. In these later episodes nominal benefits from an annuity would have better helped to mitigate the adverse effect of the decline in stock values.

Due to this recent evidence the relation between stock values and inflation does not seem to be as strong as indicated by the 1970s and 1980s. Nevertheless, to be conservative in evaluating the nominal benefits of an annuity the relationship on average over 1960-2009 is taken into account in the simulations. To do so the returns on stocks over this period each year were statistically related to unexpected inflation each year based on the fitted inflation relation. The results showed that one percentage point of unexpected inflation during a year was associated on average with a 3.0 percentage point reduction in the real return on stocks. And this relationship differs from zero with statistical significance.

To reflect this relationship, each year in the simulations the return on stocks is set equal to the sum of two components. One is a deduction equal to 3.0 times that component of inflation for the year that is a random drawing. The other component is another drawing from a normal distribution. This distribution has a mean and standard deviation so as to keep the mean and standard deviation of stock returns each year equal to the base case values of .07 and .18. This distribution has a mean of .07 and a standard deviation of .170.

Appendix 5-2

Modifying the Spreadsheet for Part-Time Earnings

Table 5-6 modifies the spreadsheet in Table 3-1 to include the minimal assumption about part-time earnings. This assumption is that earnings are received equal to 2 percent of the initial portfolio in real terms at the beginning of each of the first five years. Including the maximal assumption of receiving 4 percent for 10 years is similar.

The present value of any current or future earnings to be received as of the beginning of a year is calculated in column H. These present values are labeled in H4 as PV Earnings. The interest rate for calculating this present value is the RDR given in B2, which in this case is .08. The function to calculate the present value is PV(v, w, x, y, z). The first argument v is the RDR in B2. The next argument w is the remaining number of earnings flows to be received. This is equal to the total number of flows at the beginning given in H3 less the number of the row given in column A plus 1. The argument x is the negative of the entry in H2, which is the value of the earnings in the years in which they are received. The argument y is any extra flow when the flows terminate, which is zero in this case. And the argument z is a 1 when the flows are received at the beginning of a year as assumed.

As in the spreadsheet in Table 3-1, column C gives the value of the investment at the beginning of each year. This is before a withdrawal is made or any earnings received. To calculate this value its prior value is adjusted for earnings in the years in which earnings are received. This is in addition to the adjustment for the withdrawal in the prior year and the return earned on the invested balance over the prior year.

Column D calculates the upper limit on the value of the withdrawal at the beginning of each year. This calculation is the same as in Table 3-1 except for an adjustment to the value of the investment available to make withdrawals from column C. This investment value is increased by any present value of earnings available from column H for each row.

Table 5-1 reports the median value of the investment at ages 75, 85, and 95 in addition to the expected withdrawals and withdrawal probabilities at those ages. To calculate the median investment values insert =C16, =C26, and =C36 respectively in E54, F54, and G54. The medians can then be calculated by inserting Median(E55:E10054), Median(F55:F10054), and Median(G55:G10054) respectively in E10056, F10056, and G10056.

Table 5-6

Modification ofTable 3-1 to Include Part-Time Earnings*

	A	C	D	H
1				
2				2
3				5
4				PV of Earnings
5				
6	1	100	=PMT($B$2,$D$2-A6+1,-C6-H6,0,1)	=PV($B$2,$H$3-A6+1,-$H$2,0,1)
7	2	=(C6-B6+$H$2)*(1+E6)	- -	- -
8	3	- -	- -	- -
9	4	- -	- -	- -
10	5	- -	=PMT($B$2,$D$2-A10+1,-C10-H10,0,1)	=PV($B$2,$H$3-A10+1,-$H$2,0,1)
11	6	=(C10-B10+$H$2)*(1+E10)	=PMT($B$2,$D$2-A11+1,-C11,0,1)	0
12	7	=(C11-B11)*(1+E11)	- -	0
13	8	- -	- -	- -
14	9	- -	- -	- -

*Cell entries not shown in this table are the same as in Table 3-1 except for B2, which for this simulation is .08, and B6, which for this simulation is 7.5.

Appendix 5-3

Modifying the Spreadsheet for Nominal Annuity Benefits

Table 5-7 modifies the spreadsheet given in Table 5-6 to include annuitizing 50 percent of the investment when the annuity each year has a nominal benefit of 7.5 percent. The present value of the expected real benefits at any time is calculated in column I. To do so future benefits are discounted for each year in the future until they are received by the expected future inflation rate of .03. They are also discounted by the RDR of .08. This is equivalent to discounting by the combined rate 1.03(1.08)-1 given in I3. The nominal benefit each year is half of 7.5 given in I2. As the benefits are received for life the total number to be received as of age 65 is 45 as given by D2 in Table 3-1.

To calculate the real present value of the future benefits at any time the present values given in column I must be deflated for simulated actual inflation up until that time. These discount factors for each year are calculated in column J from the annual inflation rates generated in column K. As discussed in Appendix 5-1 expected inflation each year is .75 of prior inflation plus .25 of the long run expected inflation of .03. Actual inflation each year is this expected value plus a random drawing generated in column L. It is assumed that inflation in the year prior to the initial year of the plan is .025.

The discount factor for cumulated inflation at any time given in column J is used to get the real values of the nominal benefits for the calculations in columns C and D. In column C the nominal value of the benefit in I2 is multiplied by the cumulated inflation discount factor in column J to get the real value of the invested balance at the beginning of each year. In column D the expected real present value of the benefits looking forward at any time is put on a real basis and added to the value of the investment at that time to get the limit on the withdrawal.

As discussed earlier, unexpected inflation given by the entry in column L is assumed to have a negative effect on the expected return on stocks equal to 3.0 times its value. The random drawings for stock returns in this simulation are given in column E by this value plus a drawing from a normal distribution set to keep the mean return each year equal to .07 and the standard deviation equal to .18.

Table 5-7

Modification of Table 5-6 to Include Nominal Annuity Benefits*

	A	C	D	E
1				
2				
3				
4				
5				
6	1	50	=PMT($B$2,$D$2-A6+1,-C6-H6-J6*I6,0,1)	=-3*L6+NormInv(Rand(),.07,.17)
7	2	=(C6-B6+$H$2+J6*$I$2)*(1+E6)	- -	=-3*L7+NormInv(Rand(),.07,.17)
8	3	- -	- -	- -
9	4	- -	- -	- -
10	5	- -	=PMT($B$2,$D$2-A10+1,-C10-H10-J10*I10,0,1)	- -
11	6	=(C10-B10+$H$2+J10*$I$2)*(1+E10)	=PMT($B$2,$D$2-A11+1,-C11-J11*I11,0,1)	- -
12	7	=(C11-B11+J11*$I$2)*(1+E11)	- -	- -
13	8	- -	- -	- -
14	9	- -	- -	- -

*Assumes 50% of initial portfolio used to buy annuity with 7.5% nominal benefit. Cell entries not shown in this table are the same as in Table 5-6.

Table 5-7

Modification of Table 5-6 to Include Nominal Annuity Benefits Continued

	I	J	K	L
1				
2	3.75			
3	(1.08)*(1.03)-1			
4	PV Annuity Benefits			
5			.025	
6	=PV($I$3,$D$2-A6+1,-$I$2,0,1)	1	=.75*K5+.25*(.03)+L6	=NormInv(Rand(),0,.02)
7	- -	=J6/(1+K6)	=.75*K6+.25*(.03)+L7	=NormInv(Rand(),0,.02)
8	- -	=J7/(1+K7)	- -	- -
9	- -	- -	- -	- -
10	- -	- -	- -	- -
11	- -	- -	- -	- -
12	- -	- -	- -	- -
13	- -	- -	- -	- -
14	- -	- -	- -	- -

Appendix 5-4

Modifying the Spreadsheet to Include a Mixed Portfolio

Table 5-8 modifies the spreadsheet given in Table 3-1 to include an allocation of the portfolio to fixed income issues. In particular, at the beginning of each year the portfolio is reallocated without cost to have 25 percent of its value in intermediate government issues. The remainder is in stocks whose returns have the same mean and standard deviation each year as before. Column M gives the return each year on the intermediate governments. As discussed in the text this is a random drawing from a normal distribution with a mean of .03 and a standard deviation of .07.

Table 5-8

Modification of Table 3-1 to Include a 25% Fixed Income Allocation*

	A	E	M
1			
2			
3			
4			
5			
6	1	=.25*M6+.75*NormInv(Rand(),.07,.18)	=NormInv(Rand(),.03,.07)
7	2	=.25*M7+.75*NormInv(Rand(),.07,.18)	=NormInv(Rand(),.03,.07)
8	3	- -	- -
9	4	- -	- -

*Cell entries not shown in the table are the same as Table 3-1 except for B2, which for this simulation is .08, and B6, which for this simulation is 7.5.

Appendix 5-5

Modifying the Spreadsheet for Deferred Social Security

Table 5-9 modifies the spreadsheet in Table 3-1 to include Social Security benefits. Initially, it is planned that these benefits will start at age 70, but there is an exception. The benefits start before age 70 if the annual benefit that can be received is a quarter or more of the value of the investment at that time.

The value of the annual Social Security each year when the benefits start is in column W. For instance, if the benefits start at age 66 the benefit received at the beginning of each year starting at age 66 is given in W7 as 3.21. The value of the annual Social Security being received each year is given in column X. A benefit is not received at age 64, so X5=0.

Benefits begin before age 70 if both of the following conditions are satisfied for an earlier year. One is that a benefit was not received for the prior year. The other is that the benefit that would be received if benefits were to start that year is equal to or greater than a quarter of the value of the investment at that time.

These two conditions are satisfied when both of the arguments of the logical function, And(x,y), are true and its arguments are specified as follows. In particular, consider their specification at age 66. In this case, the first argument is X6=0, which says that a benefit was not received in the prior year. The second argument is W7>=.25*(C7+$H$2+J7*.66*$I$2), which says that the benefit has exceeded its limit relative to the size of the investment. Note in the latter expression that the earnings and the annuity benefit for the year have been included in the value of the investment.

The value of the Social Security received each year before age 70 is given by the logical function, If(x,y,z), when its arguments are specified as follows. In particular, consider again its specification at age 66. In this case, the first argument is And(x,y) as just specified above, the second argument is W7, and the third argument is X6. This says that when And(x,y) is true because both of its arguments are true that X7 is equal to W7 because Social Security starts at that time. When And(x,y) is false X7 is equal to its prior value of X6.

At age 70, Social Security starts at that time if benefits were not received in the prior year, which is true when X10=0. If Social Security was received in the prior year the same benefit as before is received at age 70. Thus, X11 is given by: If(X10=0,W11,X10). In years subsequent to age 70 the same benefit is received each year as the year before.

In these simulations, 33 instead of 50 percent of the initial investment is annuitized in expectation that Social Security will begin at age 70. This is because if the benefits begin at age 70 about 17 percent of the initial investment will be used to replace the deferred Social Security. Thus, in these simulations the value in C6 is 67. Also, in these simulations the value of any Social Security each year in column X is added to the value of the investment in Column C to get the value of the investment in the following year.

In these simulations the present value of the future Social Security benefits is added to the value of the investment in calculating the limit on the withdrawal each year in column D.

This present value is calculated each year in column Y using the RDR in B2 as the rate of interest. Suppose Social Security is not being received in a year prior to age 70. In this case, the benefits are assumed to start at age 70 and to continue to age 110 in calculating the present value. Otherwise, the current benefit is assumed to be received each year to age 110.

Table 5-9

Modification ofTable 3-1 to Include Deferred Social Security*

	A	B	C	D
1				
2		.08		45
3				
4				
5				
6	1	=Min(10.5,D6)	67	=PMT($B$2,$D$2-A6+1,-C6-H6-J6*.66*I6-Y6,0,1)
7	2	=Min(B6,D7)	=(C6-B6+X6+$H$2+J6*.66*$I$2)*(1+E6)	=PMT($B$2,$D$2-A7+1,-C7-H7-J7*.66*I7-Y7,0,1)
8	3	=Min(B7,D8)	=(C7-B7+X7+$H$2+J7*.66*$I$2)*(1+E7)	- -
9	4	-	- -	- -
10	5	-	- -	=PMT($B$2,$D$2-A10+1,-C10-H10-J10*.66*I10,0,1)
11	6	-	=(C10-B10+X10+$H$2+J10*.66*$I$2)*(1+E10)	=PMT($B$2,$D$2-A11+1,-C11-J11*.66*I11,0,1)
12	7	-	=(C11-B11+X11+J11*.66*$I$2)*(1+E11)	- -
13	8	-	- -	- -

*Assumes case of minimal earnings and that Social Security is planned to begin at age 70 unless the benefit earlier is more than a quarter of the value of the investment at the beginning of a year. An annuity with an annual benefit of 7.5% is purchased initially with 33% of the investment.

Table 5-9

Modification of Table 3-1 to Include Deferred Social Security Continued

	W	X	Y
1			
2	=PV($B$2,40,−W11,0,1)		5
3			
4			
5		0	
6	3.00	=If(And(X5=0,W6>=.25*(C6+$H$2+J6*.66*$I$2)),W6,X5)	=If(X6=0,PV($B$2,$Y$2-A6+1,0,-$W$2,1), PV($B$2,$D$2-A6+1,-X6,0,1))
7	3.21	=If(And(X6=0,W7>=.25*(C7+$H$2+J7*.66*$I$2)),W7,X6)	=If(X7=0,PV($B$2,$Y$2-A7+1,0,-$W$2,1), PV($B$2,$D$2-A7+1,-X7,0,1))
8	3.47	- -	- -
9	3.73	- -	- -
10	3.99	=If(And(X9=0,W10>=.25*(C10+$H$2+J10*.66*$I$2)),W10,X9)	=If(X10=0,PV($B$2,$Y$2-A10+1,0, -$W$2,1), PV($B$2,$D$2-A10+1,-X10,0,1))
11	4.24	=If(X10=0,W11,X10)	=PV($B$2,$D$2-A11+1,-X11,0,1)
12		=X11	- -
13		=X12	- -

6

Including a Pension

Many workers begin retirement with a pension as well as an investment portfolio. If they have a pension in effect a portion of their investment is already annuitized. The pension needs to be taken into account in determining the withdrawals that they can make. And their pension must be considered in determining any additional annuitization or allocation to fixed income issues that is desirable.

This chapter assumes that the benefits of a pension are fixed in nominal terms like those of the annuities considered in the last chapter. This assumption seems appropriate for the pensions of most private sector workers. Many pensions for workers from the public sector, however, receive at least some adjustment for inflation on a regular basis.

In the period of high inflation in the 1970s the pensions of private sector workers frequently received some special upward adjustment for inflation. Since then, however, any adjustments for inflation have been unusual and relatively small if they have occurred. It seems prudent for most private sector workers to assume that their pensions will not be adjusted upward for inflation.

The presence of a pension alters the risk characteristics of retirement assets. It might seem therefore that a pension will affect the choice of an RDR, especially if the pension is relatively large. Surprisingly, however, the presence of a pension has little effect on the choice of an RDR. The argument for choosing an RDR of .08 is just about the same if retirees start out with just a pension or just an investment portfolio.

Suppose retirees are beginning retirement at age 65 in good health with the same assumptions as to stock returns and inflation as earlier. If they are using an RDR of .08 it will be shown that they should add 75 percent of any annual pension benefit to their allowed withdrawal. This is in addition to 7.6 percent of the value of their investment portfolio. Also, 10 times their annual pension benefit should be added to their investment portfolio as equivalent annuitized value.

This is in deciding how much of the portfolio should be annuitized or allocated to fixed income issues.

Other than Social Security the retirement assets of some are limited largely to a pension. It would be best for them to invest savings from their early pension benefits in stocks to provide for later erosion in their pension benefits due to inflation. But those with no experience in stock investments may be averse to stocks and prefer fixed incomes. The last part of this chapter shows that these retirees should use an RDR of .05. Such a reduction in the RDR for a pension, however, requires significantly less retrenchment than the same reduction in the RDR for stocks.

6.1 Allowable Pension Withdrawals

When there is a pension the Retrenchment Rule is applied as it was for an annuity in Appendix 5-1 of the last chapter. Future nominal benefits are put on a real basis by discounting them by the expected average annual rate of inflation. This is for each year in the future until the benefits are received. Appendix 5-1 argued that viewed from 2010 a reasonable value for this expected average annual rate of inflation is .03.

After putting the future stream of nominal benefits on a real basis they are discounted by the assumed discount rate for the Retrenchment Rule to get their present value. This present value is then treated the same as the value of an investment to determine the largest withdrawal allowed by the pension.

As an example, suppose that retirees are beginning retirement at age 65 in good health with a limit on life expectancy of age 110. Suppose that they have a pension that pays a benefit of 100 at the beginning of each year including the initial one. Suppose also that they are using a discount rate for the Retrenchment Rule of .08.

The first step is to discount each of the future pension benefits for expected annual inflation of .03 for each year in the future until they are received. The next step is to calculate the present value of these inflation adjusted benefits using an interest rate equal to the assumed discount rate of .08. Calculating the present value of the inflation adjusted benefits, however, can be carried out in one step by using an interest rate of .1124. This is because using an interest rate of .1124 is equivalent to discounting a future benefit by .03 and by .08 each year since (1.03)(1.08)=1.1124.

The present value of a stream of 45 annual benefits of 100 using an interest rate of .1124 is 981. This is about 10 times the annual benefit of 100. This result is easily verified using a handheld calculator.

It is assumed that the benefits are paid at the beginning of each year so the calculator must be set for this mode. Input n=45, i=11.24, PMT=100, and FV=0. The PV obtained is a multiple of the value of PMT equal to 9.81 or about 10. And this multiple is independent of the value assumed for PMT.

For an RDR of .08 at age 65 it was established in Chapter 4 that the largest allowed annual withdrawal from an investment is 7.6 percent. As stated earlier the present value of the future pension benefits is treated as if it is the value of an investment in using the Retrenchment Rule each year. Thus, the largest allowed annual withdrawal from the pension at age 65 is 7.6 percent of its present value.

It was just established that this present value at age 65 is a multiple equal to 9.81 of the annual benefit of the pension. Taking 7.6 percent of the multiple of 9.81 shows that 75 percent of the annual benefit of the pension can be withdrawn. This is because .076(9.81) =.75.

For a discount rate of .08 the largest allowed annual withdrawal of 7.6 percent from an investment and 75 percent from a pension benefit apply only to those in good health at age 65. These percentages gradually increase as retirees become older. For instance, suppose that they reach age 75 and that the limit on their life expectancy continues to be age 110. For a discount rate of .08 the largest allowed annual withdrawal from an investment becomes 7.9 instead of 7.6 percent. And the largest allowed withdrawal from a pension benefit becomes 77 instead of 75 percent. Despite this rising percentage the real value of the withdrawal from the pension is expected to decline over time, however, due to erosion in the real value of the benefits because of inflation.

The last chapter discussed the best way to allocate an investment between stocks and an annuity or fixed income issues. The best allocation depends on the withdrawal required to cover expenses as a percentage of the value of the investment. When there is a pension its present value is added to the value of the investment in calculating this percentage. And the present value of the pension as a percent of the total value of these assets is taken into account in deciding on any additional annuitization or allocation to fixed income issues that is required.

6.2 An Example

As an example, suppose a retiree in good health at age 65 has an investment portfolio of $400,000 and a pension with an annual benefit of $20,000 in nominal terms. The largest allowed withdrawal is 7.6 percent of $400,000 plus 75 percent of $20,000. This is a total of about $45,000.

The combined value of the assets is the sum of 10 times the annual pension benefit of $20,000 and the value of the investment of $400,000. This is a total of $600,000. Suppose the required withdrawal to cover essentials is $45,000. This is 7.5 percent of the combined value of the assets of $600,000.

When the required withdrawal is as large as 7.5 percent Chapter 5 showed that the sustainability of the withdrawals could be significantly improved by annuitizing about half of the investment, and seeking part-time work. Here about a third of the value of the assets is already effectively annuitized by the pension. To increase the annuitization to a half of the value of the assets, $100,000 of the investment should be annuitized.

Suppose the required withdrawal to cover expenses is only $25,000 instead of $45,000. Now the withdrawal as a percentage of the combined value of the assets is only a little over 4 percent. Based on the results in Chapter 5 for a reasonably sustainable withdrawal from an investment, it may be desirable to allocate only about 25 percent of the combined value of the assets to fixed income issues. The pension, however, is already about a third of the combined value of the assets. Thus, no allocation to fixed incomes or further annuitization may be desirable in this case.

Suppose instead that the annual pension benefit is only $5,000, with a required withdrawal to cover expenses of $18,000. Now the combined value of the assets is $450,000. The required withdrawal of $18,000 is 4 percent of the value of the assets, and the desired allocation to fixed incomes may still be only 25 percent.

In this case, the present value of the pension of $50,000, however, is only a little over 10 percent of the asset value of $450,000. If the desired allocation to fixed incomes is 25 percent of \$450,000, this is equal to \$112,500. Allowing for the present value of the pension of \$50,000, an amount equal to \$62,500 of the investment portfolio should then be allocated to fixed incomes initially. The amount of fixed incomes in the future is determined similarly depending on the total value of the assets and the present value of the pension at that future time.

6.3 Selecting the RDR for a Pension

The preceding calculations assumed a discount rate of .08 is used when applying the Retrenchment Rule to a pension. It remains to show as asserted earlier that the argument for using an RDR of .08 for a pension is the same as for a stock portfolio. This is done by showing that the argument for using an RDR of .08 when there is just a pension at the beginning of retirement is the same as when there is just a stock portfolio.

To demonstrate this proposition the simulations in Chapter 4 are rerun starting with just a pension. Starting with just a pension, however, a stock portfolio immediately begins to accumulate as the Retrenchment Rule allows only a portion of the pension benefits to be spent. It is assumed that this investment is a well diversified portfolio of stocks with the same returns as assumed for the stock portfolio in Chapter 4. The effect of inflation on the real value of the nominal pension benefits is taken into account in the same way as described for the annuity benefits in Appendix 5-1.

The streams of expected withdrawals for discount rates ranging from .04 to .12 are shown in Table 6-1. These are based on averages for 10,000 replications of the simulations. The streams are in real terms as a percentage of the initial annual pension benefit. The pension benefit is used as the base so that the streams for different discount rates are comparable. The streams are not comparable for different discount rates when the present value of the benefits is used as the base because the present value depends on the discount rate.

Table 6-1

Expected Withdrawals from Nominal Pension Benefits
Base Case Stock Returns and Inflation*

Discount Rate	Expected Withdrawals**							
	65	70	75	80	85	90	95	100
.04	67	64	62	61	59	58	58	57
.06	71	68	66	64	62	60	59	58
.08	75	72	69	66	64	62	60	58
.10	78	75	71	68	64	62	59	57
.12	81	77	73	69	65	61	58	55

*Inflation simulated as specified in Appendix 5-1 with initial inflation of .025. Annual stock returns for normal valuation each year except adjusted for unexpected inflation as specified in Appendix 5-1.
**In real terms as a percent of the initial annual pension benefit.

Note that the streams in Table 6-1 look just about the same relative to each other as those in Table 4-1 for a stock portfolio. Most importantly, as in Table 4-1, the stream for a discount rate of .08 is above that for .06 at all ages except for age 100 where the expected withdrawals are the same. Thus, based on these streams of expected withdrawals all retirees will prefer a discount rate of .08 to .06 or to lower discount rates just as in Table 4-1.

Next compare the stream for a discount rate of .10 to that for .08. In Table 6-1 there is a small disadvantage for .10 late in retirement as the stream for .10 drops slightly below that for .08 at ages 95 and 100. In Table 4-1 there is more of a disadvantage for .10 late in retirement. The stream for .10 drops further below that for .08 and the disadvantage begins at age 90 instead of 95. To compensate, however, in Table 4-1 there is more of an advantage for .10 early in retirement. In Table 4-1 the stream for .10 is further above that for .08 than in Table 6-1.

The disadvantage of choosing .10 is less late in retirement in Table 6-1, but the advantage of choosing .10 is also less early in retirement. The later disadvantage of .10 relative to its earlier advantage is about the same in either Table 6-1 or

Table 4-1. Based on the streams of expected withdrawals the choice of an RDR is very similar if retirement assets consist of just a pension or just a stock portfolio. And in general it can be inferred that the presence of a pension has little effect on choosing an RDR based on the streams of expected withdrawals.

It remains to see whether the choice of an RDR might be affected by differences in the risk of low withdrawals due to a pension. Table 6-2 shows the risk of future low withdrawals when starting with a pension. In particular, it shows the probability for ranges of future withdrawals in real terms as a percentage of the initial annual pension benefit. These ranges are from 5 percentage points below to 5 above the numbers at the top of the columns in Table 6-2. For instance, the probabilities for 50 are for the withdrawal being between 45 and 55 percent of the initial pension benefit in real terms. These results for a pension compare with those for a stock portfolio in Tables 4-2 & 4-3.

Compare the effect of increasing the discount rate on the results for a pension and for a stock portfolio. For a pension there is less of an increase in the expected withdrawals early in retirement and less of an increase in risk late in retirement. The later increase in risk relative to the earlier increase in expected withdrawals looks about the same, however, for either a pension or a stock portfolio.

Suppose the discount rate is increased from .06 to .08. For either the pension or the stock portfolio the benefit from the increase in expected withdrawals appears to easily be more than enough to outweigh the increase in risk later in retirement. Suppose the discount rate is increased from .08 to .10. In this case for either the pension or the stock portfolio the increase in the expected withdrawals early in retirement has the cost of a small decrease in the expected withdrawals late in retirement. For both the pension and the stock portfolio there is also some increase in the risk of low withdrawals later in retirement.

The benefit from the higher expected withdrawals earlier in retirement relative to the later costs generally looks similar for either the pension or the stock portfolio when the discount rate is increased from .08 to .10. In either case some retirees may see a net benefit and others a net cost, or be indifferent. The general point, however, is that taking risk into account the choice of a discount rate continues to look very similar for the pension and the stock portfolio. This is when the discount rate is increased either from .06 to .08 or from .08 to .10.

Table 6-2

Withdrawal Probabilities for Nominal Pension Benefits
Base Case Stock Returns and Inflation*

Age	Discount Rate	Withdrawal Probability**						
		80	70	60	50	40	30	20
75	.12	.51	.30	.15	.04	0	0	0
	.10	.45	.33	.18	.04	0	0	0
	.08	.28	.46	.21	.05	0	0	0
	.06		.66	.26	.07	.01	0	0
	.04		.47	.41	.11	.01	0	0
85	.12	.33	.20	.21	.16	.08	.02	0
	.10	.32	.23	.20	.16	.07	.02	0
	.08	.21	.33	.22	.16	.07	.01	0
	.06		.51	.25	.16	.07	.01	0
	.04		.39	.35	.18	.07	.01	0
95	.12	.26	.14	.16	.17	.16	.09	.02
	.10	.27	.17	.17	.16	.14	.07	.02
	.08	.19	.26	.19	.17	.12	.06	.01
	.06		.46	.21	.17	.10	.05	.01
	.04		.36	.32	.18	.10	.04	0

*Same as Table 6-1.

**Probability that withdrawal is in a range from 5 above to 5 below 80, 70, ..., or 20. Withdrawals are in real terms, and as a percent of the initial annual pension benefit.

The choice of an RDR appears to be very similar irrespective of whether retirement starts with Social Security and either just a stock portfolio or just a pension. From this it can be inferred that in general the mix of retirement assets between a stock portfolio and a pension does not affect the choice of an RDR. The argument for using an RDR of .08 is the same irrespective of whether or not a retiree has a pension of any given size.

The existence of a pension, however, does have an effect on the sustainability of an initial withdrawal. Much of this effect disappears, however, as an appropriate portion of a stock portfolio is annuitized or allocated to fixed income issues. This is depending on the sustainability of the required withdrawal to cover living expenses.

The size of a pension depends on the retirement plans where retirees have worked, their pay while employed there, and the duration of this employment. Even under favorable circumstances, however, a pension is unlikely to be large enough to sustainably cover a preretirement standard of living. In fact, even after including Social Security, the largest allowed withdrawal by the Retrenchment Rule from a pension may well be insufficient to avoid some painful retrenchment after retirement.

Whether they will have a pension or not retirees must accumulate investments to provide a reasonably sustainable standard of living in retirement commensurate with the one they enjoyed beforehand. The next chapter considers how much must be accumulated to achieve varying degrees of sustainability. In making such an assessment any pension benefits that are expected to be available are taken into account along with Social Security.

6.4 Investing in Fixed Incomes

Those who start retirement with just a pension are in effect fully invested in a fixed income issue. Accumulating a portfolio of stocks with savings from the near-term benefits therefore provides a better allocation. But those who start retirement largely dependent on a pension likely have little or no experience with investing in stocks.

Suppose they agree that they need to save some of their near-term benefits to provide additional income in the future. This is to supplement their pension benefits after the benefits have become significantly eroded by inflation. But without any experience with stocks they may have a strong preference for investing in fixed income issues.

The same analysis can be carried out assuming the savings from the benefits are invested in fixed incomes instead of stocks. In particular, suppose that the fixed income investments are represented by the returns on the intermediate government issues considered in the last chapter. The real return on the investment each year is then a random drawing from a normal distribution with a mean of .03 and a standard deviation of .07.[1]

Suppose the future streams of withdrawals are simulated as before for a series of discount rates. The streams of expected withdrawals assuming funds are invested in fixed income issues are shown in Table 6-3. The relationship of these streams to each other differs significantly from that in Table 6-1.

Note first that the initial withdrawals at age 65 are the same in both tables. This is because the initial withdrawals are independent of the expected return on the investment. They depend only on the value of the discount rate and the assumed limit on life expectancy.

Subsequent expected withdrawals for a given discount rate are lower in Table 6-3 due to the lower expected return on the fixed incomes. Also, due to the lower expected returns, a stream for a higher discount rate in Table 6-3 is declining more rapidly relative to a stream with a lower discount rate.

Consequently, in Table 6-3 the stream for a discount rate of .08 is now below that for .06 at ages 95 and 100. Also, the stream for a discount rate of .06 is below that for .05 at age 100. In Table 6-3 the discount rate must be reduced to .05 to give a stream with the same dominance over the streams for lower discount rates as the discount rate of .08 has in Table 6-1.

In Table 6-3 the argument for choosing a discount rate of at least .05 for the RDR is much the same as for choosing at least .08 for the RDR in Table 6-1. Reducing the expected return and volatility by investing in fixed incomes reduces the RDR from .08 to .05. And the lower RDR causes a reduction in the largest percentage of the initial benefit that can be withdrawn to avoid painful retrenchment.

If retirees want to invest in fixed incomes instead of stocks their initial allowed withdrawal to avoid painful retrenchment is limited to 69 instead of 75 percent of the initial benefit. And their stream of expected withdrawals in the future is also less than if they invest in stocks. For instance, the expected withdrawal is 56 percent at age 95 for fixed incomes versus 60 percent for stocks in Table 6-1.

Table 6-3

Expected Withdrawals from Nominal Pension Benefits
Savings Invested in Fixed Income Issues*

Discount Rate	Expected Withdrawals**							
	65	70	75	80	85	90	95	100
.04	67	64	62	60	58	57	56	55
.05	69	66	64	62	59	58	56	55
.06	71	68	65	63	60	58	56	54
.08	75	72	68	65	62	58	55	53

*Real returns on fixed income issues are the same as simulated for intermediate government issues in Chapter 5 except for adjustment each year for unexpected inflation as specified in Note 1 of this chapter.
**In real terms as a percent of the initial annual pension benefit.

Suppose the risk of low withdrawals is simulated for fixed incomes as shown for stocks in Table 6-2. The risk of low withdrawals for fixed incomes is higher than for stocks, but the difference is very small. For instance, consider the chance that the withdrawals will be less than 45 percent at age 95. For fixed incomes the chances are .21 versus .19 for stocks.

Investing in stocks gives a higher stream of expected withdrawals, and slightly reduces the risk of low withdrawals. After seeing these results those whose inclination is to invest in fixed incomes instead of stocks may change their mind. The differences in the results, however, are not as compelling as for some of the earlier choices involving retrenchment.

Suppose Louise in the scenario in Chapter 1 has a pension with a $60,000 annual benefit instead of a $600,000 investment portfolio. Investing in stocks makes her allowable initial withdrawal to avoid painful retrenchment 75 percent of $60,000, or $45,000. With her $20,000 of social Security this gives her as much as $65,000 to meet her $60,000 requirement.

If she invests in fixed incomes instead of stocks her allowable initial withdrawal is reduced. Now it is limited to 69 percent of the $60,000 benefit, or $41,400. With the Social Security this is $61,400, which is only $3,600 less than her allowable for investing in stocks of $65,000.

Even if her requirement were $65,000 instead of $60,000, however, the $3,600 required retrenchment might not be sufficient to overcome her reluctance to invest in stocks. There is a good argument for investing in stocks. But changes in the discount rate do not have as large an impact on the withdrawals from a pension as for an investment portfolio.

6.5 Conclusions

Many individuals begin retirement with a pension as well as an investment portfolio and Social Security. For those who have worked in the private sector the future benefits of the pension are almost always fixed in nominal terms like the annuities considered in the last chapter. Suppose the withdrawals for different discount rates are simulated starting with a pension just as they were earlier when starting with a stock portfolio. The argument for choosing an RDR of .08 when starting with a pension is the same as when starting with the stock portfolio.

Starting in good health at age 65 and using an RDR of .08 retirees can withdraw as much as 75 percent of an annual pension benefit to avoid painful retrenchment. And they should add 10 times the annual pension benefit to their investment portfolio in equivalent annuitized value. This is to determine whether additional annuitization or allocation to fixed incomes is desirable depending on the sustainability of the total withdrawal needed to cover expenses.

Those who begin retirement with just a pension and Social Security should accumulate savings in stocks to offset future erosion in the value of their benefits due to inflation. But those with just a pension may be averse to investing in stocks and strongly prefer investing in fixed incomes. If they do so, for these retirees an RDR of .05 is equivalent to an RDR of .08 for those who invest in stocks. And their initial withdrawal from the benefit to avoid painful retrenchment is limited to 69 instead of 75 percent.

Note

1. The real return on intermediate governments tends to decline when there is unexpected inflation. A similar relationship for stock returns was discussed in Appendix 5-1. This negative relationship needs to be taken into account in the simulations because it tends to reinforce the negative effect of lower returns and higher inflation on the withdrawals. In particular, since the early 1960s one percentage point of unexpected inflation has been associated with a 2.2 percentage point reduction in the real return on the intermediates. To reflect this relationship in the simulations the return on the intermediates each year is set equal to the sum of two components. One is a deduction equal to 2.2 times that component of inflation for the year that is a random drawing. The other component is another drawing from a normal distribution set to keep the mean and standard deviation of the annual real return on intermediates equal to the base case values of .03 and .07. The mean and standard deviation of this latter distribution are respectively .03 and .0536.

7

Saving Enough for Retirement

During retirement unsustainable investment withdrawals to cover expenses may be justified to avoid painful retrenchment. But before retirement a sufficiently large investment can be accumulated to make it unlikely that unsustainable withdrawals will be necessary. The question is how large an investment is required at the beginning of retirement to make a desired standard of living sufficiently sustainable?

This chapter presents a schedule that shows how the sustainability of the desired standard of living improves as a larger investment is accumulated. Looking at this schedule individuals and their advisors can determine how much must be accumulated to achieve a minimally sufficient degree of sustainability. And they can also see the benefit of accumulating more than this minimal level. Using the schedule individuals can see the benefit of increasing their savings and decide whether the cost in terms of a reduced preretirement standard of living is justified.

This chapter first presents such a schedule based on the simulated investment returns used earlier in this book. But retirees face another major uncertainty besides the future returns they will earn on their investments. This is the possibility that large extra withdrawals may be needed in the future to cover emergencies. This is in addition to the withdrawals to cover normal living expenses that have been considered so far.

Suppose, for instance, that water incursion requires major home repairs at some time in the future. Or suppose a child is in dire need and there is a compelling reason to provide major financial assistance. Covering such emergencies could have the same effect on the investment portfolio as a financial bear market. But unlike a bear market there is no possibility that such losses will later be reversed.

These sorts of emergencies are frequently not even on the radar at the beginning of retirement. And even if they are recognized, insurance for such risks is frequently not available or considered too costly. All that can be done with respect to such a diverse set of risks is to self-insure by saving more. But how much more savings to meet such needs is reasonable?

To provide an answer this chapter assumes there is a very small chance each year that an emergency will require a very large extra withdrawal. Withdrawals are then simulated that include both the risk of these very large extra withdrawals and the uncertainty of future investment returns considered earlier. A new schedule is obtained that includes both of these uncertainties. Suppose retirees and their advisors think that the simulated risk of such emergencies should be considered. They should then use the second schedule instead of the first to gauge savings requirements.

Another possible reason for large extra outlays over retirement is the possibility of elevated health care costs. This possibility differs from the earlier emergencies in several respects. The possibility of elevated health costs later in retirement typically is on the radar at the beginning of retirement, and a wide range of insurance is available for such contingencies. And, of course, almost all retirees at age 65 and over in the U. S. have insurance from Medicare to cover many medical problems.

Medicare, however, is widely recognized to have limited benefits for covering assisted care later in retirement. The Retrenchment Rule recognizes this problem by incorporating some self-insurance specifically tailored to this need. In particular, in projecting future withdrawals for the rule at any age an unusually long lifespan is assumed. Specifically those believed to be in as good health as can be expected for that age are assumed to have a limit on their life expectancy of age 110.

It is virtually certain, of course, that their health will take a turn for the worse at an earlier age, and very likely much earlier. And when this happens a reduction in the limit on their remaining lifespan becomes appropriate. The reduction in their lifespan increases the largest withdrawal allowed by the Retrenchment Rule. More funds are then available to provide some assistance in the tasks of daily living if that should become necessary.

At some point, of course, full time care may be required. At such a time those in the middle income range are unlikely to be able to cover the cost with the withdrawals allowed by the Retrenchment Rule. The rule will have to be ignored and the expense covered by the withdrawals that are necessary to do so.

Normally those following the Retrenchment Rule never run out of funds. This is because they have retrenched and reduced their standard of living well before that may happen. If it becomes necessary to cover full time nursing care, however, even those following the rule could run out of funds.

Simulations later in this chapter for those following the rule, however, show that running out of funds for this reason is very unlikely. The simulations show the chances the extra outlays could continue for various lengths of time. This is based on the size of the investment portfolio remaining for those using the rule before the full time care becomes necessary. The length of time care can be provided is then related to data on the probability of nursing home stays of varying length. Middle income retirees following the rule and saving enough for sizable sustainable withdrawals appear to have chances of running out of funds for this reason that are very low. For single retirees additional savings for this purpose do not appear necessary.

Finally, this chapter looks at the increase in savings requirements for those who want to retire early. Suppose individuals in the middle income range want to retire at age 55 instead of 65. Doing so may increase their savings requirement by 50 percent or more. One reason for the increase is to provide a comparably sustainable stream over the longer withdrawal period. For those in the middle income range, however, most of the increase is to cover the absence of Social Security benefits over the early part of their retirement.

The analysis in this chapter assumes that retirees are starting retirement in good health. It also assumes that asset valuations and inflation at the beginning of retirement are at a normal level. And it also ignores taxes. Chapter 9 considers how poor health at the beginning of retirement reduces savings requirements. Chapter 11 considers the extent to which abnormal asset valuations at the beginning of retirement increase or decrease savings requirements. Chapter 13 shows how an income tax increases savings requirements especially when a large portion of the initial portfolio is in a traditional IRA.

The analysis in this chapter assumes that individuals are normally planning to begin their retirement at age 65. Chapter 5 discussed why those who retire at 65 nevertheless have an incentive to defer the start of their Social Security until age 70. To simplify in this chapter, however, it is convenient to assume for those retiring at age 65 that their Social Security also begins at that time. The possibility that they will actually defer the start of their Social Security means that the results for their withdrawals are somewhat better than shown.

7.1 Investment Size and Sustainability

In the analysis in earlier chapters the size of the investment at the beginning of retirement is fixed. What varies is the size of the standard of living that can be obtained from that investment. If the percentage withdrawn from the investment declines a corresponding decline occurs in the standard of living provided by the given investment.

In this chapter the size of the desired standard of living is fixed. What varies is the size of the investment at the beginning of retirement to provide that standard of living. For instance, in earlier chapters a decline in the initial withdrawal from 6 to 3 percent reflected a substantial decline in standard of living. In this chapter there is no change in the standard of living when the initial withdrawal declines from 6 to 3 percent. In this chapter when the initial withdrawal declines from 6 to 3 percent the investment is twice as large.

Due to this difference the results of the simulations in this chapter are presented in a different format. Future withdrawals in this chapter are presented as a proportion of their initial value. When these proportions are the same the standard of living being provided by the withdrawals is the same irrespective of the size of the initial investment.

Suppose, for instance, that the initial annual withdrawal to cover expenses is $30,000. The value of the portfolio for a 3 or 4 percent withdrawal is then respectively $1,000,000 or $750,000. This is because 3 or 4 percent of these respective amounts is equal to $30,000. In the future the 3 and 4 percent withdrawals provide the same amount when they both decline by the same proportion of their initial value. Thus, suppose the 3 and 4 percent withdrawals each decline by a half to 1.5 and 2 percent respectively. In this case both future withdrawals are the same and equal to $15,000. The future withdrawals are therefore reported in this chapter as half of their initial value to make them the same for differing percentages of the initial withdrawal.

Simulated future withdrawals on this basis are shown in Table 7-1. This is for a series of initial withdrawals ranging from 3 to 6 percent. Note that the expected future withdrawals at ages 75, 85, and 95 in this table are given as a proportion of their initial value. And the probabilities for future withdrawals are given as ranges for their proportion of initial value. For instance, the probabilities given for .6 in the table are the chances that a withdrawal has declined to from .5 to .7 of its initial value.

Table 7-1

Effect of Portfolio Size on the Sustainability of Withdrawals

Base Case for Investment Returns and Inflation*

Annuity Rate 7.5% RDR .08

Age	Withdrawal Age 65**	Stocks/IntGovts/ Annuities	Withdrawal/Initial Value***						
			Expected	1.0	.8	.6	.4	.2	0
75	3.0	75/25/0	1.00	.99	.01	0	0	0	0
	3.5	75/25/0	.99	.97	.02	.01	0	0	0
	4.0	75/25/0	.98	.94	.04	.02	0	0	0
	5.0	75/0/25	.93	.76	.14	.08	.02	0	0
	6.0	50/0/50	.87	.52	.31	.16	.01	0	0
85	3.0	75/25/0	.98	.95	.03	.01	.01	0	0
	3.5	75/25/0	.96	.90	.04	.04	.02	0	0
	4.0	75/25/0	.94	.84	.06	.06	.03	.01	0
	5.0	75/0/25	.85	.63	.13	.13	.09	.02	0
	6.0	50/0/50	.78	.39	.25	.23	.12	.01	0
95	3.0	75/25/0	.97	.93	.02	.02	.02	.01	0
	3.5	75/25/0	.94	.86	.04	.04	.04	.02	0
	4.0	75/25/0	.90	.78	.06	.07	.06	.03	0
	5.0	75/0/25	.80	.57	.12	.13	.13	.05	0
	6.0	50/0/50	.72	.34	.21	.22	.19	.04	0

*Assumptions about investment returns and inflation are the same as in Tables 5-2 and 5-3.

**Same initial expenses are covered by investments of varying size.

***Probability that withdrawals in real terms as a proportion of their initial value are from .1 below to .1 above .8, .6, .4, or .2, or from 1.0 to .9 or 0 to .1.

Other than the change in the format of the presentation these simulations are similar to those presented earlier. The assumptions about the returns on investment and inflation are the same as in Chapter 5. The rate on the annuity is also the same as in Chapter 5. And the results are based on 10,000 replications.

Chapter 5 argued that allocating 25 percent or more of the portfolio to fixed incomes is appropriate when the initial withdrawal is reasonably sustainable. And the returns on fixed incomes were simulated to resemble those of the intermediate government issues reported in the SBBI Yearbook. As initial withdrawals of 4 percent or less are reasonably sustainable it is assumed that the portfolio in these cases in Table 7-1 is allocated 25 percent to fixed incomes at the beginning of each year. And these returns are simulated to resemble those of intermediate government issues as before. Chapter 5 also argued that half of the investment should be annuitized when the initial withdrawal has poor sustainability. For the 6 percent withdrawal half of the initial portfolio has therefore been annuitized. For the 5 percent initial withdrawal 25 percent has been annuitized as an intermediate case.

As expected, the sustainability of the future stream of withdrawals improves in Table 7-1 as the initial percentage withdrawal declines. At later ages the expected withdrawals decline less. Also, there is an increasing chance that the initial withdrawal will be sustained to a later age and there is less risk of very low withdrawals.

7.2 Optimal Savings

The commonly recommended initial annual withdrawal to provide a sustainable standard of living is 4 percent. Table 7-1 shows, however, that 4 percent is at best at the upper end of the range of initial withdrawals that might be considered as reasonably sustainable under these conditions. At age 75 there is high assurance that 4 percent can be sustained and reasonable assurance at age 85. At age 95, however, the sustainability is not very good. There is a .22 chance that the withdrawal will be less than .9 of its initial value, and a .09 chance that it will be less than half of its initial value.

For high assurance of sustainability at age 95 only 3 percent can be withdrawn initially. For a 3 percent initial withdrawal there is only a .07 chance that the withdrawal will be less than .9 of its initial value at age 95. And there is only a .03 chance that it will be less than half of its initial value.

How much to save for retirement, however, depends on the costs as well as the benefits. Table 7-1 shows the benefits of saving more. But these benefits must be weighed against the cost of additional savings in terms of the effect on the preretirement standard of living.

Assessing an optimal level of savings starts with an estimate of the spending necessary to provide a desired standard of living in retirement. This includes spending for recurring activities each year and a normal level for non-recurring expenses that are uncertain. Possible major outlays for the sorts of emergencies discussed earlier are taken into account in the next section of this chapter.

An estimate of the Social Security that will be available is deducted from the expected normal expense. The required investment is obtained by grossing up the expenses not covered by Social Security for the required initial withdrawal percentage. This is the withdrawal percentage required to obtain an acceptable degree of sustainability.

Suppose that there is a pension and that retirement is expected to begin at about age 65. Based on the discussion in the last chapter for an RDR of .08 the expected annual real benefit of the pension is multiplied by 10 to get the equivalent value it contributes to the required investment. Suppose there are other expected inflows or outflows. The present value of the expected real value of these future flows is calculated using the RDR as the rate of interest. The required investment is then adjusted further to reflect these present values.

The next step is to assess how difficult it will be to accumulate the estimated required investment after any applicable adjustments. If saving this much appears too difficult the next step is to consider reducing the desired standard of living and/or the acceptable degree of sustainability. The difficulty of accumulating the reduced investment is assessed and the process repeated if necessary. As just described achieving sufficient sustainability is an iterative process that takes into account both the costs and benefits of achieving it. Table 7-1 shows just the benefits of additional savings. To determine optimal savings the increased benefits from more savings must be weighed against the increased cost of achieving those additional savings.

7.3 Emergencies and Required Savings

Table 7-1 shows the effect on sustainability of uncertainty about future investment returns. But there is also another major risk. As discussed earlier this risk is the possibility that one or more very large extra withdrawals may be required to cover emergencies. And frequently these possibilities are not even on the radar before the start of retirement. And even if their nature has been identified their timing and severity are highly uncertain.

To illustrate some of the possibilities suppose when away from home that a water pipe bursts. Beyond any insurance that may exist, the cost of repairing the damage could have the same effect on the investment portfolio as a financial bear market. Moreover, unlike a financial bear market the effect of the cost of the repairs is not reversible in the future. Similar damage could arise from the overflow of a local stream, a mudslide, or a buildup of mold behind the walls from an unknown leak. Hurricanes, tornados, and earthquakes may be on the radar in some areas, but the severity and location of such events sometimes surprises.

As another type of emergency suppose that a child develops a serious medical problem. The child has insurance that will cover part of the cost, but there is nowhere near enough to cover what is desirable for a full recovery. As a result suppose a compelling need arises to make a financial contribution to the child comparable in size to the cost of the repairs for the earlier damage.

Perhaps a major emergency arises, but the expense is not as large as for the earlier problems. But together with a number of other smaller items cumulative extra withdrawals may be required that are as large. Suppose one year, for instance, that wind damage requires roof repairs of $30,000. Suppose another year that a couple of dental implants are required at a cost of $8,000. Sometimes it may be possible to offset some of these necessary extra expenses by reducing discretionary items, but such cuts are likely to be nowhere near sufficient.

As with the occurrence of financial bear markets the severity of such emergencies, how many there are, and when they will occur are unknown. And these uncertainties are an important part of the risk that needs to be simulated to realistically evaluate the sustainability of investment withdrawals. To do so it will be assumed that there is a very small chance of an emergency occurring each year.

Under this assumption there is a reasonable chance that no emergency will occur over retirement. But there is also a reasonable chance that there will be one or two emergencies, or a small chance that there will be even more. Moreover, as in accord with reality these emergencies can occur at any time over a retirement.

In particular, suppose each year that there is a .05 chance that an emergency will occur. Over a 20 year period the chances that a given number of emergencies will occur under this assumption can be calculated using the binomial distribution. These chances appear realistic. There is a .36 chance that there will not be any emergencies. There is a .38 chance of one, a .19 chance of two, a .06 chance of three, and a .01 chance of more than three. On average over the 20 years one emergency is expected.

The cost of an emergency of the type described earlier is likely to represent a significant portion of the initial investment. For instance, the cost of major home repairs will be proportional to the value of the home, which in turn will be related to the value of the investment accumulated for retirement. But the expenditure for an emergency may have to be limited if the investment portfolio has become unduly depleted at the time the emergency occurs.

In view of this latter consideration it will be assumed that the outlay for the emergency does not exceed 25 percent of the value of the investment in real terms at the time the emergency occurs. On the other hand, if sufficient funds are available without violating this limit, it will be assumed that the outlay for the emergency is equal in real terms to 20 percent of the initial value of the investment. Thus, as earlier, the emergency if it occurs has a comparable effect on the value of the investment as a financial bear market. But retirees will limit the expenditure on the emergency if necessary to provide sufficient funds for future living expenses.

When an emergency occurs the Retrenchment Rule may require a significant reduction in the withdrawals that are allowed and in the standard of living. On the other hand, if investment returns have been favorable a large extra withdrawal for an emergency may be accommodated with little difficulty. By increasing the risk of low withdrawals later in retirement the possibility of emergencies could make it desirable to use a lower discount rate for the RDR. This possibility is considered in Appendix 7-1. Appendix 7-2 discusses the modification of the spreadsheet to include possible emergencies.

Based on Table 7-1 presumably most individuals and their advisors will conclude that enough should be accumulated to allow normal living expenses to be covered by an annual withdrawal from investments of no more than 4 percent.

The effect of emergencies on future sustainability will therefore be examined only for withdrawals of 4 percent or less. The effect of including the risk of the emergencies on the simulated withdrawals is shown in Table 7-2.

To facilitate comparison the results without the emergencies in Table 7-1 are also repeated in Table 7-2. These results are shown where No appears in the second column from the left. The results when the risk of the emergencies is included in the simulations are shown where Yes appears in the second column.

Without the risk of the emergencies a 4 percent withdrawal appears to be at the upper limit of what might be considered as reasonably sustainable. When the risk of the emergencies is included there is no way that a 4 percent withdrawal can still be considered as reasonably sustainable. There is now a .37 chance that the withdrawal will be less than .9 of its initial value at age 95. And there is a .22 chance that it will be less than .5 of its initial value.

When the risk of the emergencies is included suppose it is desired to limit the risk that the withdrawals will be less than .5 of initial value at age 95 to .09, which is the risk for a 4 percent withdrawal without the emergencies. Table 7-2 shows that only 3 percent can then be withdrawn. To see that this is true compare the 3 percent withdrawal for Yes and the 4 percent withdrawal for No immediately above it in Table 7-2. The chances in both cases are .09 that the withdrawal will be less than .5 of initial value at age 95. Similar comparisons give similar results at ages 75 and 85. Besides a low risk of low withdrawals, however, retirees also want a high probability of being able to sustain their initial withdrawal. To assess the sustainability of the initial withdrawal look at the chances in Table 7-2 that the future withdrawals will be at least .9 of their initial value. For the 4 percent withdrawal without emergencies these chances are the same when the withdrawal with the emergencies is between 3 and 3.5 percent.

Thus, with the emergencies a somewhat higher withdrawal than 3 percent is possible to achieve the same probability that the initial withdrawal will be above .9 of initial value. But the withdrawal must be less than 3.5 percent to achieve this comparability. Taking into account that only 3 percent can be withdrawn to achieve the same risk of low withdrawals the following appears to be a fair conclusion.

Table 7-2

Effect of Emergencies on Reasonably Sustainable Withdrawals
Investment Returns for Normal Valuation Each Year
Stocks/IntGovts 75/25 RDR .08

Age	Extras*	Withdrawal Age 65		Withdrawal / Initial Value**					
			Expected	1.0	.8	.6	.4	.2	0
75	No	3.0	1.00	.99	.01	0	0	0	0
		3.5	.99	.97	.02	.01	0	0	0
		4.0	.98	.94	.04	.02	0	0	0
	Yes	3.0	.99	.97	.02	.01	0	0	0
		3.5	.98	.94	.03	.02	.01	0	0
		4.0	.96	.88	.07	.03	.02	0	0
85	No	3.0	.98	.95	.03	.01	.01	0	0
		3.5	.96	.90	.04	.04	.02	0	0
		4.0	.94	.84	.06	.06	.03	.01	0
	Yes	3.0	.96	.89	.04	.04	.02	.01	0
		3.5	.92	.81	.06	.07	.04	.02	0
		4.0	.87	.71	.09	.09	.08	.03	0
95	No	3.0	.97	.93	.02	.02	.02	.01	0
		3.5	.94	.86	.04	.04	.04	.02	0
		4.0	.90	.78	.06	.07	.06	.03	0
	Yes	3.0	.91	.83	.04	.04	.05	.04	0
		3.5	.86	.73	.05	.07	.09	.05	0
		4.0	.80	.63	.07	.08	.12	.09	0

*For Yes there is a .05 chance each year of an extra withdrawal equal to the smaller of 25% of the value of the portfolio when it occurs or 20% of the initial portfolio in real terms.
**Same as Table 7-1.

With the emergencies only close to 3 percent can be withdrawn to achieve the same sustainability as 4 percent without the emergencies. The conventional belief is that saving enough to cover living expenses with an annual withdrawal of 4 percent from investments will provide a sustainable standard of living. Based on Table 7-1, 4 percent appears to be at the upper end of such withdrawals when possible emergencies are ignored. When the risk of possible emergencies is included Table 7-2 shows that individuals should be thinking in terms of saving enough for an annual withdrawal of close to 3 percent, not 4 percent.

7.4 Providing for Elevated Health Costs

The earlier simulations assume that retirees are in good health and at age 65 when they begin retirement. In using the Retrenchment Rule retirees are also assumed to have a limit on their life expectancy of age 110. Furthermore, as a base case, they are assumed to remain in as good health as can be expected as they grow older so that the limit on their life expectancy remains at age 110. Thus, in using the rule each year they plan on continuing to make withdrawals for each year up to and including the year in which they are 109.

It is virtually certain, of course, that their health will take a turn for the worse at an earlier age, and very likely much earlier. When health begins to deteriorate a reduction in the limit on their remaining lifespan becomes appropriate. And when this reduction is taken into account in using the Retrenchment Rule increased withdrawals are allowed. Funds are released to cover assistance that may become necessary for some of the tasks of daily living. Additional funds are also released by the accelerated slowing in lifestyle that occurs with the deterioration in health.

Note that the Retrenchment Rule by assuming a longer than usual lifespan has in effect created a reserve to cover a significant amount of elevated health care needs later in retirement. This is apart from any of the earlier emergencies that may arise. Moreover, this reserve is well suited to this particular problem. The earlier the age at which health takes a turn for the worse the larger is the reserve available. This is appropriate because the earlier assistance becomes necessary the longer is it likely to be required,

Often when health first takes a turn for the worse retirees will be able to remain at home with limited assistance. Some aid may be available from close relatives or friends. In addition home health aide or homemaker/ companion services are available from agencies.

A survey by MetLife indicates the cost of such services in 2008 averaged about $20 per hour in the U.S. There was a range of from $12 to $28 depending on the area (MetLife 2008a). With cuts in other expenses many in the middle income range should be able to afford a modest amount of assistance at home. With 8,750 hours in a year, however, around the clock care is clearly out of the question except for a very short period.

Those who anticipate that they may need more care for a significant period will have to move to where such care is affordable. The first step in doing so is an independent residence in an assisted living community. For those owning a home its sale in making such a move provides funds to help cover the cost.

A survey by MetLife indicates that the base rate for such assisted living services in 2008 for the U.S. averaged about $3,000 per month (MetLife 2008b). There was a range of from $2,000 to $4,800 depending on the area. An increase of $500 per month or more may be applicable to those requiring services not included in the base rate. There may also be an initial admission fee of $60,000 to $120,000.

When more extensive care becomes necessary on a 24 hour basis a move becomes necessary to a nursing home facility. And a significant increase occurs in cost. In some cases there is a nursing home facility attached to the assisted living community.

A MetLife survey for nursing homes in the U.S. for 2008 shows a daily average rate of about $200. Excluding Alaska there was a range of from about $125 to $350 depending on the area. For most in the middle income range this care will exceed their normal living expenses and their withdrawal allowed by the Retrenchment Rule.

No attempt will be made to simulate the various possibilities that may occur. A simple way, however, to depict the essential problem is the following. Suppose retirees follow the Retrenchment Rule up until a given age. At that time suppose nursing home care becomes necessary for as long as they survive. The chances of providing such care for various lengths of time from the remaining portfolio at that age can be simulated.

Simulations of the possible need for nursing home care start under the same conditions as the earlier simulations that tested the effect of emergencies. Now, however, beginning at a preset future age withdrawals of a preset amount occur for nursing home care. These withdrawals continue each year until the portfolio runs out of funds. The computer keeps a record of whether that withdrawal is still being made for a given number of years after it begins. At the end of the simulations the computer reports the proportion of runs for which the withdrawal was still being made for a given number of years.

The preset withdrawal to cover the cost of care depends on an estimate of how much nursing home care will cost in a given area at a future time. As a percentage of the initial investment it also depends, of course, on the initial value of the investment. Suppose the only sources of funds other than the portfolio are Social Security and any remaining funds from the sale of a home. Social Security is deducted from the estimated cost of the care and the residual expressed as a percentage of the initial investment. Any contribution that might be available from home equity if the portfolio runs out of funds is considered separately.

As an illustration consider the case of Louise Logan in the introductory scenario in Chapter 1. Suppose her annual care in the future is estimated to be $80,000 in real terms. Deducting her Social Security of $20,000 gives a required withdrawal of $60,000 to cover the care. This is 10 percent of her initial portfolio of $600,000. In the simulations it is therefore assumed that an annual withdrawal of 10 percent is made when full time nursing care is assumed to start. The appropriate percentage of this withdrawal in other cases will, of course, depend on the circumstances in those cases. Modification of the spreadsheet to include the possibility of full time nursing care is discussed in Appendix 7-2.

Table 7-3 shows the probability of sustaining the 10 percent withdrawal for at least the number of years given at the top of the columns on the right. The initial withdrawal at age 65 and the age at which the care first becomes necessary are shown on the left. The other conditions are the same as those in Table 7-2 without the emergencies.

Table 7-3

Covering Nursing Home Care for Sustainable Withdrawals Age 65
Investment Returns for Normal Valuation Each Year
Stocks/IntGovts 75/25 RDR .08

Withdrawal Age 65	Age Care Starts	Probability Portfolio Sufficient Years After Care Starts*				
		2	4	6	8	10
3.0	75	1.00	.97	.91	.83	.75
	85	.97	.93	.88	.82	.77
	95	.94	.90	.86	.82	.79
3.5	75	1.00	.96	.89	.80	.71
	85	.96	.89	.83	.77	.72
	95	.91	.85	.80	.76	.72
4.0	75	.99	.95	.87	.76	.66
	85	.95	.85	.78	.71	.66
	95	.87	.79	.74	.69	.66

*When care starts 10% of initial investment in real terms is withdrawn each year as long as possible.

7.5 Adequacy of Savings for Care

In order to assess the adequacy of the care provided in Table 7-3 estimates are needed of the chances such care will be needed for various lengths of time. Jeffrey Brown and Amy Finkelstein (2008) report some estimates that can be used for this purpose. They attribute these estimates in part to well known but unpublished work of James Robinson that is widely used in the insurance industry. These estimates are as follows.

Suppose a 65 year old woman is in sufficiently good health to be eligible to purchase long-term care insurance. The chances that she will spend from 1 to 3,

3 to 5, or more than 5 years in a nursing home are respectively .09, .04, and .05. The chances she will spend less than a year are .26.

The simulations assume that the care continues till the end of life, but the nursing home care in these data can end for other reasons. Presumably, however, in these other cases the care is most likely to be for less than a year. Also, Table 7-3 indicates that stays of less than a year are very likely to be covered by the portfolio. And if the portfolio is not sufficient additional funds are likely to be available from home equity. For these reasons stays of less than one year will be ignored.

The reported average age for first entering a nursing home for these data is 84. This includes those who will not stay till the end of life, which may tend to lower the average. Nevertheless, it will be assumed that these estimates are reasonably representative for those in Table 7-3 whose care begins at age 85.

Those who first begin care much earlier than age 85 will presumably tend on average to have longer stays than the estimates just cited. Table 7-3 shows, however, that those starting at age 75 also have a significantly higher chance of providing care from their portfolio for a given length of time. Thus, these factors tend to be offsetting for those starting care much earlier than age 85. They tend to need care for a longer time, but their portfolio tends to be larger and to provide care for a longer time. Similarly, those starting much later than age 85 will presumably tend to have shorter stays. But Table 7-3 shows that those starting at age 95 also have an offsetting lower chance of providing care from their portfolio for a given length of time.

For women starting at age 65 the earlier estimate says that .09 of them should expect to spend from 1 to 3 years in a nursing home, and therefore require on average about 2 years of care. Suppose that they have withdrawn 4 percent initially so that the lower panel of three rows is applicable. For starting care at age 85 under these conditions Table 7-3 shows a .95 chance that the portfolio will cover at least 2 years of care. Thus, on average only about .05 of the .09 will need to cover part of the care from other sources than their portfolio. This is equal to only .0045 of them as .05(.09)=.0045.

The earlier estimate also says that .04 of the women at age 65 will need care for from 3 to 5 years, or for 4 years on average. Table 2 indicates on the same basis that the chances of providing at least 4 years of care from the portfolio are

.85. Thus, on average only .15 of the .04 will not be able to cover all of the care from their portfolio. This is only .0060 of them as .15(.04)=.0060.

Finally, the earlier estimate says that .05 of the women at age 65 on average will need care for more than 5 years. Suppose on average that this is 8 years of care. Table 7-3 indicates that the chances are .71 that at least 8 years of care will be available from the portfolio. Thus, on average .29 of the .05 will require funds for part of their care from other sources. This is equal to only .0145 of them as .29(.05)=.0145.

The chances that women at age 65 will need care from sources other than their portfolio under these conditions are the sum of the chances for the three cases just examined. These chances are only about .025 as .0045+.006+.0145=.025. It is certainly possible to question the way averages were used to arrive at this estimate. Nevertheless, these chances are clearly very small. Moreover, it is likely that funds will also remain from sale of a home to cover care if the portfolio is exhausted. The chances that women under these conditions will eventually have to depend on Medicaid to cover care are therefore even smaller.

For men the estimated chances of spending the same periods of time in a nursing home are significantly less. At age 65 the chances of spending from 1 to 3, 3 to 5, or more than 5 years in a nursing home are respectively .06, .02 and .01. Suppose the same analysis is carried out for men. The chances that men will have to depend on sources other than their portfolio for nursing home care under otherwise the same conditions are less than half that for women.

Suppose that middle income retirees follow the Retrenchment Rule and have saved enough to cover living expenses with sizable reasonably sustainable investment withdrawals. It appears that these retirees have only a very small chance of running out of funds due to the need to cover full time nursing care. Retirees concerned about running out of funds for this reason can purchase insurance to help avoid such a possibility. Brown and Finkelstein in the paper cited earlier, however, discuss why some may not purchase such insurance because they are willing to rely on Medicaid if such a contingency occurs. And funds from the equity in their home may also remain. It should also be noted that savings allocated for this particular purpose are not available to cover the general types of emergencies discussed earlier.

Where long-term care insurance is of particular importance is for couples. For a couple covering elevated health care costs for one of them from their portfolio depletes the funds needed for living expenses for the other. And Medicaid may not be available to cover the cost of care until most of the assets are depleted.

For single retirees long-term care insurance will help maintain the value of their estate in the event that covered costs for care are incurred. Without such insurance, however, it appears very likely that they will nevertheless be able to cover elevated health care costs later in retirement. This is if they are following the Retrenchment Rule and have saved enough to cover normal living expenses with a sizable reasonably sustainable initial withdrawal. Additional savings for this purpose do not appear necessary.

7.6 Early Retirement

So far it has been assumed that retirement begins at age 65. But suppose that individuals want to retire at an earlier age. For instance, how much more savings would be required to retire at age 55?

Significant increases in savings are required at age 55 for two reasons. One is that a larger investment is required to provide a comparably sustainable stream of withdrawals over the longer withdrawal period. The other reason is the need to cover the absence of Social Security benefits for a number of years when retiring at age 55.

To consider the effect of the longer withdrawal period suppose withdrawals start at either age 55 or 65. And suppose the real value of the investment is the same in either case as are the subsequent distributions of the returns on the investment. Suppose also that the real value of the initial withdrawal is the same in either case, and that subsequent withdrawals are made using the Retrenchment Rule.

Under these conditions the chances are higher that the withdrawals starting at age 65 will exceed a given value at any subsequent age than the withdrawals that start at age 55. The only way to get a comparably sustainable stream of withdrawals after age 65, when starting at age 55, is to start with a larger investment. With a larger investment the sustainability of the withdrawals starting at age 55 deteriorates at a slower rate. Thus, as the investment at age 55 increases eventually the withdrawals from that stream will have better sustainability at age 95 and subsequently. The withdrawals starting at age 65, however, will still have better sustainability at earlier ages.

Suppose, however, that further increases occur in the investment at age 55. At some point the better sustainability later in the period of the withdrawals starting at age 55 will be sufficient to compensate for their worse sustainability earlier in the period. The increase in the investment necessary to achieve this balance can be considered as the additional savings necessary to achieve a comparably sustainable stream of withdrawals starting at age 55.

As just described a significant increase in savings is required to make a comparably sustainable withdrawal of the same amount when starting at age 55 compared to age 65. But additional increases in savings are also required to provide the same standard of living at age 55. This is because larger withdrawals must be made for a number of years to cover the absence of Social Security benefits when starting at age 55.

Suppose retirees at age 65 will make a 4 percent withdrawal from their investment. Suppose also at age 65 that there are three possibilities with respect to their Social Security benefits. In one they do not have any Social Security. In the other two cases their Social Security benefit each year will be equal to either 2 or 4 percent in real terms of their investment at age 65.

Suppose starting at age 55 that a withdrawal is made of the same size as the funds that will be provided from the investment and the Social Security in each case at age 65. The question is how large an investment is required to provide comparable sustainability for the withdrawals from both the investment and the Social Security when starting at age 55 instead of age 65? To find the answer some modifications are required in the simulations.

Before the Social Security begins the present value of the expected future benefits is calculated each year using the RDR as the rate of interest. This present value is added to the value of the investment each year to determine the largest withdrawal allowed by the Retrenchment Rule. Before the Social Security begins, however, an additional limit is also required.

Table 7-4

Comparable Withdrawals for Starting Retirement at Ages 55 and 65

Investment Returns for Normal Valuation Each Year

Stocks/IntGovts 75/25 RDR .08

Portfolio*		Withdrawal*		Soc. Sec.*								
Age	Age	Age	Age	Age	Age	Withdrawal / Initial Value**						
55	65	55	65	65		Expected	1.0	.8	.6	.4	.2	0
	100		4	0	75	.98	.94	.04	.02	0	0	0
					85	.94	.84	.06	.06	.03	.01	0
					95	.90	.78	.06	.07	.06	.03	0
118		4		0	75	.97	.91	.04	.03	.02	0	0
					85	.94	.86	.05	.04	.04	.01	0
					95	.92	.84	.04	.04	.05	.03	0
	100		4	2	75	.99	.95	.04	.01	0	0	0
					85	.96	.86	.09	.05	0	0	0
					95	.93	.80	.09	.09	.02	0	0
138		6		2	75	.98	.92	.05	.03	0	0	0
					85	.96	.87	.06	.06	.01	0	0
					95	.94	.84	.07	.07	.02	0	0
	100		4	4	75	.99	.97	.03	0	0	0	0
					85	.97	.88	.10	.02	0	0	0
					95	.95	.82	.12	.04	.02	0	0
158		8		4	75	.98	.92	.07	.01	0	0	0
					85	.97	.88	.08	.04	0	0	0
					95	.96	.86	.08	.06	0	0	0

*Portfolios, withdrawals, and Social Security are percentages of the value of the investment at age 65.

**Probability that withdrawals in real terms as a proportion of their initial value are from .1 below to .1 above .8, .6, .4, .2, or from 1.0 to .9 or 0 to .1.

This additional limit is a precaution to make sure that there will be enough cash to make the withdrawals before Social Security begins. This second limit is the annuity that the investment would provide each year up until the expected start of Social Security. This is given that the investment earns a return equal to the RDR. There is virtually no chance, however, that this second limit will reduce the withdrawals in cases where early retirement may be viable.

Starting at age 55 instead 65 could also affect the choice of the RDR. Chapter 9 shows, however, that the length of the horizon has little effect on the selection of the RDR. An RDR of .08 will therefore be used for the rule when starting from either age 55 or 65.

The results of the simulations are shown in Table 7-4. By trial and error the size of the investment is determined at age 55 that makes the distribution of the withdrawals at age 85 about the same as when starting at age 65. In all cases this makes the sustainability of the withdrawals starting at age 55 somewhat worse at age 75 and somewhat better at age 95 than the withdrawals when starting at age 65. On balance, however, over ages 75, 85, and 95 the sustainability of the withdrawals starting at either age appears to be about the same over retirement.

Table 7-4 shows that the investment must be increased by about 18 percent to get comparable withdrawals when starting at age 55 when there is no Social Security. When there is Social Security a further increase in the investment is required that is about equal to the cumulative real value of the benefits up until the time they begin. Thus, when the Social Security benefits are equal to 2 percent each year this cumulative value is 20 percent of the value of the investment at age 65. The required investment for equivalence at age 55 is therefore 38 percent higher than at age 65. When the benefits are 4 percent the required investment for equivalence is 58 percent higher.

For those in the middle income range Social Security benefits will generally be in the range shown in the table, and require very large increases in savings to retire at age 55. For instance, in the scenario in Chapter 1 Louise Logan's $20,000 of Social Security was equal to 3.3 percent of her $600,000 investment. A 4 percent withdrawal plus the $20,000 of Social Security provided her with $44,000 to cover expenses each year. To provide $44,000 with comparable sustainability at age 55 based on Table 7-4 would require about a 50 percent larger investment, or $900,000 instead of $600,000. Note that this is to cover only $44,000 of expenses each year in real terms, not her anticipated need of $60,000 to avoid painful retrenchment.

Another way of pointing out the substantial additional needs for savings at age 55 is to compare the withdrawal rates. Even without any Social Security the withdrawal rate at age 55 required to get comparable sustainability to 4 percent at age 65 is 3.4 percent, as 4/118=.034. With Social Security of 2 or 4 percent of the investment at age 65 the withdrawals are respectively 4.4 and 5.1 percent of the required investment at age 55. This compares to withdrawals of 6 and 8 percent of the investment at age 65 when the Social Security is included in these cases.

7.7 Conclusions

The first step in determining the savings needed for retirement is to estimate the annual withdrawal from the savings needed to fund the desired standard of living. The next step is to determine the amount of savings necessary to provide this withdrawal with sufficient sustainability over all of retirement. Making this latter assessment requires a schedule. This schedule shows the sustainability of a series of possible initial annual percentage withdrawals. As the size of the investment increases the percentage withdrawn to fund a given standard of living declines and the sustainability of the withdrawal improves.

This schedule shows the benefit of saving more in terms of improved sustainability. But saving more may have an unacceptable cost in terms of reducing the preretirement standard of living. Determining optimal savings is therefore an iterative process. A withdrawal with a minimally acceptable degree of sustainability is determined from the schedule. An estimate is then made of the effect on the preretirement standard of living to achieve the necessary savings at retirement. This is to fund the necessary withdrawal for the desired standard of living with a sufficiently large investment to provide the required sustainability.

Suppose the cost of the required savings in terms of reducing the preretirement standard of living is deemed too large. Some tradeoffs are then necessary. Some reduction is necessary in the standard of living to be funded over retirement and/or some increase in the percentage withdrawal on the schedule. If the percentage withdrawal is increased there is, of course, a corresponding reduction in sustainability. The tradeoffs continue until the most acceptable compromise is found.

This chapter has focused on providing the schedule that shows the relationship between the percentage withdrawn initially and the sustainability of future withdrawals. Two schedules have been provided. One assumes the same uncertainty about future investment returns as in the earlier simulations. In this schedule the commonly recommended "sustainable" annual withdrawal of 4 percent under these conditions is at best at the upper end of what might be considered a reasonably sustainable range.

The other schedule includes additional uncertainty in the form of a very small chance each year of a large extra withdrawal to cover a major emergency. With this additional uncertainty only close to 3 percent can be withdrawn to get the same sustainability as a 4 percent withdrawal in the first schedule.

Another possible need for additional savings is to fund elevated health care needs later in retirement. The Retrenchment Rule in effect provides a reserve for this possibility by assuming an unusually long lifespan for those in good health. When health takes a turn for the worse the lifespan is appropriately reduced freeing up additional funds for assisted care if it should become necessary.

If full time care becomes necessary, however, those in the middle income range may no longer be able to cover the expense with the withdrawals allowed by the Retrenchment Rule. The possibility then arises of running out of funds. An analysis indicates, however, that running out of funds for this reason is very unlikely. Those who save enough for a sizable and reasonably sustainable withdrawal to cover living expenses should have enough to meet elevated health care needs later in retirement.

If individuals want to retire at age 55 instead of 65 savings requirements for those in the middle income range may rise by 50 percent or more. One reason is to provide for comparably sustainable withdrawals over the longer period. The other reason is to cover the absence of Social Security benefits for a number of years. For those in the middle income range the absence of Social Security accounts for most of the required increase.

The schedules derived in this chapter assume individuals are beginning retirement in good health. Asset valuations at the beginning of retirement are assumed to be at a normal level. Taxes have been ignored. Later chapters consider the effect of starting in poor health, starting when asset valuations are abnormal, and the effect of an income tax on savings requirements.

References

Brown, Jeffrey R., and Amy Finkelstein. 2008. "The Interaction of Public and Private Insurance: Medicaid and the Long-Term Care Insurance Market." *American Economic Review*, 98(3): 1083-1102.

MetLife Mature Market Institute. 2008a. "MetLife Market Survey of Adult Day Services & Home Care Costs 2008." http://metlife.com.

MetLife Mature Market Institute. 2008b. "MetLife Market Survey of Nursing Home & Assisted Living Costs 2008." http://metlife.com

Appendix 7-1

Effect of Emergencies on the RDR

The withdrawals with the emergencies have been simulated assuming the Retrenchment Rule is used with an RDR of .08. But the possibility of the emergencies significantly increases risk. And the higher risk could make it desirable to use a lower RDR to reduce the risk of low withdrawals later in retirement. To see whether this is true the simulations used to choose the RDR in Chapter 4 need to be rerun including the risk of the emergencies.

When this is done the argument for choosing a discount rate of .08 over .06 for the RDR is not as strong as in Chapter 4. Nevertheless, it is strong enough to indicate that even with the emergencies that almost all retirees will still want to choose an RDR of at least .08. When emergencies are considered, however, the need for reducing risk with part-time work and the purchase of a lifetime annuity becomes even more compelling than indicated in Chapter 5.

Table 7-5 shows the streams of expected withdrawals with the emergencies for a series of discount rates. And for ease of comparison the streams without the emergencies given earlier in Table 4-1 are also provided. With the emergencies the spread of the stream for .08 over .06 has narrowed somewhat. And the expected withdrawal for .08 at age 100 is now slightly less than that for .06 instead of being slightly higher.

The argument for choosing .08 over .06 in the lower panel of Table 7-5 is not as strong as in the upper panel. But there is still a strong argument for choosing .08 in the lower panel. In the lower panel the stream for .08 dominates that for .06 up through age 95. And there is a significant spread in favor of .08 early in retirement. Moreover, most retirees will not survive long enough for the withdrawals beyond age 95 to be relevant.

Table 7-5

Effect of Possible Emergencies on Expected Withdrawals

Stock Returns for Normal Valuation Each Year

Extras*	Discount Rate	Expected Withdrawals**							
		65	70	75	80	85	90	95	100
No	.04	4.6	3.9	3.7	3.5	3.5	3.4	3.4	3.3
	.06	6.1	5.0	4.5	4.3	4.1	4.0	3.9	3.8
	.08	7.6	6.0	5.2	4.8	4.4	4.2	4.0	3.9
	.10	9.2	6.9	5.8	5.0	4.5	4.1	3.8	3.5
Yes	.04	4.6	3.8	3.5	3.3	3.2	3.1	3.0	3.0
	.06	6.1	4.8	4.3	3.9	3.7	3.5	3.3	3.2
	.08	7.6	5.8	4.9	4.3	3.9	3.6	3.3	3.1
	.10	9.2	6.6	5.3	4.4	3.8	3.3	3.0	2.7

*Chance of emergency each year is .05. Extra withdrawal for an emergency is 20% of initial investment in real terms or 25% of current portfolio value, whichever is smaller.

**Expected withdrawals are in real terms as a percent of initial investment value.

Recall also that Chapter 4 argued that some retirees would likely prefer the stream for .10 to that for .08. Note in the upper panel that the stream for .10 is below that for .08 starting at age 90. But early in retirement the expected withdrawals for .10 are significantly above those for .08. Some retirees may be willing to accept the risk of the lower expected withdrawals late in retirement to achieve the improvement in standard of living earlier in retirement when survival is more likely.

Note in the lower panel, however, that the stream for .08 relative to .06 is significantly more favorable than is the stream for .10 relative to that for .08 in the upper panel. Clearly, many more will prefer .08 to .06 in the lower panel than will prefer .10 to .08 in the upper panel. And it is not unreasonable to believe that almost all will prefer .08 to .06 in the lower panel.

Table 7-5, however, considers only the streams of expected withdrawals. There is the possibility in the lower panel that a discount rate of .06 reduces the risk of low withdrawals sufficiently to justify its selection despite the lower expected withdrawals it provides. Chapter 4 showed that .06 did reduce the risk of low withdrawals later in retirement relative to .08. But the reduction in risk appeared to be nowhere near enough to compensate for the lower stream of expected withdrawals provided by .06 earlier in retirement.

Table 7-6 shows the risk of low withdrawals that was shown earlier in Chapter 4, and also the risk when the possible emergencies are included in the simulations. The emergencies significantly increase the risk of very low withdrawals late in retirement. For instance, for a discount rate of .08 the risk that the withdrawals will be less than 3 percent at ages 85 and 95 rises respectively from .30 and .39 to .42 and .53.

But there is also a significant increase in this risk for a discount rate of .06. For .06 the risk that the withdrawals will be less than 3 percent rises from .29 and .35 to .39 and .47. The emergencies cause a significant increase in risk for both discount rates. The emergencies, however, provide only a small improvement in the risk reduction provided by the lower discount rate. The emergencies make choosing .06 somewhat more attractive since the emergencies increase somewhat more the reduction in risk later in retirement provided by choosing .06. But the reduction in risk later in retirement still does not appear sufficient to warrant the lower withdrawals that .06 provides earlier in retirement.

Table 7-6

Effect on Withdrawal Probabilities of Possible Emergencies
Stock Returns for Normal Valuation Each Year

Age	Extras*	Discount Rate	Withdrawal Probability**					
			10	8	6	4	2	0
75	No	.10	.12	.20	.27	.29	.12	0
		.08		.23	.32	.32	.13	0
		.06			.43	.41	.16	0
	Yes	.10	.10	.16	.25	.31	.18	0
		.08		.19	.28	.34	.19	0
		.06			.37	.40	.22	.01
85	No	.10	.08	.12	.18	.27	.30	.05
		.08		.17	.23	.30	.27	.03
		.06			.35	.36	.27	.02
	Yes	.10	.06	.09	.13	.24	.39	.09
		.08		.13	.18	.27	.35	.07
		.06			.28	.33	.34	.05
95	No	.10	.06	.09	.14	.23	.34	.14
		.08		.15	.19	.27	.31	.08
		.06			.32	.33	.30	.05
	Yes	.10	.05	.06	.09	.17	.38	.25
		.08		.11	.15	.21	.36	.17
		.06			.25	.28	.36	.11

*Same as Table 7-5.

**Probability that withdrawal is in a range from one above to one below 10, 8, 6, 4, or 2, or from 0 to 1. Withdrawals are in real terms as a percentage of initial investment.

Using a lower discount rate than .08 is therefore not an effective way of reducing the risk of low withdrawals later in retirement. But clearly this risk does need to be reduced. Chapter 5 showed that most of the risk of very low withdrawals could be eliminated by investing half of the portfolio in a lifetime annuity and achieving significant part-time earnings. In the example of doing so in Chapter 5 the risk that the withdrawals will be less than 3 percent at ages 85 and 95 was reduced from .30 and .39 to .04 and .12.

With the emergencies significant reductions in risk can be obtained in the same way. With the emergencies under the same conditions the risk is reduced from .42 and .53 to .09 and .23. As to be expected, the risk remains higher with the emergencies, but it is now much more reasonable. Any further reduction in risk requires saving more before the start of retirement.

Appendix 7-2

Modifying the Spreadsheet for Emergencies and Assisted Care

To modify the spreadsheet in Table 3-1 to incorporate the extra withdrawals for emergencies that have been specified a new column is introduced to calculate whether an emergency occurs in any year. And the relations for investment value in column C are rewritten. This is to reflect the change in value of the investment that is available to make the regular withdrawals for living expenses if an emergency does occur.

Whether an emergency occurs can be calculated in column N. To do so insert in cell N6

=If(Rand() ≤.05,20,0)

and copy it to lower rows in column N to N50. The relation, If(x, y, z), is a logical function in Excel that is equal to y when x is true and z otherwise. As specified this relation generates a value of 20 with probability .05 and 0 with probability .95.

The value of the investment available at the beginning of year 2 for making regular withdrawals in C7 is rewritten to be:

=Max((C6-B6)*(1+E6)-N6,.75*(C6-B6)*(1+E6)).

This reduces the investment by the smaller of 20% of the initial investment or 25% of the value of the investment if an emergency occurs. This is the specified value of the extra withdrawal in the event of an emergency. This relation is then copied to lower rows in column C to C50. The other cells in Table 3-1 remain the same with the possible exception of the discount rate and initial withdrawal. Similar modifications are made in Table 5-8 when annuitization or part-time earnings are included in the simulations.

To modify the spreadsheet in Table 3-1 to make 10 percent withdrawals for full time nursing care starting at a given age the cells for that age and later ages are rewritten in column B. And the calculation of the probabilities for the withdrawals at the bottom of Table 3-1 are rewritten.

Suppose it is desired to determine the chances a 10 percent withdrawal for care can be sustained for a given number of years starting at age 75. The entry in cell B16 is then replaced by: =Min(10,C16) and copied to lower rows to B50. Note that if this entry becomes equal to the value of the cell in column C that the subsequent values of the cells in column C are equal to 0 as are the subsequent values of the cells in column B.

To calculate the probability that 10 is withdrawn in 2 years replace cell B54 in Table 3-1 with =B18, and cell B10056 with:

=(Countif(B55:B10054,"10")-Countif(B55:B10054,"<10"))/ Count(B55:B10054).

The probabilities that 10 continues to be withdrawn for 4, 6, 8, and 10 years are calculated similarly as are the probabilities that care can be sustained starting at ages 85 and 95. When earnings and annuitization are included similar modifications are made to Table 5-8.

8

Voluntary Extra Withdrawals

With more leisure time suppose retirees would like to buy a cabin in the woods or a beach house. Or suppose they already own a property for part-time use and would like to make a major contribution to a non-profit organization with which they have been involved. The last chapter considered the possibility of involuntary extra withdrawals that turned out to be necessary to provide an existing standard of living. This chapter considers the possibility of voluntary extra withdrawals that enhance the existing standard of living.

In particular this chapter shows that buying a property with 20 percent of their investment portfolio is affordable if they can sustain their living expenses with a reasonably sustainable withdrawal before the purchase. On the other hand, making a contribution equal to 20 percent of their portfolio is not affordable. This is unless they can cover their living expenses with a far more sustainable withdrawal than when buying the property.

The difference is that the property can be sold if retrenchment becomes necessary. The loss is limited to the return that would have been earned if the funds had remained in the portfolio. A large contribution, on the other hand, effectively causes a substantial increase in the percentage withdrawal necessary to cover living expenses. This effective increase in the withdrawal rate significantly reduces sustainability.

Suppose retirees have existing living expenses that are providing significant satisfaction, but are not really sufficiently important to be very painful to eliminate. Withdrawals to cover these desirable but non-essential continuing expenses can be viewed as voluntary extra withdrawals. This chapter shows that withdrawals are allowed to cover non-essential existing expenses when the total withdrawal required is reasonably sustainable.

Thus, a reasonably sustainable withdrawal can effectively be viewed as a budget for an existing standard of living. Existing expenses can be covered that are making a reasonable contribution to satisfaction. Suppose, on the other hand, that a withdrawal is allowed by the Retrenchment Rule, but cannot be considered as reasonably sustainable. Such a withdrawal should only be used to cover expenses that would be painful to eliminate. In this case any non-essential expenses should be eliminated.

The difference is that with an unsustainable withdrawal it is likely that painful retrenchment will eventually be required. And continuing to spend on non-essentials is increasing the future painful retrenchment that will be required because the investment is being further depleted. Cutting non-essentials is therefore desirable when the withdrawal is unsustainable even when very painful cuts should be deferred.

In general, the Retrenchment Rule assumes that withdrawals are made only to cover the existing standard of living. Sometimes, however, as in the last chapter emergencies occur in which extra withdrawals become necessary to cover vital needs. But the extra withdrawals in these cases do not really represent an increase in standard of living. They reflect large unexpected expenses to provide the existing standard of living.

The reason that the withdrawals allowed by the Retrenchment Rule in general cover only the existing standard of living is the following. Withdrawals that increase the standard of living reduce the investment. The lower investment tends to increase any future retrenchment that may be required. But retirees are set in their ways and much more sensitive to reductions in their standard of living than increases. Thus, for retirees it is assumed that any increased satisfaction from increases in their standard of living is outweighed by the possibility it causes of more drastic retrenchment in the future.

When withdrawals are sufficiently sustainable, however, some voluntary extra withdrawals may be desirable to increase the standard of living. When withdrawals are sufficiently sustainable it is very likely that moderate increases in spending can be sustained. And the lower value of the investment is unlikely to make retrenchment in the future more drastic because there is little chance that retrenchment will be necessary. The voluntary extra withdrawals mentioned earlier that can be made satisfy this condition.

The cases examined in this chapter occur at or near the beginning of retirement. But voluntary extra withdrawals may also be desirable later in retirement when the withdrawal to cover the standard of living at that time is sufficiently sustainable. These possibilities have not been considered in running earlier simulations. But a future extra withdrawal will have little or no effect on the sustainability of an initial withdrawal when that future extra withdrawal occurs only when it has little or no effect on future sustainability.

Such future extra withdrawals will reduce the value of the investment available for an estate. But these reductions will occur only for very large values of the investment. This is because the extra withdrawals will be made only when the investment has become large enough to make the future withdrawals highly sustainable. Thus, there will be little effect on the median investment values that have been reported for earlier simulations.

8.1 Buying a Property

Many retirees may already own a property for seasonal or recreational use. With additional leisure time those who do not may want to consider whether buying such a property is affordable. Simulations of the sustainability of future withdrawals with and without purchasing the property provide a basis for making a decision.

Suppose that a property is purchased initially. Over time it is assumed that this property maintains its value in real terms. Also, to simplify suppose that owning the property allows a reduction in other leisure time expenses so that there is no net change initially in the annual withdrawals to cover expenses. Another possibility is that the property is rented out part-time to cover some of its upkeep. These assumptions can easily be modified when appropriate.

Each year as long as the property is retained its value is added to that of the portfolio to determine whether retrenchment is required. If retrenchment is required on this basis it is assumed that the property is sold and added to the value of the portfolio. While the property is retained its value is also considered as part of the investment available to cover emergencies or assisted care and for an estate.

When the property is purchased and retained the portfolio provides less income each year. The simulations with the property show the effect of this lower income on the sustainability of the withdrawals later in retirement, and on the future median value of the investment. The simulations are also set up to show the chance that the property is still retained in selected future years. The probability that the property is retained is the benefit of buying the property. This benefit must be weighed against the cost in terms of any reduced sustainability for the withdrawals and any lower future value for the investment.

Table 8-1

Effect of 20% Initial Withdrawal to Buy a Property
Property Sold When Retrenchment Is Necessary
Base Case Investment Returns and Inflation* RDR .08

Initial Withdrawal	Buy	Age	Withdrawal/Initial Value** Expected	1.0	.8	.6	.4	.2	0	Median** Investment	Prob.*** Retain
4	No	75	.98	.94	.04	.02	0	0	0	112	NA
		85	.94	.84	.06	.06	.03	.01	0	128	NA
		95	.90	.78	.06	.07	.06	.03	0	155	NA
	Yes	75	.99	.97	.02	.01	0	0	0	98	.94
		85	.94	.83	.08	.06	.03	0	0	94	.77
		95	.88	.72	.10	.08	.07	.03	0	90	.66
5	No	75	.93	.76	.14	.08	.02	0	0	83	NA
		85	.85	.63	.13	.13	.09	.02	0	90	NA
		95	.80	.57	.12	.13	.13	.05	0	104	NA
	Yes	75	.94	.81	.13	.05	.01	0	0	71	.69
		85	.85	.60	.17	.14	.08	.01	0	67	.48
		95	.78	.50	.16	.15	.14	.05	0	63	.40

*Portfolio for 4% withdrawal is allocated 25% to intermediate governments at the beginning of each year. For 5% withdrawal 25% of initial portfolio is invested in an annuity with a 7.5% nominal benefit each year. Returns are the same as for Tables 5-2 and 5-3.

**Withdrawals are in real terms and as a proportion of their value at age 65. Probabilities for withdrawals are for ranges of the proportions from .1 above to .1 below .8, .6, .4, or .2, or from 1.0 to .9 or 0 to .1. Investment values are in real terms as a percentage of their value at age 65 before any withdrawals and include the value of the property when it is retained.

***Probability property continues to be retained at the stated age when it is purchased initially.

Table 8-1 shows the effect of buying a property at age 65 equal to 20 percent of the initial value of the portfolio. Results are shown for initial withdrawals of 4 and 5 percent with and without buying the property. Comparable declines in standard of living in both cases are shown by equal percentage declines in the withdrawals from their initial values. As in Chapter 7 the future withdrawals are therefore shown as proportions of their initial values. In particular, probabilities are shown for ranges of the proportions about midpoints given at the top of the table. For instance, the probabilities given for .6 are for withdrawals ranging from .5 to .7 of the initial value of the withdrawal. The possibility of emergencies has not been included in these results.

Recall that the property is sold when retrenchment becomes necessary. The column on the far right gives the probability that it is retained at a future age when it has been purchased initially. As long as the property is retained its value is available for the estate or to cover possible emergencies or assisted care. Thus, when it is retained its value is included with the median value of the portfolio in the median investment values reported in the table.

The results when the property is not purchased are the same as those reported earlier in Table 7-1 for initial withdrawals of 4 and 5 percent. For the 4 percent withdrawal it is assumed as earlier that 25 percent of the portfolio is allocated to intermediate government issues at the beginning of each year. For the 5 percent withdrawal it is assumed that 25 percent of the initial investment is used to purchase an annuity that pays a nominal benefit at the beginning of each year equal to 7.5 percent of the amount purchased. Modification of the spreadsheet to include buying a property is discussed in Appendix 8-1.

Note first that purchasing the property has very little effect on the sustainability of the withdrawals. The expected future withdrawals and the chances of low withdrawals later in retirement remain just about the same after the property is purchased. There is some reduction in the chances of sustaining the initial withdrawal later in retirement. But there is also a slight increase in the chances of sustaining the initial withdrawal early in retirement.

Buying the property has little effect on sustainability because it effectively provides additional diversification. It is assumed that the property has no change in real value over time. Thus, it has a zero real return, but it also has zero volatility. The net effect is that holding the property causes little change in the sustainability of the withdrawals. This is when the initial withdrawal is either 4 or 5 percent.

The cost of the zero real return on the property is a decline in the future value of the investment. Buying the property results in a significant decline in the future median investment values. For the 4 percent initial withdrawal these median values decline at ages 85 and 95 respectively from 128 and 155 to 94 and 90. For the 5 percent initial withdrawal the declines are from 90 and 104 to 67 and 63. These reductions mean that fewer funds are available later in retirement for possible emergencies or assisted care. And there will be a smaller estate.

Those with their eye on a beach house or a cabin in the woods may not be too concerned about the impact on their estate. But they will have some concern about the reduced availability of funds for possible emergencies or assisted care. To cover this cost they will want assurance that they can retain the property over the years when it is likely they can make good use of it.

For those who require a 4 percent initial withdrawal there is such assurance. The chances that they will retain the property at ages 75 and 85 are respectively .94 and .77. For those with a reasonably sustainable withdrawal buying the property appears affordable.

On the other hand, for those with a 5 percent withdrawal buying the property is more of a borderline proposition. The chances that the property will be retained at ages 75 and 85 decline respectively to .69 and .48. And they already have a smaller value of their investment later in retirement to cover possible emergencies and assisted care.

8.2 Making a Donation

Suppose now that the extra 20% initial withdrawal is not reversible. Now the funds have been irrevocably committed to some purpose such as a donation to a non-profit organization or the educational expense of grandchildren. With the permanent loss of the funds the costs in this case are significantly larger. Irrespective of the desirability of such a commitment retirees seem unlikely to find it affordable if their required withdrawal to cover expenses is 4 percent. To make it affordable they will need to have accumulated enough to require a much lower initial withdrawal.

One cost of such a donation is a reduction in any future estate by a much larger amount. The recipients of the estate may well be the same as those of the earlier donation. Retirees, however, may see a major benefit in being able to actually experience and observe the effects of the earlier donation. This is compared to having to imagine what the effects may be after they are gone. Thus, they may view an earlier smaller donation as of more value than a later bequest even if the later bequest is much larger. A good example is contributing to educational expenses. Such judgments, however, depend on the size of the reduction in the future estate caused by the earlier donation.

Table 8-2 shows the results for initial withdrawals of 3 and 4 percent when the initial donation is an extra withdrawal equal to 20 percent of the investment. Possible emergencies are not included in these results. The initial extra withdrawal reduces the median portfolio values at age 85 by an amount equal to about 52 percent of the initial investment. That is over 2.5 times the initial donation of 20 percent. Nevertheless, this gain in value by deferring the bequest to the estate seems unlikely to be decisive. What will limit an earlier donation is if the cost turns out to be too high in terms of reducing the sustainability of the withdrawals to cover living expenses.

The simulations show that this cost does appear to be too high when the initial withdrawal is 4 percent. With the donation the chances that the withdrawal will be above .9 of its initial value at ages 85 and 95 decline respectively from .84 and .78 to .64 and .57. The chances that the withdrawal will be less than half of its initial value increase respectively from .04 and .09 to .11 and .20. These costs are not surprising as a 20 percent initial donation effectively converts a 4 to a 5 percent withdrawal, as 4/80 = .05.

On the other hand, the cost of the reduced sustainability appears tolerable when the initial withdrawal is 3 percent. With the donation the chances that the initial withdrawal will be above .9 of its initial value at ages 85 and 95 decline respectively only from .95 and .93 to .88 and .83. The chances that the withdrawal will be less than half of its initial value increase respectively only from .01 and .03 to .03 and .07. Note also that the probabilities for sustaining the 3 percent withdrawal with the donation are still somewhat better than for sustaining the 4 percent withdrawal without the donation. This is not surprising as a 20 percent initial donation effectively converts a 3 percent withdrawal to 3.75 percent, as 3/80 = .0375.

Table 8-2

Effect of 20% Initial Withdrawal to Make a Donation
Investment Returns for Normal Valuation Each Year
Stks/IntGovts 75/25 RDR .08

Initial Withdrawal	Give	Age	Withdrawal/Initial Value* Expected	1.0	.8	.6	.4	.2	0	Median* Portfolio
3	No	75	1.00	.99	.01	0	0	0	0	126
		85	.98	.95	.03	.01	.01	0	0	164
		95	.97	.93	.02	.02	.02	0	0	227
	Yes	75	.99	.96	.03	.01	0	0	0	93
		85	.95	.88	.05	.04	.03	0	0	110
		95	.92	.83	.05	.05	.05	.02	0	136
4	No	75	.98	.94	.04	.02	0	0	0	112
		85	.94	.84	.06	.06	.03	.01	0	128
		95	.90	.78	.06	.07	.06	.03	0	155
	Yes	75	.94	.80	.12	.06	.01	0	0	79
		85	.85	.64	.12	.13	.06	.02	0	76
		95	.79	.57	.10	.13	.11	.08	0	73

*Same as Table 8-1

8.3 Non Essential Continuing Expenses

Non-essential continuing expenses are those that provide some satisfaction, but are not important enough to cause significant pain if they are eliminated. If retrenchment is required non-essentials will be the first to go. But should non-essentials be eliminated if they can be covered by the withdrawal allowed by the Retrenchment Rule?

The answer depends on the sustainability of the withdrawal required to cover expenses including the non-essentials. If a withdrawal that covers the non-essentials is reasonably sustainable and the non-essentials are providing a reasonable amount of satisfaction they should be retained. If a withdrawal that covers the non-essentials is unsustainable the non-essentials should be eliminated. This is even if they can be covered by a withdrawal allowed by the Retrenchment Rule.

The reason that non-essentials should be eliminated for unsustainable withdrawals is that there is a good chance that they will soon have to be eliminated anyway. This is because the rule is likely to soon be requiring some retrenchment. And withdrawals to cover non-essentials are depleting investment value that will likely be needed later to cover more important expenses. Thus, by covering non-essential expenses there is a good chance retirees are increasing painful retrenchment that will be required later with respect to essential expenses.

Withdrawals to cover non-essential expenses can be viewed as voluntary extra withdrawals. As for the earlier voluntary extra withdrawals in this chapter simulations can be used to help determine their costs and benefits. Their cost is the deterioration they cause in the future withdrawals for covering essential expenses. Their benefit depends on how long the non-essential spending will continue, and the satisfaction it provides.

Table 8-3

Effect of Extra 20% Initial Withdrawal for Non-Essential Expenses
Extra Withdrawal Reduced First If Retrenchment Is Required
Base Case Investment Returns and Inflation* RDR .08

Initial Withdrawal Total	Initial Withdrawal Essentials	Age	Essentials/Initial Essentials** Expected	1.0	.8	.6	.4	.2	0	Expected Extra/ Initial Extra
4.0	3.2	75	.99	.98	.01	.01	0	0	0	.94
		85	.96	.89	.06	.03	.02	0	0	.83
		95	.93	.83	.06	.05	.04	.02	0	.77
3.2	3.2	75	1.00	.98	.02	0	0	0	0	NA
		85	.98	.94	.03	.02	.01	0	0	NA
		95	.96	.90	.03	.04	.02	.01	0	NA
5.0	4.0	75	.97	.91	.06	.03	0	0	0	.80
		85	.91	.75	.10	.09	.05	.01	0	.64
		95	.85	.66	.10	.10	.09	.05	0	.57
4.0	4.0	75	.98	.94	.04	.02	0	0	0	NA
		85	.94	.84	.06	.06	.03	.01	0	NA
		95	.90	. 78	.06	.07	.06	.03	0	NA
6.25	5.0	75	.91	.70	.18	.10	.02	0	0	.47
		85	.82	.57	.18	.16	.11	.02	0	.35
		95	.76	.46	.15	.17	.15	.07	0	.31
5.0	5.0	75	.93	.76	.14	.08	.02	0	0	NA
		85	.85	.63	.13	.13	.09	.02	0	NA
		95	.80	.57	.12	.13	.13	.05	0	NA

*For the3.2% and 4% withdrawals for essentials the portfolio is allocated 25% to intermediate governments at the beginning of each year. For the 5% withdrawal for essentials 25% of the initial investment is invested in an annuity with a nominal benefit each year equal to 7.5% of the amount purchased.

**Same format as Table 8-1.

When there are non-essentials included in expenses the Retrenchment Rule assumes that the non-essentials are eliminated first when retrenchment is required. A record is kept at future times of the withdrawals being made for spending on both essentials and non-essentials. Modification of the spreadsheet for the simulations to segregate the future withdrawals in this way is discussed in Appendix 8-2. Possible emergencies are not included in these results.

Results for these simulations are shown in Table 8-3 for initial withdrawals with different degrees of sustainability. In each case it is assumed that 20 percent of the initial withdrawal is for non-essentials. The future withdrawals for the essentials are compared when the non-essentials are eliminated initially and when they are not. The expected future withdrawals for non-essentials are shown assuming this spending is eliminated first when any retrenchment is required in the future.

In particular, Table 8-3 considers cases in which the initial withdrawal required to cover existing living expenses is 4, 5, or 6.25 percent. Twenty percent of the expense covered by these withdrawals, however, is for non-essentials. Thus, the initial required withdrawal for essential expenses in these cases is respectively 3.2, 4.0, or 5.0 percent.

Suppose the non-essentials are eliminated initially. The withdrawals for essentials of 4 or 5 percent initially are then the same as for the 4 or 5 percent withdrawals given in Table 7-1, or in Table 8-1 when the property is not purchased. As in those earlier cases it is assumed that 25 percent of the portfolio at the beginning of each year is allocated to intermediate governments for the 4 percent withdrawal. For the 5 percent withdrawal it is assumed that 25 percent of the initial investment is used to purchase an annuity that pays a nominal benefit at the beginning of each year equal to 7.5 percent of the amount purchased.

The top panel of three rows in the table shows the sustainability of the withdrawal of 3.2 percent for essentials when an initial withdrawal of 0.8 percent is also made for non-essentials. Future withdrawals for essentials are shown as a proportion of the initial withdrawal for essentials. This is both for the expected value of the proportion and the probabilities of ranges for the proportion at ages 75, 85, and 95. The second panel from the top of three rows shows the sustainability of the withdrawals for essentials when the non-essentials are eliminated initially. The column on the far right shows the expected withdrawal for non-essentials as a proportion of the initial withdrawal for non-essentials.

In the top two panels where the initial withdrawal is reasonably sustainable there is little cost to withdrawing enough to cover the non-essentials. In going from the first to the second panel there is little improvement in the sustainability of the withdrawals to cover essentials. For instance, eliminating the non-essentials reduces the chances that the withdrawal for essentials will be less than .7 of its initial value at age 85 only from .05 to .03. At age 95 the reduction is from .11 to .07.

There is also a substantial benefit with respect to being able to continue to cover the non-essential expenses. Even at age 85 the expected spending on non-essentials is .83 of its initial value. And at age 95 it is .77.

Individual retirees will have to consider how much they value continuing to enjoy the non-essentials. This is relative to the small increased risk that continuing to cover them causes of additional retrenchment with respect to essentials. It appears likely that the non-essentials will be of sufficient value to more than compensate for this small increase in risk.

Suppose retirees have saved enough to cover their expenses with a reasonably sustainable withdrawal. There is then no need for them to retrench with respect to expenses that are providing a reasonable degree of satisfaction, even if doing so would not be painful. The situation is quite different for those who have not saved enough to cover their expenses with a sustainable withdrawal.

The bottom two panels of three rows each show that covering non-essential expenses is no longer advisable when the initial withdrawal is unsustainable. In this case, covering the non-essentials requires an initial withdrawal of 6.25 percent. In this case, first note that there is much less benefit to continuing the spending on the non-essentials. It is expected that over half of this spending will have to be eliminated anyway by age 75, and about two-thirds by ages 85 and 95.

Moreover, continuing the spending on non-essentials now causes a more significant reduction in the sustainability of the spending on essentials. For instance, the chances decline that the withdrawal for essentials will be above .9 of its initial value at ages 75, 85, and 95. Respectively, these chances decline from .76, .63, and .57 to .70, .53, and .46. And even without the extra spending the sustainability for the essentials is much less than at the top of the table.

To make a decision individual retirees again have to consider how much they value the non-essentials relative to the essentials. In this case, however, the decision seems fairly easy. Much of the non-essential spending will have to be eliminated anyway. And there is a significant cost in reduced sustainability for essentials. Most retirees will presumably decide it is prudent to eliminate the non-essentials initially in this case.

And the argument strengthens for eliminating the non-essentials initially as the initial withdrawal becomes less sustainable. Those who have to withdraw as much initially as allowed by the Retrenchment Rule will surely want to eliminate most if not all of their non-essential expenses. This is the assumption that was made earlier for those making withdrawals at the limit.

The two panels of three rows each in the middle of the table cover a borderline situation. In this case the initial withdrawal including the non-essentials is 5 percent. In this case retirees will have to consider their spending priorities more carefully. And they may decide to eliminate some non-essential existing expenses but not others.

8.4 Conclusions

In general the Retrenchment Rule assumes that withdrawals are made only to cover the existing standard of living. This is because a larger withdrawal reduces the investment, which tends to increase any retrenchment that may be required in the future. And any satisfaction from the current increase is viewed as insufficient to compensate for the additional painful retrenchment in the existing standard of living that may be required later. Suppose, however, that the current standard of living is sufficiently sustainable to make future retrenchment unlikely. In such cases it is reasonable to consider voluntary extra withdrawals that enhance the standard of living.

It has been shown that it is reasonable to use about 20 percent of the initial portfolio to purchase a property for part-time use when the initial withdrawal is reasonably sustainable. To afford making a donation equal to 20 percent of the initial portfolio, however, the withdrawal to cover existing living expenses must be highly sustainable. The difference is that the property can be sold if retrenchment becomes necessary. The donation, on the other hand, significantly increases the effective withdrawal rate.

Suppose retirees have existing expense that is providing satisfaction, but cannot really be considered as sufficiently vital to be painful to eliminate. Covering such non-essential expense can be considered as a voluntary extra withdrawal. If these non-essentials can be covered with a reasonably sustainable withdrawal it is reasonable to continue these outlays. On the other hand, they should be eliminated if doing so requires an unsustainable withdrawal even if the withdrawal is allowed by the Retrenchment Rule.

Appendix 8-1

Modifying the Spreadsheet for Buying a Property

To modify the spreadsheet in Table 3-1 to incorporate buying a property a new column is introduced. The cell for a year in this column has the value 1 when the property is held over that year and the value 0 when it is not. Suppose this column is O. O6 for year 1 is equal to 1 if the property is purchased initially and 0 if it is not.

The property is sold at the beginning of year 2 if O6 =1 and retrenchment is required at the beginning of year 2. Retrenchment is required when the prior withdrawal, B6, exceeds the limit for year 2 given by D7. The logical function in Excel, And(O6=1,B6>D7), is true if both of its arguments are true and false otherwise.

The logical function in Excel, If(x,y,z), is equal to y if x is true and to z otherwise. The value of O7 is therefore given by: =If(And(O6=1,B6>D7),0,O6). If the first argument is true the property is sold at the beginning of year 2 and O7=0. If the first argument is false the property is held or not in year 2 as it was in year 1 so O7=O6. This relation is copied to the following rows through O50 as it applies each year whether or not retrenchment first occurs in year 2.

The value of the property each year is 20 because it is assumed to have a constant real value equal to 20 percent of the initial value of the investment of 100. The initial value of the portfolio in C6 if O6=1 is 80. If retrenchment is required at the beginning of year 2 the property is sold without cost and added to the portfolio invested over year 2. The relation in C8 gives the value of the portfolio at the beginning of year 3 before any withdrawals and is equal to:

If(And(O6=1,B6>D7),(C7–B7+20)*(1+ E7),(C7-B7)*(1+E7))

And this relation is copied to the following rows through C50 as it applies to future years whether or not retrenchment is first necessary at the beginning of year 2.

When O6=1 the limit on the withdrawal at the beginning of year 2 determined in D7 depends on the value of the portfolio in C7 plus the value of the property. If O6=0 it depends only on C7. The third argument of PMT in D7 is therefore replaced by: –If(O6=1,C7+20,C7). And this modified relation for PMT is copied to the following rows through D50.

The value of the property is added to that of the portfolio at the beginning of year 2 to get what is available for the estate before any transactions. To record this value a new column P is introduced in which P6 is 100 and P7 is set equal to: =If(O6=1,C7+20,C7). And this is copied to the following rows through P50. The median value of the investment available for the estate at ages 75, 85, and 95 is calculated respectively as discussed in Appendix 5-2 from P16, P26, and P36.

The probability that the property is retained over the year at age 75 is the average value of O16 given by the simulations. To calculate this average enter: =O16 in O54 and: =Average(O55:O10054) in O10056. The probability the property is retained at age 85 or 95 is obtained similarly.

When the initial withdrawal is 4 percent it is assumed that 25 percent of the portfolio is allocated to intermediate government issues at the beginning of each year. Thus, in this case the modification in Table 5-8 must also be made to Table 3-1. For the initial withdrawal of 5 percent the modifications for an annuity in Table 5-7 must also be added to Table 3-1.

Appendix 8-2

Modifying the Spreadsheet for Non-Essential Expenses

To modify the spreadsheet in Table 3-1 to incorporate non-essential expenses two new columns are introduced. These columns calculate the spending on essentials and non-essentials each year. Suppose these columns are respectively Q and R. Q6 and R6 are set equal respectively to the initial withdrawals required to cover essential and non-essential expenses. B6 is set equal to the sum of Q6 and R6.

Q7 is given by: =Min(B7,$Q$6) and copied to the following lower rows through Q50. This relation says that the initial expenditure on essentials is covered as long as it is covered by the total withdrawal given in column B. When the total withdrawal becomes less than the initial expenditure on essentials the expenditure on essentials is equal to the total withdrawal. R7 is given by: =Max(B7-$Q$6,0) and copied to lower rows through R50.

The averages and probabilities of the ranges for Q16, Q26, and Q36 or R16, R26, R36 are calculated in a similar way as earlier. The modifications to Table 3-1 given in Tables 5-7 & 5-8 are also made to incorporate initially investing 25 percent in an annuity or allocating 25 percent of the portfolio each year to intermediate governments as applicable.

9

Shorter Horizons

The simulations for choosing an RDR have assumed that individuals are in good health when they begin retirement. But poor health is one of the reasons that some have to retire before accumulating sufficient savings. Does a much shorter expectation for the longest they might possibly live affect their choice of an RDR?

This chapter shows that a shorter horizon has little effect on the discount rate chosen for the RDR. A shorter horizon, however, does significantly affect the strategy for reducing the risk of low withdrawals later in retirement. For those in good health Chapter 5 showed that an effective strategy for reducing this risk is to annuitize a large portion of the investment and seek part-time employment. But those in poor health should not buy a lifetime annuity. And those in poor health may find part-time work more onerous, or not feasible at all.

The good news for those in poor health is that there is much less risk of low withdrawals in the latter part of their retirement. This is because of the shorter period. And due to the shorter period this risk can be further reduced by allocating a portion of their portfolio to fixed income issues. Also, due to their shorter horizon those in poor health can withdraw a larger percentage of their investment to avoid painful retrenchment. And they also need to have saved less to provide a reasonably sustainable standard of living.

Chapter 5 advised that those in good health should annuitize about half of their portfolio if they require an unsustainable withdrawal to avoid painful retrenchment. Those in poor health who require an unsustainable withdrawal may want to allocate only a quarter of their portfolio to fixed income issues. Nevertheless, this is sufficient to give them about the same risk of low withdrawals late in their retirement as those in good health who annuitize half of their portfolio and achieve part-time earnings. Thus, those in poor health are not necessarily at a disadvantage to those in good health even though they cannot make use of lifetime annuities.

Suppose those in poor health can cover their expenses with a reasonably sustainable initial withdrawal. These retirees should allocate about a half of their portfolio to fixed income issues. Those with a less sustainable initial withdrawal may want to allocate as little as a quarter to fixed incomes. This is because these latter retirees have more need for the higher expected return on stocks.

Those in poor health have a shorter horizon at the beginning of their retirement. Those who remain in as good health as can be expected, however, necessarily have a shorter horizon when they reach old age. This chapter later argues that the results for those in poor health at the beginning of their retirement also apply to those who remain in as good health as can be expected when they reach old age. Thus, they should continue to use the same RDR as earlier. And if initially they were allocating a quarter of their portfolio to fixed incomes, by age 90 they should have increased the allocation to about a half, if their withdrawal remains reasonably sustainable.

The last part of this chapter considers the possible benefit of using a shorter budget interval. It is shown that budgeting on a quarterly basis provides a small improvement in the withdrawals. This improvement, however, appears insufficient to warrant the more frequent disruptions and the extra effort.

9.1 Shorter Horizon at Age 65

Earlier it was assumed that retirees are in good health at age 65, and that the longest they might possibly live is to age 110. Now suppose that they are still age 65, but that they have a medical problem. This problem reduces their average life expectancy by about a half. Instead of a maximum life expectancy of age 110, the longest they might possibly expect to live now is to age 85. Does this much shorter horizon affect the choice of an RDR? Or should the maximum withdrawal at age 65 continue to be calculated with the shorter horizon and the same RDR?

As before the RDR is selected by simulating the use of the Retrenchment Rule over a hypothetical retirement period using a series of possible discount rates. The rate that gives the best withdrawals is chosen as the RDR. As before the largest initial withdrawal that can be made to avoid retrenchment for a given discount rate is given by an annuity calculation. It is the largest fixed annuity that can be obtained over the retirement period when the investment earns a return equal to the discount rare.

Now, however, the investment at age 65 needs to provide only 20 withdrawals instead of 45. The fixed annuity provided by any discount rate, and the largest allowed withdrawal at age 65, is therefore larger than before. For discount rates from .04 through .12 these are the withdrawals shown for age 65 in Table 9-1. As an example of the effect of the shorter horizon note that the withdrawal at age 65 for a discount rate of .08 is now 9.4 instead of 7.6 percent. Subsequent withdrawals are the averages for 10,000 replications assuming that the last possible withdrawal occurs when the retiree reaches age 84. Relative to life expectancy ages 70, 75, and 80 are now comparable to ages 75, 85, and 95 for retirees in good health at age 65.

The key point to note in Table 9-1 is the relationship of the streams of expected withdrawals to each other. The streams of expected withdrawals for the different discount rates look just about the same relative to each other as when retirees are in good health at age 65 in Table 4-1. For instance, when retirees were in good health the spread narrowed over time for the stream of .08 versus .06. The expected withdrawals for .08, however, were never less than those for .06, even late in the period. On the other hand, late in the period the expected withdrawals for .10 were slightly less than those for .08.

Table 9-1

Expected Withdrawals Maximum Life Age 85

Stock Returns for Normal Valuation Each Year

Discount Rate	Expected Withdrawals*			
	65	70	75	80
.04	7.1	6.0	5.7	5.5
.06	8.2	6.7	6.2	5.9
.08	9.4	7.4	6.5	6.0
.10	10.7	8.0	6.7	5.9
.12	12.0	8.5	6.7	5.7

*Expected withdrawals are as a percentage of the value of the investment at age 65, and are in real terms.

Table 9-1 shows the same pattern for these streams when retirees have a short horizon at age 65. The spread of .08 over .06 narrows over time, but the expected withdrawals for .08 are never lower. On the other hand, late in the period the expected withdrawals for .10 are slightly less than for .08. Thus, based on the expected withdrawals all retirees will prefer a discount rate of .08 to .06, and lower discount rates. It cannot be said, however, that all retirees will necessarily prefer .10 to .08. This is because .10 has slightly lower expected withdrawals late in the period than .08.

Table 9-1, however, shows only that .08 will give a larger standard of living than .06 each year over retirement on average. It is possible that .06 has a sufficiently lower risk of low withdrawals to more than compensate for the lower stream of expected withdrawals that it provides. Table 9-2 shows, however, that .06 does not lower risk sufficiently to do so.

Similar to Table 4-2, Table 9-2 shows the probability of the withdrawals for different discount rates at ages 65, 70, 75, and 80. Probabilities are given for withdrawals of 1, 3, 5, 7, and 9 percent as shown at the top of the table. As for Table 4-2 these values represent ranges for the withdrawals from one below to one above the stated number. For instance, the probabilities given for a withdrawal of 5 percent cover withdrawals that are in a range of from 4 to 6 percent.

There are some important points to note in Table 9-2. One is that there is some risk of very low withdrawals, especially later in the period. The chances of very low withdrawals, however, are only about half the chances for retirees in good health at age 65 when they reach comparable ages. For instance, in Table 9-2 with a discount rate of .08 there is a .15 chance that the withdrawal will be less than 4 percent at age 75. Earlier in Table 4-2 for those in good health at age 65 there was a .30 chance that the withdrawal would be less than 3 percent at age 85.

The other important point to note in Table 9-2 is that the risk of very low withdrawals is not appreciably reduced by choosing a lower discount rate than .08.

Choosing .06 instead of .08 does not reduce the chances that the withdrawals will be less than 4 percent at age 75. And at age 80 the chances are reduced only from .24 to .21.

Table 9-2

Withdrawal Probabilities Maximum Life Age 85
Stock Returns for Normal Valuation Each Year

Age	Discount Rate	Withdrawal Probability*				
		9	7	5	3	1
65	.08	1.00	0	0	0	0
	.06	1.00	0	0	0	0
	.04	0	1.00	0	0	0
70	.08	.43	.34	.19	.04	0
	.06	.31	.39	.25	.05	0
	.04	0	.59	.33	.08	0
75	.08	.31	.28	.26	.14	.01
	.06	.25	.32	.28	.14	.01
	.04	0	.57	.33	.15	.01
80	.08	.27	.24	.25	.20	.04
	.06	.23	.29	.27	.17	.04
	.04	0	.49	.31	.17	.03

*Probability that withdrawal is in a range from one above to one below 9, 7, 5, 3, or 1percent. Withdrawals are in real terms, and as a percentage of the investment at age 65.

Few if any retirees seem likely to find this reduced risk for .06 sufficient to compensate for the lower stream of expected withdrawals it provides in Table 9-1. For instance, .08 provides an initial withdrawal of 9.4 percent, whereas .06 provides only 8.2 percent. Note also in Table 9-2 that choosing .06 instead of .08 also reduces the chances of keeping the initial withdrawal above 8 percent.

Thus, whether they are in poor health or good health virtually all retirees will want to choose a discount rate for their RDR that is at least equal to .08. Lower discount rates do not provide enough risk reduction later in retirement to compensate for the lower expected standard of living that they provide over all of retirement. In effect, whatever their health, discount rates less than .08 require retirees to undertake too much retrenchment.

9.2 Risk Reduction for Shorter Horizons

Suppose those in good health at the beginning of retirement require an unsustainable withdrawal to avoid painful retrenchment and this withdrawal is allowed by the Retrenchment Rule. Chapter 5 advocated that these retirees reduce their risk of future low withdrawals by annuitizing a large portion of their portfolio and seeking part-time work. Chapter 5 also looked at the alternative of investing the portfolio in fixed income issues instead of annuitizing. The fixed incomes provided somewhat better results early in retirement, but much worse results late in retirement.

Those in poor health at the beginning of retirement who require an unsustainable withdrawal will likely find working part-time more onerous, if it is feasible at all. And lifetime annuities are not attractive for those in poor health. But with a shorter horizon they can take advantage of fixed income issues to reduce their risk of low withdrawals. The results in Chapter 5 showed that fixed incomes were unattractive for those in good health late in their retirement, but those in poor health do not expect to live that long.

Table 9-3 shows that investing in fixed incomes is attractive for reducing risk when those in poor health have to make an unsustainable withdrawal at the beginning of retirement. It is assumed that they are using an RDR of .08 and withdrawing the largest amount allowed of 9.4 percent with their short horizon.

The first row at each age shows the results when they invest just in stocks. The lower rows assume they allocate 25 or 50 percent of their portfolio to intermediate government issues at the beginning of each year.

The real returns on the intermediates each year are assumed to be the same as in Chapter 5. They are drawings from a normal distribution with a mean of .03 and a standard deviation of .07. And these drawings each year are independent of the drawings to obtain the returns on stocks.

Table 9-3 shows that allocating 25 percent of the portfolio to the intermediates is clearly attractive. The chances that the withdrawals are less than 4 percent at ages 70, 75, and 80 are reduced respectively from .04, .15, and .24 to .01, .09, and .19. And at all ages the expected withdrawals increase and there is only a slight reduction in the chances that the withdrawals will be larger than 8 percent. Also, there is only a modest reduction in the median portfolio values, which is easily more than compensated for by the improvement in the withdrawals.

Whether it pays to increase the allocation further to 50 percent is more questionable, but such an increase may be desirable. A further increase to 50 percent further lowers the risk of low withdrawals at all ages. But later in retirement this improvement is accompanied by deterioration in other measures of performance.

Increasing the allocation of intermediates from 25 to 50 percent reduces the risk that the withdrawals are less than 4 percent respectively from .01, .09, and .19 to .00, .04, and .14. But at age 80 there is some decline in the expected withdrawal. And at ages 75 and 80 there is a decline in the chances that the withdrawals will be greater than 8 percent. Also, there are further moderate declines in the median portfolio values at all ages.

Thus, it can be said without doubt that those in poor health should allocate at least 25 percent of their portfolio to fixed incomes. There is also an argument for further increasing the allocation from 25 to 50 percent to reduce the risk of low withdrawals. But that additional reduction in risk has some costs. Other measures of performance later in retirement are reduced.

Even if they allocate only 25 percent to fixed incomes, however, those in poor health are able to reduce their risk of low withdrawals late in retirement to make it about the same as those who are in good health. This is when those in good health annuitize a large portion of their investment and achieve a meaningful level of part-time earnings. Thus, the fact that those in poor health cannot take advantage of lifetime annuities does not put them at a disadvantage relative to those who can take advantage of annuities.

Table 9-3

Effect of Fixed Incomes for 9.4% Short Horizon Withdrawal Age 65
Investment Returns for Normal Valuations Each Year,* RDR .08

Age	Stocks/ IntGvts	Expected Withdrawal	Withdrawal Probability**					Median Portfolio
			9	7	5	3	1	
70	100/0	7.40	.43	.34	.19	.04	0	82
	75/25	7.61	.45	.39	.15	.01	0	78
	50/50	7.74	.45	.46	.09	0	0	75
75	100/0	6.53	.31	.28	.26	.14	.01	63
	75/25	6.72	.30	.33	.28	.09	0	58
	50/50	6.73	.24	.41	.31	.04	0	52
80	100/0	6.04	.27	.24	.25	.20	.04	44
	75/25	6.16	.25	.26	.30	.18	.01	36
	50/50	6,02	.17	.30	.39	.14	0	28

*Returns for fixed income issues are based on those for intermediate government issues and are the same as for Table 5-3.
**Same as Table 9-2.

Suppose those in poor health at age 65 can cover their expenses with a reasonably sustainable withdrawal of 6 percent. In this case, increasing the allocation to fixed incomes from 25 to 50 percent is clearly advisable. And doing so eliminates almost all of the risk of future low withdrawals.

The results for a 6 percent withdrawal for those in poor health are shown in Table 9-4 for conditions that are otherwise the same as for Table 9-3. Increasing the allocation from 25 to 50 percent reduces the chances that the withdrawal will be less than 5 percent at ages 70, 75, and 80 from respectively .03, .11, and .17 to .00, .05 and .11. And there is also an increase in the expected withdrawals at all ages, and an increase in the chances that the withdrawals will be sustained. The only cost for these improvements is a moderate decline in the median portfolio values.

Table 9-4

Effect of Fixed Incomes for 6% Short Horizon Withdrawal Age 65

Investment Returns for Normal Valuations Each Year,* RDR .08

Age	Stocks/ IntGvts	Expected Withdrawal	Withdrawal Probability** 6	4	2	0	Median Portfolio
70	100/0	5.81	.92	.07	.01	0	97
	75/25	5.93	.97	.03	0	0	94
	50/50	5.98	1.00	0	0	0	91
75	100/0	5.54	.82	.14	.04	0	89
	75/25	5.75	.89	.10	.01	0	84
	50/50	5.88	.95	.05	0	0	79
80	100/0	5.34	.76	.15	.09	0	80
	75/25	5.58	.83	.13	.04	0	73
	50/50	5.75	.89	.10	.01	0	64

*Same as Table 9-3.

**Probability that withdrawal is in a range from 1 above to one below 6, 4, and 2, or from 0 to 1. Withdrawals are in real terms and as a percentage of the investment at age 65.

Table 9-3 shows that it is arguable as to whether the allocation should be increased from 25 to 50 percent when those in poor health are withdrawing as much as allowed by the Retrenchment Rule. As the initial withdrawal becomes more sustainable, however, the doubt about increasing the allocation to 50 percent diminishes. When the initial withdrawal has declined to as low as 6 percent it is clear that the allocation should be increased to 50 percent.

9.3 Saving Enough with a Short Horizon

Excluding the possibility of large extra withdrawals to cover emergencies, Chapter 7 showed that an annual withdrawal of 4 percent is at the upper end of the range that appears to be reasonably sustainable. To cover possible emergencies and sustain a given standard of living individuals should save enough to cover their expenses with closer to a 3 percent annual withdrawal. This is for those who plan to retire in good health at age 65.

But those who know they will be in poor health when they retire need to accumulate much less. Table 7-1 in Chapter 7 showed how much individuals need to save to achieve varying degrees of sustainability when they retire in good health at age 65. For those who know they will be in poor health those simulations need to be rerun with a short horizon.

The results for a short horizon are shown in Table 9-5. As in Table 7-1 the withdrawals in this case are measured as a proportion of their initial value. As explained in Chapter 7 this measure facilitates comparing the sustainability of a given standard of living with withdrawals from investments of varying size.

It has just been established that those withdrawing 6 percent or less should allocate at least 50 percent to fixed income issues. An allocation of 50 percent is therefore assumed for these withdrawals in the table. The allocation to fixed incomes for larger withdrawals has been reduced. Some retirees may prefer a somewhat larger allocation to fixed incomes for these larger withdrawals than that assumed in the table.

Comparing the results in Table 9-5 with those in Table 7-1 shows the significantly smaller amount of savings required to achieve a given degree of sustainability by those who will be in poor health when they retire. In Table 9-5 a withdrawal somewhat higher than 6 percent provides comparable sustainability to that achieved by a 4 percent withdrawal in Table 7-1. And a somewhat higher withdrawal than 5 percent provides the same sustainability as a 3 percent withdrawal.

Table 9-5

Effect of Portfolio Size on Short Horizon Sustainability

Investment Returns for Normal Valuations Each Year,* RDR .08

Age	Withdrawal Age 65	Stocks/ IntGovts	Withdrawal/Initial Value** Expected	1.0	.8	.6	.4	.2	0
70	5.0	50/50	1.00	1.00	0	0	0	0	0
	6.0	50/50	1.00	.99	.01	0	0	0	0
	7.0	62.5/37.5	.97	.89	.09	.02	0	0	0
	8.0	75/25	.91	.67	.24	.08	.01	0	0
75	5.0	50/50	1.00	.99	.01	0	0	0	0
	6.0	50/50	.98	.92	.06	.02	0	0	0
	7.0	62.5/37.5	.92	.73	.16	.09	.02	0	0
	8.0	75/25	.83	.50	.24	.18	.07	.01	0
80	5.0	50/50	.99	.97	.02	.01	0	0	0
	6.0	50/50	.96	.87	.07	.05	.01	0	0
	7.0	62.5/37.5	.87	.64	.16	.13	.06	.01	0
	8.0	75/25	.77	.43	.20	.21	.13	.03	0

*Same as Table 9-3

**Probability that withdrawals in real terms as a proportion of their initial value are from .1 below to .1 above .8, .6, .4, or .2, or from 1.0 to .9 or 0 to .1.

Thus, for those who will not be in good health when they retire, the earlier initial withdrawal percentages are increased by 2 percentage points or more. Even including the possibility of extra withdrawals for emergencies they can achieve reasonable sustainability if they can cover their expenses with as much as a 5 percent withdrawal.

9.4 Planning at Age 90

Suppose those in good health at age 65 survive to age 90 in as good health as can be expected for that age. Earlier at age 65 they made decisions assuming they would reach age 90 in good health. But now that they have actually done so do they have any reason to change their earlier decisions.

Suppose that conditions in financial markets are normal when they reach age 90 just as they were at age 65. In this case these retirees at age 90 face the same problem just considered for those in poor health at age 65. With a maximum life expectancy of age 110 they must consider the possibility of making 20 annual withdrawals in the future just like those in poor health did at age 65.

Thus, the simulations for different discount rates for those who reach age 90 in as good health as can be expected are the same as those shown in Tables 9-1 & 9-2. All that needs to be done is to relabel ages 65, 70, 75 and 80 in those earlier tables with ages 90, 95, 100, and 105. As earlier these retirees will want to choose an RDR at least equal to .08.

Earlier it was implicitly assumed that the discount rate remains the same as the future unfolds. It has just been demonstrated that this is a reasonable assumption. This is assuming that conditions in financial markets remain normal. Chapter 11 looks at the effect on the choice of a discount rate when conditions are abnormal.

Chapter 5 considered retirees in good health at age 65 who required either an unsustainable or a reasonably sustainable withdrawal. It was argued that those with an unsustainable withdrawal should annuitize. Those with a reasonably sustainable withdrawal, however, could allocate 25 percent or more of their portfolio to fixed income issues instead of annuitizing.

In allocating 25 percent to fixed incomes it was assumed that they maintained the 25 percent allocation over all of retirement. It has been seen in this chapter, however, that there is a good argument for those with a short horizon to increase their allocation to 50 percent when they have a reasonably sustainable withdrawal. Thus, those in good health with a sustainable withdrawal at age 65 should later increase their allocation to fixed incomes if their withdrawal continues to be reasonably sustainable. If they remain in good health by the time they reach age 90 they should have increased to 50 percent their allocation to fixed incomes.

This increase in allocation to fixed incomes is in line with the conventional wisdom that portfolios should become more conservative as retirees grow older. Suppose, however, due to unfavorable investment returns that the withdrawal later in retirement becomes unsustainable instead of reasonably sustainable. Increasing the allocation to fixed incomes later in retirement is then not appropriate.

The simulations in Chapter 5 for those in good health at age 65 did not include such variation in the allocation to fixed income issues over retirement. Doing so, however, causes little change in the results as viewed from age 65. And there is no change in the conclusions. Nevertheless, based on the simulations for a short horizon in this chapter the allocation to fixed incomes should be increased over retirement if the withdrawal remains reasonably sustainable.

Those with a short horizon and a reasonably sustainable withdrawal have little to gain and more to lose by a larger allocation to stocks. They can cover their needs without accepting more risk. Those with an unsustainable withdrawal, however, have more to gain by earning higher returns. It therefore pays for them to accept more risk.

9.5 Shorter Budget Intervals

So far this chapter has considered the effect of reductions in the longest that a retiree might possibly live. Retirees have continued to plan their budgets on an annual basis. The last topic in this chapter is to consider the effect of reducing the length of the budget interval.

Suppose, for instance, that retirees plan their budgets every quarter instead of once a year. What effect will planning more frequently have on their annual withdrawals? There are both costs and benefits to more frequent budgeting.

More frequent budgeting should improve the withdrawals later in retirement. This is because retrenchment will occur more quickly in response to unfavorable developments. But there are costs to this improvement. Sometimes retrenchment may occur on a quarterly basis that would not have been necessary on an annual basis when conditions later improve. Also budgeting is work that almost everyone would like to avoid. And frequent changes in planned activities are disruptive. Is the improvement in the withdrawals sufficient to justify these costs?

The only way to tell is to run simulations both ways under conditions that are otherwise the same. The improvement due to more frequent budgeting can then be identified. Retirees can then assess whether this improvement appears sufficient to justify the cost of more frequent budgeting.

To make such a comparison the probability distribution of the returns over a quarter needs to be put on a comparable basis to that over a year. And a comparable value of the RDR needs to be determined for quarterly budgeting. This is comparable to the RDR used for annual budgeting.

To test the effect of quarterly versus annual budgeting it is convenient to assume that stock returns are lognormally instead of normally distributed. This is because for lognormally distributed returns it is possible to specify quarterly distributions of stock returns that are consistent with an annual distribution. This is not possible when stock returns are normally distributed.

The annual returns are lognormally distributed when the natural logarithm of one plus the annual simple return is normally distributed. Consistent with the base case it is assumed that the mean of one plus the annual simple return is 1.07 and its standard deviation is .18. It is also assumed that the quarterly returns are independently and identically lognormally distributed. The mean and standard deviation of the quarterly returns can then be determined by known relationships.[1]

If retirees are budgeting quarterly the Retrenchment Rule must be reformulated to give a limit on the withdrawal that can be made at the beginning of each quarter. For annual budgeting the rule with a discount rate of .08 allows a withdrawal of as much as 7.6 percent at age 65. This is for those who are in good health with a limit of age 110 on their life expectancy.

For the first quarter at age 65 a withdrawal of 1.9 percent is equal to 7.6 percent at an annual rate, as 7.6/4=1.9. On a quarterly basis there will be 180 quarterly withdrawals up until age 110 instead of 45 annual withdrawals. A calculator shows that a fixed annuity of 1.9 percent can be obtained for 180 periods as required if the quarterly discount rate is .0187.

To compare quarterly to annual budgeting the limit on the withdrawals at age 65 should be equivalent. The test therefore assumes that an RDR of .08 is used to determine the withdrawals using the rule on an annual basis. An RDR of .0187 is used to determine the withdrawals using the rule on a quarterly basis.

Table 9-6

Effect of Budget Interval for 7.5% Withdrawal Age 65
Stock Returns for Normal Valuation Each Year*

Age	Distribution	Budget Interval	Expected Withdrawal	Withdrawal Probability**					Median Portfolio
				8	6	4	2	0	
75	Normal	Annual	5.23	.23	.32	.32	.13	0	85
	LogNormal	Annual	5.24	.22	.33	.34	.11	0	83
	LogNormal	Quarterly	5.16	.19	.37	.35	.11	0	88
85	Normal	Annual	4.41	.17	.29	.30	.27	.03	77
	LogNormal	Annual	4.42	.16	.24	.31	.27	.02	75
	LogNormal	Quarterly	4.44	.13	.27	.32	.26	.02	86
95	Normal	Annual	3.98	.15	.19	.27	.31	.08	72
	LogNormal	Annual	4.00	.14	.20	.27	.33	.06	71
	LogNormal	Quarterly	4.07	.14	.24	.29	.31	.05	89

*Stock returns are normally and lognormally distributed as discussed in text. The RDR is .08 for annual budgeting and .0187 for quarterly budgeting.

**Probability that withdrawal is in a range from one above to one below 8, 6, 4, and 2 or from 0 to 1. Withdrawals are in real terms as a percentage of the investment at age 65. Quarterly withdrawals are at annual rates for the first quarter at stated age.

Suppose annual withdrawals are simulated using the rule on an annual basis with an RDR of .08. And suppose the annual returns in these simulations are lognormally distributed as just specified. Suppose another set of simulations is made on a quarterly basis using the rule with an RDR of .0187. The quarterly distributions of the returns in these simulations are lognormally distributed so as to be compatible with the annual distributions in the first set of simulations. How to achieve this compatibility is described in the note at the end of this chapter referred to earlier. Any difference in the results for these two sets of simulations should be due to the difference in the length of the budget interval.

Suppose the initial withdrawal in the annual simulations is 7.5 percent. The initial withdrawal in the quarterly simulations is then 1.875 percent. This is 7.5 percent at an annual rate, as 7.5/4=1.875. Table 9-6 compares the results from these two sets of simulations.

The results for the quarterly withdrawals are for the first quarter at an annual rate for the stated age. The first row of results at each age in Table 9-6 repeats results given earlier for annual withdrawals when the RDR is .08 and the annual returns are normally distributed under the base case. Note first that the withdrawals on an annual basis for the normally and lognormally distributed returns are virtually the same.

The withdrawals on a quarterly basis are slightly worse than those on an annual basis at age 75. The quarterly withdrawals, however, are slightly better at age 85, and somewhat better at age 95. But the improvements seem insufficient to cover the cost of budgeting four times as often and the slightly worse withdrawals at age 75.

That the results are worse early in retirement and better later on with quarterly budgeting is not surprising. Quarterly budgeting causes more retrenchment early in retirement when unfavorable developments occur. For instance, unfavorable developments over a quarter may cause retrenchment and the unfavorable developments may later be reversed over a full year. But this earlier retrenchment provides more funds to reduce the need for retrenchment later in retirement.

Suppose the discount rate is increased slightly from .0187 to .0194. Now the expected withdrawals at age 75 are virtually the same. There is still some improvement, however, in the withdrawals later in retirement, but not as much as before. There is now no doubt that quarterly budgeting improves the withdrawals, but the improvement is not enough to compensate for the cost of more frequent budgeting.

Suppose the initial annual withdrawal is reasonably sustainable, and equal to 4 percent instead of being 7.5 percent. In this case, quarterly budgeting causes even less improvement in the withdrawals than when the initial withdrawal is unsustainable. There appears to be little reason for retirees to budget more frequently than once a year.

9.6 Conclusions

The longest possible remaining lifetime has little effect on the RDR to use for the Retrenchment Rule. Individuals in poor health at the beginning of retirement should use the same RDR as those in good health. And retirees should continue to use the same RDR over retirement as their longest possible lifetime becomes shorter as they grow older.

Those in poor health at the beginning of retirement should not annuitize and may be less able to obtain part-time work when their initial withdrawals are unsustainable. Nevertheless, by allocating a portion of the portfolio to fixed income issues they can achieve a comparable risk of low withdrawals in the latter part of their shorter retirement period. This is compared to the risk in the latter part of their longer retirement period for those in good health. This is assuming those in good health have a comparably unsustainable initial withdrawal and annuitize and achieve part-time earnings.

Reasonably sustainable annual withdrawals for those with a maximum remaining lifetime of 20 years are 2 percentage points or more above the sustainable withdrawals for those in good health at the beginning of their retirement. Those with a short horizon and a sustainable withdrawal should allocate about 50 percent of their portfolio to fixed incomes. This is irrespective of whether they are in poor health at the beginning of retirement or in good health late in retirement. Those who are in poor health and making an unsustainable withdrawal at the beginning of retirement should allocate at least 25 percent to fixed incomes. An allocation of 50 percent further reduces the risk of low withdrawals later in retirement. It also causes deterioration in other measures of performance, however, and may not be desirable.

Shortening the budget interval from a year to a quarter produces some modest improvement in the withdrawals. The improvement, however, does not appear sufficient to warrant the additional disruptions and other costs involved.

Note

1. Consistent with the earlier assumption about the distribution of annual stock returns suppose that the distribution of one plus the simple annual real return has a mean of 1.07 and a standard deviation of .18. Instead of the simple annual real return being normally distributed, however, assume now that one plus the simple annual real return is lognormally distributed. This requires that the natural logarithm of one plus the simple annual real return have a normal distribution. And the mean and standard deviation of this normal distribution have known relationships to 1.07 and .18. These relationships can be found, for instance, in Campbell, Lo, and MacKinlay (1997) pp 15&16. These relationships show that the mean and standard deviation of the normal distribution are respectively .0537 and .1671. Suppose one plus the quarterly simple real returns are independently and identically lognormally distributed. To be consistent with the normal distribution of the logarithm of one plus the annual simple real return the normal distribution of the logarithm of one plus the quarterly simple real return must have a mean and variance that is one quarter as large. These are respectively .0537/4 and $.1671^2/4$. Using the inverse of the earlier relationships the mean and standard deviation of one plus the quarterly simple returns must then be respectively 1.01706 and .0851. In the simulations with quarterly returns one plus the quarterly simple real return is assumed to have a mean of 1.01706 and a standard deviation of .0851 and to be lognormally distributed.

Reference

Campbell, John Y., Andrew W. Lo, A. Craig MacKinlay, 1997, *The Econometrics of Financial Markets,* Princeton University Press, Princeton NJ.

10

Variable Valuations

So far the annual returns on investment have assumed that the valuation of the investment at the beginning of each year is normal. But at times valuations are highly abnormal such as in the early 1980s or the late 1990s. And the expected return on an investment over a year presumably changes with its valuation at the beginning of that year. Since abnormal valuations tend to persist for a number years the sustainability of subsequent investment withdrawals at such times could be significantly affected.

Based on historical data this chapter estimates relations for the movement of valuations over time, and the dependence of returns on these valuations. The next chapter reruns earlier simulations using these returns to test their effect on earlier results. These new simulations show that the estimates for the effect of valuations in this chapter, if reasonably accurate, require major changes in some of the earlier results. Other results, however, are little affected.

What is little affected is the retrenchment decision and the choice of an RDR. Valuations do have a significant effect on the sustainability of the withdrawals for a given discount rate. But the sustainability of the withdrawals for different discount rates is affected in much the same way. Thus, there is little change in the performance of one discount rate relative to another, and the discount rate selected as the RDR.

As an approximation it can be assumed that the RDR does not change with valuations. And as an approximation this means that the RDR can be assumed to stay the same over retirement even when cyclical changes are occurring in valuations and the expected annual return on investment. Also, as an approximation the RDR selected using the earlier simulations can be used to determine allowable withdrawals even when valuations are abnormal at the beginning of retirement.

The new tests also show that when starting from normal valuations future cyclical changes in expected returns increase somewhat the risk of low withdrawals later in retirement. But as an approximation this increased risk is small enough to neglect. The earlier simulations that ignored cyclical changes in expected return appear to be reasonably valid if the withdrawals start when valuations are normal.

Valuations, however, must be taken into account when assessing the sustainability of withdrawals that start when valuations are significantly abnormal. This is assuming that the best guesses made in this chapter about the strength of the relationship between valuations and expected returns are approximately valid. In such cases, the new tests confirm that highly abnormal valuations at the beginning of retirement have a significant effect on the size of a sustainable withdrawal.

In the early 1980s the valuation of both the S&P 500 and fixed income issues was very low. On the other hand, the valuation of the S&P 500 was very high in the late 1990s. Based on tests using historical stock returns Michael Kitces (2008) has argued that larger sustainable withdrawals are possible when stock valuations are low. And the valuation dependent simulations in the next chapter confirm that the sustainable amount that could have been withdrawn from a given portfolio in the early 1980s was more than 50 percent higher than in the late 1990s. Thus, more than a 50 percent larger portfolio would have been required in the late 1990s to sustainably cover the same living expenses.

Chapter 7 considered the savings that need to be accumulated to cover a desired standard of living over retirement with acceptable sustainability. The results in Chapter 7 provide a good approximation when retirement starts from normal valuations. Suppose, however, that retirement starts at a time when valuations are abnormally high. If the estimated relationships between valuations and subsequent expected returns made in this chapter are valid significantly more savings must be accumulated. The validity of these relationships can certainly be questioned. Nevertheless, their reliability is sufficient to indicate that it is prudent to accumulate significantly more savings before retiring at a time when valuations are high.

Suppose, on the other hand, that retirement starts when valuations are abnormally low. In this case, less than the usual concern is warranted if it becomes necessary to begin retirement before accumulating as much as the normally desired amount. This is the amount required to cover living expenses with the desired sustainability when valuations are at a normal level.

Simulations in Chapter 5 based on normal valuations each year indicated that allocating about a quarter of a portfolio to fixed incomes is desirable when the initial withdrawal is reasonably sustainable. Increasing the allocation further to 50 percent provides a further small reduction in the risk of low withdrawals. But it is questionable whether this additional reduction in risk is worth the reduced portfolio values later in retirement caused by the increased allocation to fixed incomes. Chapter 9 showed, however, that further increases in the allocation to 50 percent are desirable later in retirement if the withdrawal continues to be reasonably sustainable.

With variable valuations the possibility now exists of an abnormal decline in the expected return on stocks relative to the expected return on fixed income issues. Such a decline may make it advisable to temporarily increase the allocation to fixed incomes well above 25 percent. This is even if higher allocations did not appear advisable in Chapter 5 when there was a fixed premium expected return on stocks over fixed income issues.

The next chapter formulates a rule for changing the allocation to fixed income issues under these conditions. This rule is then tested against the alternative of allocating the same fixed portion to fixed incomes each year. Suppose a reasonably sustainable withdrawal is made at the beginning of retirement and that valuations at that time are normal.

Under these conditions the tests show that the rule provides little reduction in the risk of low withdrawals compared to allocating 50 percent at the beginning of each year to fixed income issues. The rule, however, does provide significant increases in portfolio values later in retirement in this case. And meaningful increases in portfolio value are achieved even when compared to allocating only 25 percent of the portfolio to fixed incomes each year. Also, meaningful reductions in risk are obtained compared to a 50 percent allocation when retirement starts at a time when the valuation of stocks is abnormally high relative to that of fixed income issues.

The favorable results using the rule are based on what happens on average in the very large number of runs in the simulations. There will, of course, be many instances in practice, after the fact, when the rule has advised using the wrong allocation. This is not surprising. This chapter shows that changes in prior valuations account for only a very small portion of the changes in subsequent realized investment returns. Allocations based on valuations are therefore frequently going to be wrong after the fact in specific instances. This is even if they improve the results obtained on average as viewed from beforehand.

John Campbell and Luis Viceira (2005), and in earlier work, have shown how to simulate investment returns that depend on valuations and other factors using vector autoregression. Only the dependence on valuations, however, will be considered in this chapter. Valuations presumably incorporate the influence of other factors, and therefore appear to be the most important influence on subsequent returns. And developing some confidence as to the influence of just valuations on subsequent returns is difficult enough.

The first step in this chapter is to examine historical data relating the real returns on both the S&P 500 and intermediate governments to their prior valuations. Based on this evidence best guesses are made as to the change in the expected returns on these investments with their prior valuations. Relations are also estimated for the movement of the valuations over time.

Distributions are then specified for the annual real returns on these investments whose expected returns vary over time with their valuations. These returns are specified so that the annual real returns on these investments in the long run have the same distribution as the annual real returns each year in the earlier simulations. This is for any given initial valuations that are assumed.

10.1 Valuations and Stock Returns

As discussed earlier in Chapter 3 two good measures of the valuation of stocks are the dividend yield on the S&P 500 and its P/E10 ratio. The P/E10 ratio is the P/E ratio for the S&P 500 compiled by Robert Shiller where the earnings are averaged over the trailing 10 years on an inflation adjusted basis. The reciprocal

E10/P ratio is about twice as high as the dividend yield, but they both move up and down together in a similar way.

In this chapter the dividend yield will be used as the indicator of stock valuations. This is because changes in dividend yield account for a somewhat larger portion of changes in the real return on the S&P 500 over a subsequent year. Such a test is made by separately statistically relating the returns to either measure of valuation using regression analysis and comparing the results.

The key question is how much does the expected real return on the S&P 500 change over a year in response to a change in its dividend yield at the beginning of that year? This is a very difficult question to answer.

As discussed earlier in Chapter 3 at the beginning of a year the possible returns over that year have a probability distribution. And that distribution has a mean value, which is the expected return. But these probability distributions and expected returns are unknown and can never be observed. All that can be observed is the single drawing from the distribution that occurred, which is the realized return. And these realized returns are highly volatile.

The problem is shown in Chart 10-1. This chart plots the annual real return realized on the S&P 500 each year since 1960 against its dividend yield prior to that year. The chart highlights the volatility of the returns and the persistence over time of the dividend yields.

Due to the volatility of the returns it is not clear in the chart whether or not the returns move up and down with the dividend yields. At best, changes in the dividend yield account for only a very small portion of changes in the returns. It is evident that it will not be possible to estimate with any reliability the strength of any relationship that may exist.

To deal with the volatility suppose averages of the returns are compared when the dividend yield is high to when it is low. In particular, suppose the dividend yields are divided into quartiles. The highest quartile runs from 1975 through 1986 and has an average dividend yield of .047. The lowest quartile runs from 1996 through 2008 and has an average dividend yield of .016.

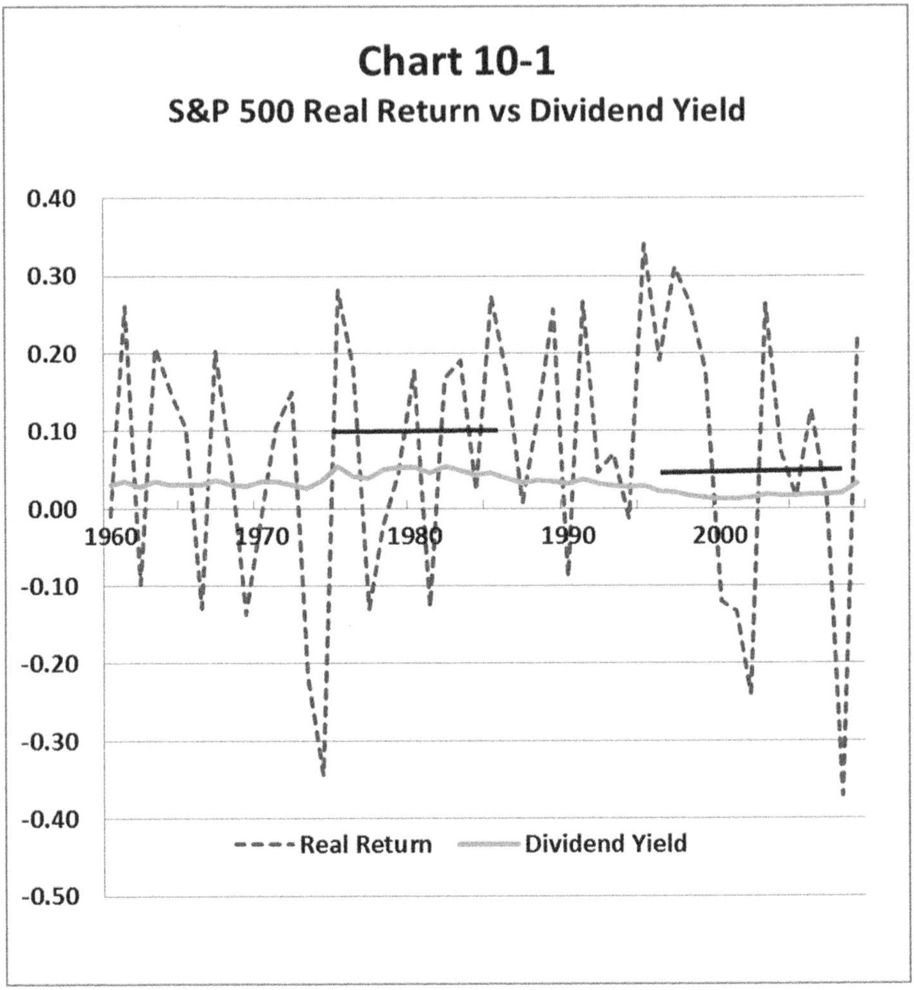

Chart 10-1. Real return realized on the S&P 500 each year in the dashed line versus its dividend yield at the beginning of each of these years in the solid line. The upper horizontal bar is the average real return over 1975 - 1986. These are the years that had the highest quartile of dividend yields over the entire period. The lower horizontal bar is the average real return over 1996 - 2008. These are the years that had the lowest quartile of dividend yields over the entire period. The real returns on the S&P 500 are those for calendar years from the *SBBIYearbook*. The dividend yields are based on the value for the prior month each year of the S&P 500 and the dividend paid for the 12 months up through that prior month. These are from the well known financial data given by Robert J. Shiller for his book, *Irrational Exuberance,* on his website.

The average real returns for these quartiles are shown by the horizontal bars in the chart. The average return shown by these bars declines from .103 to .044. Thus, the average return declines by .059 when the dividend yield declines by .031 from the highest to lowest quartile. Divide .059 by .031 getting 1.9. This estimates that the expected real return for the S&P 500 changes by 1.9 percentage points when its prior dividend yield changes by 1 percentage point.

The average dividend yield in the chart is .032. Suppose that this is the normal dividend yield for the S&P 500. And suppose when its dividend yield is at this normal level that the expected real return on the S&P 500 is .07.

By the end of the 1990s the dividend yield on the S&P 500 had declined from its normal level of .032 to .012, or by 2 percentage points. Using the estimate that was just made the expected return on the S&P 500 had then declined by 1.9 times as much or by 3.8 percentage points. Thus, the expected real return on the S&P 500 had declined from its normal level of .07 to about .03 at the end of the 1990s.

Given the very poor returns since the 1990s it is easy to believe in hindsight that the expected annual real return on the S&P 500 had fallen to .03 or possibly much lower. But there is no way of knowing for sure and some reason to question this belief. In the late 1990s a real return of close to .03 was available by rolling over T Bills. Yet investors were buying stocks at that time presumably because they believed the expected return on the stocks was significantly higher than that available on T Bills. Perhaps some did sell their shares, but all of the shares outstanding were being held by someone at the time indicating that they expected significantly better returns than on T Bills.

Another reason to question the low expected return is the unreliability of the estimate on which it is based. There is a large difference between the average returns given by the horizontal bars in the chart for the highest and lowest quartiles of the dividend yields. But the chart also shows very high volatility of the returns about these horizontal bars. This volatility indicates that the difference in the averages could be due to chance alone. It may not be due to a true difference in the expected returns caused by the difference in dividend yield.

This latter possibility is confirmed by calculating the standard deviation of the difference in the averages for the two cases assuming there is no difference in the true expected returns. Suppose the standard deviation of the returns in either case is .18. The standard deviation of the difference in the averages is then approximately equal to .072.[1]

This standard deviation is greater than the observed difference of .059. Thus, it cannot be said with statistical confidence that the true difference in expected returns is larger than zero. And there is clearly not any confidence that the true difference in the expected returns is anywhere near as large as the observed difference in the averages of .059.

These arguments call into question the reliability of the estimated relation between the dividend yield on the S&P 500 and its subsequent expected return. Nevertheless, in theory the expected return on the S&P 500 should move up and down with its dividend yield. And the estimated size of the relationship does not seem unreasonable. Theoretical support and some empirical confirmation certainly provide sufficient reason to test the implications of the estimated relationship for investment withdrawals.

Moreover, an alternative estimate of the size of the relationship shows it to be somewhat stronger. Estimating the size based on the difference in average return for the highest and lowest quartiles of dividend yields is transparent, but does not make the best use of the available data. A better estimate is obtained by statistically relating the returns on the S&P 500 to the prior dividend yields using regression analysis.

This estimate gives that the expected real return for the S&P 500 changes by 3.2 percentage points instead of 1.9 for a 1 percentage point change in dividend yield. And this coefficient has more statistical confidence being about 1.5 times its standard deviation. As it is a better best guess and provides more contrast this larger estimate will be used for simulating the returns on the S&P 500.

10.2 Valuations and Fixed Income Returns

The valuation of fixed income issues is given by the level of real interest rates. And the level of real interest rates is indicated by the yields available on TIPS. TIPS, however, have been available only since 1997. To make historical comparisons it is therefore necessary to use a proxy. For this purpose it will be assumed that the level of real interest rates at the beginning of a year is given by the real return realized by rolling over short-term T Bills in the prior year. These are the returns reported in the *SBBI Yearbook*.

How much does the expected real return on fixed income issues change in response to a change in the real return on T Bills over the prior year? To answer this question Chart 10-2 provides a comparable plot to that for the S&P 500 in Chart 10-1. In particular, Chart 10-2 plots the real return on intermediate governments each year since 1960 as given in the *SBBI Yearbook* against the real return earned by rolling over T Bills in the prior year.

The valuations given by the prior T Bill returns tend to persist over time like the dividend yields. The changes in the prior T Bill returns, however, account for a larger portion of the changes in the returns on the intermediates. Even without calculating any averages the returns on the intermediates in the chart appear to be higher when the prior T Bill returns are higher.

As in Chart 10-1 the average returns on the intermediates for the lowest and highest quartiles of prior valuations are shown by horizontal bars. From the lowest to highest quartile the average prior return on the T Bills increases from -.013 to .038, or by .051. For these quartiles the average return on the intermediates increases from -.025 to .073, or by .098.

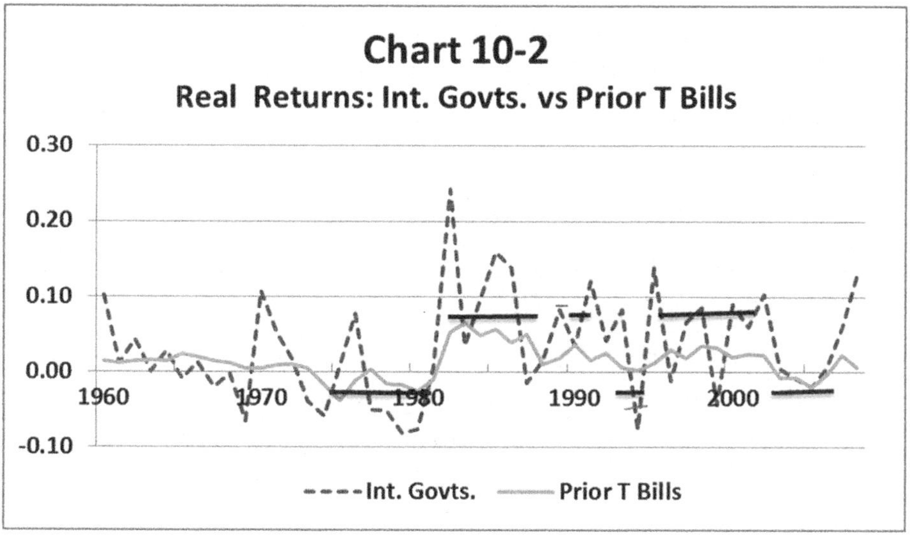

Chart 10-2. Real return realized on intermediate term U. S. government issues each year in the dashed line versus the real return realized by rolling over short term T Bills in the prior year in the solid line. The upper horizontal bars show the average real return on the intermediates over the years when the prior real return on rolling over T Bills was in its highest quartile over the entire period. The lower horizontal bars show the average real return on the intermediates over the years when the prior real return of rolling over T Bills was in its lowest quartile. The real returns for intermediate U. S. government issues are those for calendar years from the *SBBI Yearbook* as are the real returns for rolling over T Bills for the prior years.

Divide the increase in the return on the intermediates of .098 by the increase in the prior return of the T Bills of .051 getting 1.9. This estimates that a 1 percentage point change in the prior return on T Bills results in a 1.9 percentage point change in the subsequent expected return on the intermediates. Moreover, as indicated by the stronger relationship evident in the chart there is more statistical confidence about this relationship.

Suppose the standard deviation of the difference in the average returns is calculated as earlier for the average returns on the S&P 500. In this case, however, the standard deviation of the returns is assumed to be .07 in either case, and the calculated standard deviation is .028.[2] In this case the difference in the average of .098 is equal to 3.5 standard deviations, as .098/.028=3.5. This is almost twice what is necessary to show that the difference is larger than zero with customary statistical confidence.

For the S&P 500 a stronger relationship was obtained by statistically relating the returns to the dividend yield using regression analysis. For the intermediates, however, this alternative gives just about the same results as the difference in the averages for the highest and lowest quartiles.

10.3 Simulating Valuations

The next step is to estimate relations for how the valuations change over time. These estimates for the valuations can be made with much more confidence. This is because the charts show that the valuations are very persistent over time.

Consider first the dividend yield in Chart 10-1. It is clear that the dividend yield in any year is closely related to the dividend yield for the prior year. It is also clear that the dividend yields tend not to stray too far above or below their average or normal value. Thus, the dividend yields are strongly dependent on their prior value, but are also tending to revert in the long run to a normal value.

Suppose that the normal value for the dividend yield in the long run is the average in the chart of .032. To reflect its behavior in the chart it is assumed that the dividend yield each year is a weighted average of the yield in the prior year and its normal value in the long run of .032. The higher the weight of .032 in this weighted average the faster is the dividend yield tending to revert to its normal value. The dividend yield each year is equal to this weighted average plus a random drawing from a normal probability distribution with a zero mean.

The weights for the average are determined by the weights that best fit the observations in the chart based on a least squares regression. These weights are .88 for the prior dividend yield and .12 for the normal value of .032. The standard deviation for the random drawing each year is the standard deviation of the error each year between the observed value in the chart and the estimated weighted average. This standard deviation is .0055.

The relation for the real return for rolling over T Bills in the prior year is determined in a similar way. The normal prior real return of rolling over T Bills is .013 based on the average in Chart 10-2. The weighted average in this case is equal to .70 of the value for the prior year and .30 for the normal value of .013. The standard deviation of the random drawings for this valuation is .016.

The valuations at the beginning of the first year are given values. The valuations at the beginning of the second year are given by the relations just specified using these given values as the prior valuations. The valuations at the beginning of the second year as so determined become the prior valuations to use as inputs to the relations to get the valuations at the beginning of the third year. And the valuations in subsequent years are determined sequentially by continuing to use this same process.

As specified the distribution of returns for any future year depends on the year from which it is viewed and the valuation that exists for the year from which it is viewed. In general, these distributions for the returns in future years may differ significantly from those used in the earlier simulations in this book. Suppose, however, that the year being considered is sufficiently far in the future that the valuations have approximately reverted to their normal values, and are therefore no longer dependent on the valuations for the year from which they are being viewed.

The distribution of returns for a year this far in the future can be considered as the distribution of returns in the long run. And these distributions in the long run can be set equal to the distributions for the returns in the earlier simulations. This is because these distributions in the long run are independent of the year from which they are being viewed, and the valuations that exist for the year from which they are being viewed.

The distributions of the returns each year will now be specified so that the distributions of the returns in the long run are the same as for the earlier simulations in this book. When this is done any difference in the results for the simulated withdrawals can be attributed to the given initial valuations and to the cyclical variation in valuations and annual expected returns just specified.

10.4 Simulating Valuation Dependent Returns

The earlier best guess was that the expected annual real return for the S&P 500 changes by 3.2 percentage points for each one percentage point change in its prior dividend yield. Suppose the prior dividend yield is denoted by y. The expected real return on the S&P 500 each year is then equal to .07+3.2(y-.032) where .032 is the assumed normal dividend yield at the beginning of a year. This relation must hold to make the expected real return equal to .07 as assumed earlier in Chapter 3 when y is equal to its normal value of .032. And this relation must also hold to make the expected return change with y as required by the earlier best guess in this chapter for this relationship.

The simulated real return for a year adds to this expected return a drawing from a normal probability distribution with a zero mean. The standard deviation of the distribution for this random drawing is .176. The standard deviation is set equal to this value because it can be shown when this is done that the standard deviation of the annual returns then rises from .176 starting from a given year to .18 in the long run.[3] This takes into account the small increase in the random variation of the future annual returns caused by the relatively small random variation in the future dividend yields each year.

Note viewed from any year that the annual returns in the long run are normally distributed. This follows because as specified they are linear combinations of normally distributed variables and therefore also normally distributed. Thus, as specified, the annual real return on the S&P 500 in the long run is normally distributed with an expected return of .07 and a standard deviation of .18. And this is the same as the distribution each year for the S&P 500 in Chapter 4.

Now consider the real return on the intermediate governments each year. Suppose the real return of rolling over T Bills in the prior year is denoted by r. The expected real return on the intermediates each year is then equal to

.03+1.9(r-.013) where .013 is the assumed normal real return of rolling over T bills for the prior year. This relation must hold to make the real return on the intermediates equal to .03 as assumed in Chapter 5 when r is equal to its normal value of .013. And this relation must also hold to make the expected return on the intermediates change with r as required by the earlier best guess in this chapter for this relationship.

The simulated real return for the intermediates each year adds to this expected return a drawing from a normal probability distribution with a zero mean and a standard deviation of .056. The standard deviation is set equal to this value because it can be shown when this is done that the standard deviation of the annual returns then rises from .056 starting from a given year to .07 in the long run.[4] As so specified the annual real return on the intermediates in the long run is normally distributed with an expected return of .03 and a standard deviation of .07. And this is the same distribution as for the intermediates each year in Chapter 5. Moreover, as in Chapter 5 the distributions of the annual returns on the S&P 500 and the intermediates are independent.

That completes the specification of the investment returns so that they depend on their prior valuations. Modifying the spreadsheet to incorporate variation in the valuations and the expected returns over time is discussed in Appendix 10-1.

10.5 Conclusions

In theory the expected return on an investment should move up and down with its prior valuation. But the expected return on an investment cannot be observed. All that is known is the return on the investment each year that was actually realized. And these realized returns are highly volatile as they depend on many factors besides the prior valuation.

In practice, changes in valuation therefore account for only a very small proportion of changes in subsequent realized returns. And the relationship between valuations and subsequent expected investment returns cannot be reliably estimated. Despite the difficulty, however, best guesses have been made for the strength of these relationships for the S&P 500 and intermediate government issues.

Due to their persistence, relations for the movement of the valuations of these investments over time can be estimated more reliably. And using these relations the values of the future valuations of these investments can be simulated. Based on these simulated valuations and their estimated relationship to subsequent expected returns relations have been specified for simulating future returns that depend on valuations. These returns were specified so that the distribution of the annual real returns on the S&P 500 and on intermediate governments in the long run are the same as those each year for earlier simulated returns in this book.

These simulated returns can be used to test the possible effect of changes in valuation and expected investment returns. This is with respect to their effect on the retrenchment decision and the size of sustainable investment withdrawals. It is also possible to formulate a strategy for changing the allocation of a portfolio in response to changes in the relative valuation of stocks and fixed income issues, and to test its effectiveness. Such tests using the simulated returns specified in this chapter are carried out in the next chapter.

Notes

1. As an approximation for calculating the standard deviation of the difference in the averages suppose there is no serial correlation in successive returns. This is reasonable because changes in the expected returns are sufficiently small relative to changes in the returns that serial correlation in the expected returns causes little serial correlation in the returns. And, in fact, the observed returns appear to follow a random walk and not to be serially correlated. Assume the standard deviation of the returns in either case is .18. As the sample size of the quartiles is 12 and 13 the standard deviation of the difference in the averages is then approximately equal to $.18(1/12 + 1/13)^{1/2}$, or .072.

2. This is calculated in the same way as the standard deviation of the difference of the averages in Chart 10-1 using the assumed standard deviation of the returns on the intermediates of .07.

3. Consider the relation for the real return on the S&P 500 in a future year. This return is equal to an expected return plus a drawing from a normal distribution with a zero mean and a standard deviation of .176. The expected return is equal to

$.07+3.2(y-.032)$ where y is the dividend yield at the beginning of that year. The value of y is equal to an expected dividend yield plus a drawing from a normal distribution with a zero mean and a standard deviation of .0055. The expected dividend yield is equal to .88 of the prior dividend yield and .12 of its normal value of .032.

Substitute the relation for the dividend yield into the expression for the real return on the S&P 500. This now gives the return of the S&P 500 in the future year in terms of the dividend yield at the beginning of the prior year and the random drawing for the dividend yield at the beginning of the given future year. Next substitute into this latter expression for the prior dividend yield its relation in terms of the dividend yield in the next earlier year and the random drawing for the dividend yield for the prior year. Continue successively making such substitutions. This is until the return on the S&P 500 for the given future year depends on the given dividend yield for the initial year and the random drawings for the dividend yields for each of the intervening years.

Using the expression so obtained calculate the variance of the return of the S&P 500 for the given future year. Then for this variance let the given future year become arbitrarily large. In the limit this variance becomes equal to $(.176)^2+(3.2)^2(.0055)^2/(1-.88^2)$. This latter expression is equal to $(.18)^2$ as required.

4. The variance of the return in the long run for intermediate governments is calculated in a similar way to that for the return on the S&P 500. The variance in the long run in this case is equal to $(.056)^2+(1.9)^2(.016)^2/(1-.7^2)$, which is equal to $(.07)^2$ as required.

References

Campbell, John and Luis Viceira. 2005. "The Term Structure of the Risk-Return Tradeoff." *Financial Analysts Journal* 61,1: 34-44.

Kitces, Michael. 2008. "Rethinking the Safe Withdrawal Rate." *Journal of Financial Planning* 21,12 (December Supplement): 8-11.

Appendix 10-1

Modifying the Spreadsheet for Variable Valuations

The spreadsheet in Table 5-8 for a mixed portfolio is modified to incorporate expected returns that vary each year by introducing four new columns. The cells in these columns calculate the expected returns each year for stocks and fixed income issues and the respective valuations on which they depend. The given dividend yield at the beginning of the first year is put in Q6. The dividend yield for the second year is calculated in Q7 by:

=.12*.032+.88*Q6+NormInv(Rand(),0,.0055)

The dividend yields at the beginning of subsequent years are obtained by copying this relation to lower rows in column Q to Q50.

The expected return for stocks for the first year is calculated in cell R6 by:

=.07+3.2*(Q6−.032)

Expected returns for subsequent years are obtained by copying this relation to lower rows in column R to R50. And the relation in E6 in Table 5-9 is rewritten to be:

=.25*M6+.75*NormInv(Rand (),R6,.176)

and copied to lower rows of E to E50. As in Table 5-9 note that this relation assumes a fixed allocation to fixed incomes at the beginning of each year of .25. Note also that the standard deviation of the annual returns has been reduced from .18 to .176 as discussed in the text of this chapter.

Similarly, for the fixed incomes, the given real return for rolling over T Bills in the year prior to the first year is put in S6. The real return for rolling over T Bills in the first year used as the valuation for fixed incomes in the second year is calculated in S7 by:

=.30*.013+.70*S6+NormInv(Rand (),0,.016)

And this relation is copied to lower rows in column S to S50.

The expected return for fixed incomes in the first year is calculated in cell T6 by:

=.03+1.9*(S6−.013)

and this relation is copied to lower rows in column T to T50. Also, the relation in M6 in Table 5-8 is rewritten to be:

=NormInv(Rand (),T6,.056)

and copied to lower rows of M to M50. Note that the standard deviation of the annual returns has been reduced to .056 as discussed in the text of this chapter.

11

Effects of Variable Valuations

The last chapter specified annual investment valuations that vary over time, and annual distributions for investment returns that depend on these valuations. Simulated investment returns earlier in this book assumed a normal valuation each year. The distributions with the variable valuations are the same as those used earlier only in the long run when the influence of the current valuation is no longer of significance.

This chapter tests how the initial value of the valuations and their subsequent variation changes the results for the simulated withdrawals obtained earlier. The results of these tests were summarized in the introduction to the last chapter. In general, the variable valuations have little effect on the retrenchment decision. They also have little effect on savings requirements when starting retirement when valuations are normal. The variable valuations, however, do have a significant impact on savings requirements when starting retirement at a time of significantly abnormal valuations. This is assuming that the best guesses as to the relationship between valuation and expected investment returns made in the last chapter are reasonably valid.

The first step in this chapter is to test the effect of variable valuations on the retrenchment decision. Then a rule is developed to vary the allocation between stocks and fixed income issues to take advantage of any abnormal development in their relative valuations. The last step is to test the effect on savings requirements of starting retirement at a time when valuations are significantly abnormal. In doing so advantage is taken of using the variable allocation rule just developed.

11.1 Effect on Retrenchment

The Retrenchment Rule determines the most that can be withdrawn to avoid painful retrenchment at any time based on the discount rate that has been chosen as the RDR. And the RDR is chosen by simulating the use of the Retrenchment

Rule over a hypothetical retirement period using a series of possible discount rates. The discount rate that gives the best performance in these tests is selected as the RDR.

The performance of a discount rate in these tests can be significantly affected by valuation at the beginning of the retirement period. But the performance of other discount rates is affected by the valuation in the same way. Thus, the valuation has little effect on the performance of one discount rate relative to another and on the discount rate that is chosen as the RDR.

As an approximation the same RDR can therefore be used over all of retirement even if there is significant cyclical variation in the annual expected return on investment. And as an approximation the RDR can be selected assuming valuations are normal each year as earlier in this book in Chapter 4. In general, valuations have little effect on the largest withdrawals that can be made to avoid painful retrenchment even though they can have a significant effect on sustainability.

To see that valuations have little effect on the choice of an RDR the simulations made to choose an RDR in Chapter 4 are rerun in this chapter. This is for a series of possible discount rates. But now a series of runs for different discount rates is made starting from a series of possible valuations.

Results are shown in Table 11-1 for such a set of simulations. Five different valuations are assumed for the S&P 500 at the beginning of retirement. And starting from each valuation there are three streams of expected withdrawals for discount rates of .06, .08, and .10.

The top set of streams assumes that the initial valuation is very low. The dividend yield at the beginning of retirement is equal to .052, which is in the range that occurred in the early 1980s. The bottom set of streams assumes that the initial valuation is very high. The dividend yield at the beginning of retirement is equal to .012, which is in the range reached late in the 1990s.

The middle set of the five sets of streams assumes retirement starts with a normal valuation. The initial dividend yield is equal to .032. These streams are virtually the same as those shown earlier for these three discount rates in Table 4-1. The only difference is that most of the expected withdrawals later in retirement in Table 11-1 are 0.1 lower than in Table 4-1.

Table 11-1

Expected Withdrawals for Selected Initial Valuations
Expected Stock Returns Dependent on Valuations*
Selected Discount Rates

Initial Valuation	Dividend Yield	Discount Rate	Expected Withdrawals**							
			65	70	75	80	85	90	95	100
Very Low	.052	.06	6.1	5.5	5.3	5.1	4.9	4.8	4.7	4.7
		.08	7.6	6.7	6.3	5.9	5.6	5.4	5.2	5.1
		.10	9.2	7.8	7.1	6.5	6.0	5.6	5.3	5.1
Low	.042	.06	6.1	5.3	4.9	4.7	4.5	4.4	4.3	4.2
		.08	7.6	6.4	5.8	5.4	5.0	4.8	4.6	4.5
		.10	9.2	7.4	6.4	5.7	5.2	4.8	4.5	4.3
Normal	.032	.06	6.1	5.0	4.5	4.2	4.0	3.9	3.7	3.7
		.08	7.6	6.0	5.2	4.7	4.4	4.1	3.9	3.8
		.10	9.2	6.9	5.7	5.0	4.4	4.0	3.7	3.5
High	.022	.06	6.1	4.7	4.1	3.7	3.5	3.3	3.2	3.1
		.08	7.6	5.6	4.6	4.1	3.7	3.4	3.3	3.1
		.10	9.2	6.3	5.0	4.2	3.7	3.3	3.0	2.8
Very High	.012	.06	6.1	4.3	3.6	3.2	3.0	2.8	2.7	2.6
		.08	7.6	5.1	4.0	3.5	3.1	2.8	2.7	2.5
		.10	9.2	5.8	4.3	3.5	3.0	2.6	2.4	2.2

*Portfolio entirely allocated to stocks. Annual expected return depends on prior dividend yield as described in last chapter.

**Expected withdrawals are as a percentage of the value of the investment at age 65, and are in real terms.

The slightly lower expected withdrawals in Table 11-1 are not surprising. In Table 4-1 the expected real return each year is equal to its normal value of .07. But in Table 11-1 runs occur in the future of better or worse than normal expected annual real returns. When starting from a normal dividend yield, however, better or worse than normal runs are equally likely. And a run of worse than normal expected annual returns hurts the withdrawals more than they are helped by a better than normal run.

Thus, the expected withdrawals in the middle panel of Table 11-1 should be less than those for the same discount rates in Table 4-1. But the simulations show that the size of this effect is very small and of little importance. Future cyclical variation in the expected annual returns has little effect on the streams of expected withdrawals when starting from a normal dividend yield.

Now look at the panels in Table 11-1 that are just above or below the middle panel. Retirement for these panels starts at a time when the dividend yield is abnormally high or low. And for a given discount rate and age the expected withdrawals later in retirement change by from 0.5 to 0.8 relative to those in the middle panel.

An abnormal valuation in the initial year causes a change in the initial expected annual real return. And because of the persistence of the dividend yields there also tends to be a change in the annual returns expected for a number of years in the future. Later in retirement the dividend yields and annual mean returns are expected to revert to their normal levels. But the earlier changes are sufficient to significantly raise or lower the streams of expected withdrawals later in retirement.

A key point, however, is that very little change occurs in the performance of one discount rate relative to another. Relative to each other the streams for the different discount rates in each of the three middle panels look just about the same. The change in the expected annual return early in retirement affects the streams for the different discount rates in the same way. Thus, there is little change in the performance of one discount rate relative to another when the initial valuation changes. Those selecting a discount rate of .08 for their RDR in the middle panel when the initial valuation is normal will presumably also select .08 if the initial valuation is high or low.

A small change in relative performance does occur, however, for the extreme valuations at the top or bottom of the table. But these extreme valuations are likely to persist for only a short time. And at most there would be only a small loss to using the discount rate selected for a more normal valuation. This is even if some change in discount rate might be indicated if these extreme cases were expected to persist for a long time.

Consider, for instance, the panel at the bottom of the table for a very high valuation. The expected withdrawal for a discount rate of .06 at age 100 in this case is 0.1 larger than that for .08. Thus, the stream of expected withdrawals for .08 no longer dominates the stream for .06 over the entire retirement period as it does in the higher panels. Nevertheless, the argument for choosing .08 over .06 is diminished only slightly in the bottom panel.

The stream for .08 still dominates that for .06 except at age 100 in the bottom panel. And virtually all retirees seem likely to find that sufficient to still prefer the stream for .08 over that for .06. The only advantage of the stream for .06 is that it is slightly higher at age 100, but few will survive long enough to enjoy even that small advantage.

Now consider the panel at the top of Table 11-1. In this panel the stream for a discount rate of .10 dominates that for .08 just as that for .08 dominates that for .06 in the middle panel. Suppose some retirees selected .10 in the middle panel because they believed the higher expected withdrawals early in retirement more than compensated for the lower expected withdrawals later in retirement. Making such a decision in the middle panel might have been difficult. But these retirees will have no difficulty in choosing .10 in the top panel. These retirees, however, are not changing their choice of a discount rate in the upper panel due to the lower valuation. They just no longer have any difficulty in making the same choice that they did in the lower panels.

Suppose, however, that retirees prefer the stream for .08 to that for .10 in the middle panel and the panel above it. In this event they will presumably switch and prefer the stream for .10 in the top panel because the stream for .10 now dominates that for .08 over the entire retirement period. But if they preferred .08 in the lower panels switching to .10 in the top panel will provide only a small improvement. Thus, if they continue to use .08 for a short time in this extreme case in the top panel there will be only a small loss.

Thus, based on Table 11-1 a reasonable approximation is to assume that the selection of a discount rate as the RDR is unaffected by changes in valuation. Table 11-1, however, considers only the streams of expected withdrawals. It is possible that valuations affect the risk of low withdrawals sufficiently to affect the choice of an RDR.

Chapter 4 showed that virtually all retirees will prefer a discount rate of .08 to .06 even after considering the risk of low withdrawals. A discount rate of .06 does reduce the risk of low withdrawals somewhat later in retirement compared to .08. But this reduction in risk appears insufficient to compensate for the increased retrenchment and lower stream of expected withdrawals earlier in retirement required by .06.

Table 11-2 shows that changes in initial valuation can significantly affect the risk of low withdrawals later in retirement. Changes in initial valuation, however, have little effect on the reduction in this risk provided by choosing a lower discount rate. Thus, as in Chapter 4 the reduction in risk provided by choosing .06 appears insufficient to compensate for the lower expected withdrawals .06 provides earlier in retirement.

To simplify in view of the wider coverage of Table 11-2 note that withdrawal probabilities are provided only for age 85 in Table 11-2. Nevertheless, these results are sufficient to make the necessary comparisons. Note first when starting with a normal dividend yield that the withdrawal probabilities are just about the same as those obtained in Chapter 4.

In particular, in Table 11-2 the chances that the withdrawals will be less than 3 percent at age 85 for discount rates of .10, .08, and .06 are respectively .37, .32, and .30. In Chapter 4 the comparable chances at age 85 are respectively .35, .30, and .29. As expected the risk of low withdrawals is just about the same in both cases, but slightly higher in Table 11-2. Note also that the risk reduction obtained by choosing a lower discount rate is about the same in either case.

Starting with a normal valuation in the middle panel the results in Table 11-2 are very similar to those in Chapter 4. But Table 11-2 shows that abnormal valuations can have a significant effect on the risk of low withdrawals. At the top of the table the chances that the withdrawals are less than 3 percent are less than half of those for a normal valuation. On the other hand, at the bottom of the table the chances that the withdrawals are less than 3 percent are more than a half higher compared to a normal valuation.

The reduction in risk provided by choosing a lower discount rate, however, is virtually the same at the top, bottom, or middle of the table. Those who must make withdrawals with the high valuations at the bottom of the table are highly likely to have much lower withdrawals later in retirement. But choosing a lower discount rate and retrenching more initially is of no more help at the bottom of the table than in the higher panels. Whether valuations are high or low the risk of low withdrawals has no more effect on the selection of a discount rate than in Chapter 4.

In general, changes in valuation affect the withdrawals from different discount rates in the same way and have little effect on the performance of one discount rate relative to another. Changes in valuation therefore have little effect on the choice of a discount rate to use as the RDR. This has important implications.

As an approximation it is possible to use the same RDR over all of retirement. This is even if the expected annual real return each year varies in a cyclical manner. Also, suppose as earlier in this book that the RDR is selected assuming the valuation is normal each year. As an approximation this same RDR can then also be used when starting retirement when valuations are abnormal and vary over time.

11.2 A Variable Allocation Rule

Earlier tests in this book showed the effect of allocating either 25 or 50 percent of the portfolio to fixed income issues at the beginning of each year when valuations did not change. Now, however, the expected returns on stocks and fixed income issues are varying over time and relative to each other. In this case better results should be achievable by changing the allocation as changes occur in the expected returns of stocks relative to those of fixed income issues. In practice, this means changing the allocation as changes occur in the valuation of stocks relative to fixed income issues as this is the only way of gauging changes in their relative expected returns.

Table 11-2

Withdrawal Probabilities for Selected Initial Valuations
Expected Stock Returns Dependent on Valuations*
Selected Discount Rates

Initial Valuation	Dividend Yield	Discount Rate	Withdrawal Probability Age 85**					
			10	8	6	4	2	0
Very Low	.052	.06	0	0	.61	.27	.11	.01
		.08	0	.38	.28	.20	.13	.01
		.10	.22	.21	.20	.20	.15	02
Low	.042	.06	0	0	.47	.33	.18	.02
		.08	0	.26	.28	.24	.19	.03
		.10	.14	.17	.20	.23	.23	.03
Normal	.032	.06	0	0	.35	.35	.26	.04
		.08	0	.17	.23	.28	.28	.04
		.10	.07	.13	.18	.25	.31	.06
High	.022	.06	0	0	.23	.35	.36	.06
		.08	0	.10	.18	.29	.35	.08
		.10	.04	.08	.14	.26	.38	.10
Very High	.012	.06	0	0	.14	.31	.45	.10
		.08	0	.05	.13	.26	.44	.12
		.10	.02	.04	.11	.22	.45	.16

*Same as Table 11-1.

**Probability that withdrawal is in a range from one above to one below 10, 8, 6, 4, 2, or from 0 to 1. Withdrawals are in real terms and as a percentage of the investment at age 65.

Suppose y is the dividend yield on the S&P 500 at the beginning of a year. As a best guess the last chapter estimated that the expected real return over a year on the S&P 500 is equal to $.07+3.2(y-.032)$. This relation assumes that .032 is the normal dividend yield on the S&P 500 and that .07 is the expected real return when the dividend yield is at its normal level.

Suppose r is the real return of rolling over a series of T Bills in the prior year. As a best guess the last chapter also estimated that the expected real return over a year on intermediate governments is equal to $.03+1.9(r-.013)$. This relation assumes that .013 is the normal prior real return on the T Bills and that .03 is the expected real return on the intermediates when the prior real return on the T Bills is at a normal level.

The risk premium for investing in stocks is commonly considered to be the expected return on stocks less the expected return on fixed incomes. In this case the risk premium for investing in the S&P 500 instead of intermediates is the difference between $.07+3.2(y-.032)$ and $.03+1.9(r-.013)$. If y and r are at their normal values the risk premium for investing in the S&P 500 is .04. In Chapter 5 valuations were assumed to be normal at the beginning of each year and allocating 25 percent to fixed incomes at the beginning of each year gave good results. This is when the initial withdrawal is reasonably sustainable.

Suppose, however, that y and r are not at their normal values and that $3.2(y-.032)$ is less than $1.9(r-.013)$. In this case the risk premium for investing in the S&P 500 is less than the normal value of .04. Presumably now a larger portion of the portfolio should be allocated to fixed incomes than 25 percent. And the further is $3.2(y-.032)$ below $1.9(r-.013)$ the larger should be the allocation to fixed incomes.

But how much should the allocation to fixed incomes be increased when the discount from the normal risk premium increases? A possible upper benchmark for arriving at an answer is the extremely large discount that existed in the late 1990s. At that time not only were stock valuations very high, but the valuation of fixed incomes was low.

For instance, at the beginning of 1998 the dividend yield on the S&P 500 was .016 and the real return on T Bills for the prior year was .035. With these valuations the discount for the risk premium was extremely large and equal to .093 since $3.2(.016-.032)$ less $1.9(.035-.013)$ is equal to $-.093$. Instead of being equal to its normal value of .04 the risk premium had become strongly negative and equal to -.053, as .04-.093=-.053.

With such a large discount for investing in stocks instead of the normal premium of .04 it might seem that the allocation to fixed incomes should be increased to 100 percent. This would be reasonable if the relationship between valuations and expected returns was reliable. But the last chapter stressed that this relationship is highly problematic. And, in fact, very strong bull markets for stocks did occur in both 1998 and 1999 when this very high discount existed for the risk premium.

It therefore seems prudent to limit the allocation to intermediates to 75 percent even when the discount is as high as it was in the late 1990s. This represents a 50 percentage point increase from the allocation of 25 percent when the premium is at its normal level of .04. Suppose the discount for the premium is multiplied by a constant factor to get the amount to add to the allocation to the intermediates. If this factor is equal to 5.4 an increase of 50 percentage points occurs for the valuations in early 1998 as 5.4(.093)=.50.

The behavior of stocks in the late 1990s shows that caution should be used in raising the allocation of fixed incomes too high even when there is an extremely large discount for the risk premium. There is also reason not to reduce the allocation of fixed incomes too much even when the premium for stocks is well above its normal level. For instance, the premium at the beginning of 1974 was very high as the dividend yield was .036 and the real return for T Bills in the prior year equal to -.017. But despite the large premium at the beginning of the year there was a severe bear market for stocks in 1974.

Thus, the allocation to fixed incomes will not be reduced below 25 percent when the risk premium for stocks is above its normal level of .04. In view of the poor reliability of the relation between expected returns and valuations the allocation to fixed incomes will be kept between 25 and 75 percent. In summary the allocation rule to be tested is the following.

Suppose the valuations indicate that the risk premium for stocks is at a discount to its normal level. This discount is multiplied by 5.4 and added to .25 to get the proportion allocated to fixed incomes at the beginning of the year.

The proportion allocated to fixed incomes, however, cannot exceed .75. If the premium for investing in stocks is at its normal level of .04 or higher a proportion of .25 is allocated to fixed incomes.

As has been indicated this rule did not perform well in the late 1990s or at times in the1970s. But since the 1990s it has performed reasonably well. For instance, the dividend yield on the S&P 500 continued to be quite low at the beginning of 2000, 2001, and 2002. And the allocation over those years would have remained close to 75 percent protecting against the major bear market that occurred over those years. And those were also years with strong real returns on intermediates following their abnormally low valuation in the late 1990s.

By the beginning of 2003 the valuation of the S&P 500 had decreased, but its dividend yield was still abnormally low being equal to .018. A major change had occurred in the valuation of intermediates by 2003, however, as it was now abnormally high instead of being low. As a result the allocation advised by the rule for 2003 had declined to 29 percent. This would have been a favorable shift as a strong rebound occurred in stocks in 2003 following the bear market of 2000-2002.

Based on the rule the allocation to intermediates would have remained near its lower limit over the next several years as there was little change in the dividend yield and the valuation of fixed incomes remained high. By early 2008, however, the valuation of fixed incomes had declined somewhat and the rule advised an allocation to intermediates of 40 percent. This was of some help in protecting against the severe bear market for stocks in 2008, but an even higher portion in fixed incomes would, of course, have been even more helpful.

Following the major bear market for stocks in 2008 the dividend yield on the S&P 500 was back to normal at the beginning of 2009, and the valuation of fixed incomes was also close to normal. The rule advised an allocation for intermediates of close to 25 percent for 2009. This was, of course, highly desirable in view of the sharp rebound in stocks that occurred in 2009. Thus, over the period since the 1990s the allocation rule has proved to be generally helpful, if far from ideal.

Table 11-3

Variable versus Fixed Allocations for 4% Withdrawal Age 65
Expected Returns Dependent on Valuations*
Selected Allocations** RDR .08

Initial Conditions	Age	Fxd. Inc. Alloc.	Expected Withdrawal	Withdrawal Probability*** 4	3	2	1	0	Median Portfolio
Normal	75	.25	3.92	.94	.05	.01	0	0	112
		.50	3.98	.98	.02	0	0	0	105
		Var.	3.95	.96	.03	.01	0	0	117
	85	.25	3.71	.83	.08	.06	.03	0	127
		.50	3.82	.88	.07	.04	.01	0	112
		Var.	3.81	.88	.06	.05	.01	0	144
	95	.25	3.51	.76	.08	.09	.06	.01	155
		.50	3.62	.80	.07	.08	.05	0	119
		Var.	3.68	.83	.06	.07	.04	0	190
Year 2000	75	.25	3.75	.82	.12	.05	.01	0	79
		.50	3.92	.95	.04	.01	0	0	85
		Var.	3.93	.95	.04	.01	0	0	94
	85	.25	3.30	.62	.15	.15	.08	0	69
		.50	3.58	.73	.14	.10	.05	0	75
		Var.	3.69	.80	.11	.07	.02	0	99
	95	.25	2.99	.54	.12	.16	.16	.02	62
		.50	3.25	.62	.12	.16	.10	0	63
		Var.	3.47	.73	.09	.11	.07	0	110

*Portfolio allocated to stocks and fixed incomes with valuations and expected annual returns as specified in Chapter 10. For "Normal" initial conditions the initial dividend yield is .032 and the real return on T Bills in the prior year is .013. For "Year 2000" the initial dividend yield is .012 and the real return on T Bills for the prior year is .020.

**Allocation to intermediates is either .25 or .50 at the beginning of each year or variable. Variable allocations are .25 plus 5.4 times the difference between 3.2(.032-y) and 1.9(.013-r) when this difference is positive, but the total allocation to intermediates cannot exceed .75. The values y and r are respectively the dividend yield at the beginning of the year on the S&P 500 and the real return of rolling over T Bills in the prior year.
***Similar to Table 11-2.

Changing the allocation of a portfolio in response to changes in the relative valuation of stocks and fixed incomes issues frequently turns out to be counterproductive after the fact. This is not surprising as changes in valuation account for only a very small portion of changes in realized investment return. The question, however, is how well do such shifts perform on average over a very large number of runs of simulated history. That question is considered next. Modifying the spreadsheet to incorporate variable allocations is discussed in Appendix 11-1.

11.3 Effect of Variable Allocation

The performance of the variable allocation rule just formulated will now be compared to resetting the same allocation at the beginning of each year. The results of these tests are shown in Table 11-3. For these tests retirement is assumed to begin at age 65 with a reasonably sustainable withdrawal of 4 percent.

The top half of the table assumes that valuations are normal for both stocks and fixed incomes at the beginning of retirement. The bottom half assumes at the beginning of retirement that the valuations are the same as at the beginning of 2000. At that time the valuation of stocks was very high with the dividend yield on the S&P 500 equal to only .012. And the valuation of fixed incomes was somewhat low with the real return of rolling over T Bills for the prior year equal to .020.

Starting from normal valuations the variable rule has about the same risk of low withdrawals as a fixed allocation each year of 50 percent. But the variable rule provides significantly larger portfolio values later in retirement. At ages 85 and 95 the median portfolio values increase respectively from 112 and 119 to 144 and 190. This is in real terms as a percent of the initial value of the portfolio.

Suppose valuations at the beginning of retirement instead of being normal are very high for stocks and somewhat low for fixed incomes. These were the conditions for the year 2000 shown in the bottom half of the table. In this case the variable rule provides a meaningful reduction in risk later in retirement as well as significantly increasing portfolio values.

Compared to the 25 percent allocation the variable rule provides more risk reduction. But the increase in portfolio values from using the rule is smaller starting from the normal valuations in the upper half of the table. Nevertheless, the increase in portfolio values is still meaningful.

Thus, the rule performs well. Under the conditions of the tests there is little cost to using the rule. And there are significant benefits compared to the fixed allocations.

When the rule is applied in practice, however, there will be costs in the form of transaction fees and taxes. And the transactions seem likely to be larger when using the rule than a fixed allocation. If so, these higher costs for using the rule will offset some of the benefits.

It is possible, however, to keep any transaction fees quite small by appropriately selecting the investments. And taxes will not be a problem in tax-free accounts. In taxable accounts the benefits seem large enough to cover some unfavorable tax consequences. No tests have been attempted, however, to evaluate the general effect of taxes on these results.

A risk to relying on the results of the tests is that the relation between valuations and expected investment returns may not be as strong as estimated. In this case the benefits will not be as large as indicated in the tests. But, of course, the relationship could also be stronger than estimated and the benefits of using the rule larger.

Perhaps the most important caveat for using the rule, however, is the problem discussed earlier. It is clear from the historical data that changes in valuation at best account for only a very small proportion of changes in realized return. After the fact, therefore, there are likely to be many instances in practice when the rule has given very poor advice as to the best allocation. Thus, there will frequently be regrets in using the rule after the fact even if it improves performance on average viewed from beforehand.

11.4 Effect on Required Savings

Variable valuations and expected returns on investment have little effect on savings requirements when retirement starts at a time of normal valuations. When retirement starts at a time of significantly abnormal valuation, however, there is a significant effect on savings requirements. It will be shown shortly that over 50 percent more savings would have been required in early 2000 or 2010 when valuations were high than in 1982 when valuations were low. This is to fund the same withdrawal with reasonable sustainability. This is providing that the best guesses made as to the relationship between valuation and expected return in the last chapter are reasonably valid.

The first step is to show that when starting from normal valuations that cyclical variation in valuations and expected returns has little effect on savings requirements. Thus, when starting from normal valuations the savings requirements indicated earlier in Table 7-1 are approximately valid. This is even though these earlier results assumed there was a normal valuation each year.

This result can be established by comparing the results for a 4 percent withdrawal in Table 5-4 with a constant valuation to those for a 4 percent withdrawal in the upper half of Table 11-3 with a variable valuation. Either table shows what happens under these conditions when there is a fixed allocation each year of either 25 or 50 percent. In Table 11-3 there is somewhat more risk of low withdrawals, but the increase is small enough to ignore as an approximation.

In particular, for a 25 percent allocation Table 5-4 shows at ages 85 and 95 that the risk the withdrawals will be less than 3 percent are respectively .07 and .14. For the same conditions except for variable instead of constant valuations Table 11-3 shows the same risks are .09 and .16. For a 50 percent allocation the same risks increase from .03 and .09 in Table 5-4 to .05 and .13 in Table 11-3.

Thus, when starting from normal valuations cyclical variation in future valuations causes some increase in the risk of low withdrawals later in retirement as expected. But the increase in risk is small enough that it can be ignored as an approximation when planning savings requirements that start from normal valuations. When starting from significantly abnormal valuations, however, valuations cannot be ignored.

Table 11-4

Effect of Valuation on Size of Comparably Sustainable Withdrawals

Expected Returns Depend on Valuations*

Variable Allocation** RDR .08

<u>Initial Conditions</u>

Div. Yield	Prior T Bills	Withdraw Age 65	Age	Withdrawal/ Initial Value** Expected	1.0	.8	.6	.4	.2	0
.032	.013	4.0	75	.99	.96	.03	.01	0	0	0
			85	.95	.87	.05	.05	.03	0	0
			95	.92	.82	.05	.06	.05	.02	0
.054	.053	5.5	75	.98	.94	.04	.02	0	0	0
			85	.95	.86	.06	.05	.03	0	0
			95	.92	.82	.05	.06	.05	.02	0
.012	.020	3.5	75	.99	.98	.01	.01	0	0	0
			85	.96	.89	.04	.05	.02	0	0
			95	92	.83.	.05	.05	.05	.02	0
.020	−.026	3.3	75	.99	.96	.03	.01	0	0	0
			85	.95	.87	.06	.04	.03	0	0
			95	.92	.82	.05	.05	.06	.02	0

*Portfolio allocated to stocks and fixed incomes with valuations and expected annual returns as specified in Chapter 10.

**This is the variable allocation specified earlier and used in Table 11-3.

***Probability that withdrawals in real terms as a proportion of their initial value are from .1 below to .1 above .8, .6, .4, .2, or from 1.0 to .9 or 0 to .1.

To demonstrate that valuations must be considered in this latter case the simulations will be rerun assuming retirement starts with different valuations. In particular it will be shown how the size of the initial investment changes to get the same sustainability as a 4 percent withdrawal starting from normal valuations. And since Table 11-3 shows that the variable allocations give good results it is assumed that this rule is being used in these tests.

The results of these tests are shown in Table 11-4. As a standard the top panel in the table shows the sustainability of a 4 percent withdrawal starting from normal valuations. These are essentially the same results as provided in Table 11-3 for a 4 percent withdrawal starting with normal valuations and using a variable allocation. But Table 11-4 presents the results in a different format. As in Table 7-1, Table 11-4 shows future withdrawals as a proportion of their initial value. As earlier, this format makes it possible to compare the sustainability of initial withdrawals of different size.

In the second panel from the top in Table 11-4 the initial valuations are assumed to be very low for both the S&P 500 and intermediate governments. These are the same valuations that existed at the beginning of 1982. The dividend yield is equal to .054 and the real return on rolling over T Bills in the prior year is equal to .053.

The initial withdrawal of 5.5 percent for these initial conditions was determined by testing a series of initial withdrawals. This is to see which withdrawal gives about the same sustainability as the 4 percent withdrawal in the top panel of Table 11-4. Note that the expected withdrawals at ages 85 and 95 are the same for both of the top two panels. And the chances of low withdrawals at ages 85 and 95 are also the same for these two panels.

For the third panel from the top the valuation for the S&P 500 is very high with the dividend yield equal to .012. On the other hand, the valuation for the intermediates is somewhat low with the real return of rolling over T Bills in the prior year equal to .020. These were the valuations that existed at the beginning of 2000.

Following the same procedure an initial withdrawal of 3.5 percent gives just about the same sustainability in this case as the 4 percent withdrawal starting from normal valuations. The very high valuation for stocks in this case reduces the withdrawal that can be obtained with the same sustainability. But the effect of the very high valuation of the stocks is mitigated somewhat by the somewhat low valuation of the intermediates.

At the beginning of 2010, however, the valuation of fixed incomes was high. This was as the Federal Reserve kept short-term interest rates as low as possible for an extended period to promote recovery from the financial crisis and major recession of 2008-2009. The high valuation of fixed incomes at that time was indicated not only by the negative real return of rolling over T Bills in the prior year but also by the yields on long-term TIPS. In early 2010 these yields were about .02 versus being about .04 10 years earlier.

The valuation of stocks 10 years later was high. But it was not as extreme as in 2000. But ten years later the high valuation of stocks was reinforced by a high valuation for the intermediates. Ten years later only 3.3 percent could have been withdrawn initially to give the same sustainability as starting with a 4 percent withdrawal and normal valuations.

Thus, based on these results significantly more savings are required to cover the same expenses when valuations are high than when they are normal. And more than 50 percent additional savings were required at the beginning of 2000 or 2010 than when valuations for both stocks and fixed incomes were very low in 1982.

The last chapter stressed, however, that the relationship of valuations to subsequent expected investment returns cannot be estimated with much confidence. Thus, it is the general qualitative implications of these results that are of most importance. Suppose individuals are considering whether they have enough to retire. The then current level of investment valuations is a factor to consider.

Suppose valuations are high. It is then prudent to defer retirement unless more than might normally seem sufficient has been accumulated. And if valuations are very high significantly more than might normally seem sufficient is desirable.

On the other hand, suppose it becomes necessary to retire with savings well short of what would normally seem sufficient. And suppose that valuations are high. Based on the results earlier in this chapter there is then little change in how much can be withdrawn to avoid painful retrenchment. But the sustainability of these withdrawals may have been reduced due to the high valuations. And it has therefore become even more important than normally to reduce the risk of low withdrawals later in retirement as advised in Chapter 5. This is by annuitizing a large portion of the portfolio and seeking part-time work.

Suppose valuations are low instead of high. In this case there is also little change in how much can be withdrawn to avoid painful retrenchment. And the risk of low withdrawals later in retirement should still be reduced by annuitizing a large portion of the portfolio and seeking part-time work. But if valuations are low there may be less risk to avoid. Somewhat less concern about this risk is therefore warranted than would normally be the case.

11.5 Conclusions

Suppose the relationship between the dividend yield on the S&P 500 at the beginning of a year and its expected return over the year estimated in the last chapter is reasonably accurate. Abnormal valuations at the beginning of a year then significantly affect the sustainability of the withdrawals obtained using a given discount rate. The discount rate selected as the RDR, however, is little affected. The reason is that the withdrawals from different discount rates are affected in the same way so there is little change in the performance of one discount rate relative to another.

As an approximation the same RDR can therefore be used over all of retirement even if cyclical changes are occurring in the annual expected returns. And valuations have little effect on the largest amount that can be withdrawn to avoid painful retrenchment. Moreover, the argument for choosing an RDR using the simulations earlier in this book is little affected by cyclical variation in valuations and expected returns.

Suppose retirement starts at a time when valuations are reasonably normal. The savings required to achieve a sufficiently sustainable withdrawal to cover expenses are then little affected by future cyclical changes in valuations and expected returns. This is even if the estimates made in the last chapter are reasonably accurate. If these estimates are correct, however, starting retirement at a time of abnormal valuations has a significant effect on savings requirements. Over 50 percent more savings would have been required at the beginning of 2000 or 2010, when valuations were high, than in 1982 when they were low to provide a stream of real withdrawals of the same sustainability.

Suppose the initial withdrawal is reasonably sustainable and 25 to 50 percent of the portfolio is allocated to fixed income issues at the beginning of each year. Doing so provides a meaningful reduction in the risk of low withdrawals at the cost of a future reduction in portfolio values. Suppose instead of a fixed allocation that the allocation to fixed incomes is increased from 25 to as much as 75 percent as the expected return on stocks appears to have fallen abnormally below that on fixed incomes as indicated by valuations.

When initial valuations are normal the variable allocations do not reduce the risk of low withdrawals versus a fixed allocation of 50 percent, but the variable allocations do significantly increase future portfolio values. And the variable allocations do reduce the risk of low withdrawals when starting at a time when stock valuations are very high relative to those of fixed incomes. Since changes in valuation account for only a very small portion of the changes in realized returns, however, such a strategy frequently advises the wrong allocation after the fact. This is even if such shifts in allocation improve results on average viewed from beforehand.

Appendix 11-1

Modifying the Spreadsheet for Variable Allocations

The spreadsheet in Table 5-8 for a mixed portfolio is modified to incorporate the variable allocation rule specified in this chapter by introducing a new column. The cells in this column calculate each year the allocation to fixed income issues at the beginning of the year as specified in Section 11.2 of this chapter. This allocation then replaces the fixed allocation of .25 assumed in Table 5-8.

The allocation for the first year is calculated using the valuations for stocks and fixed incomes at the beginning of the first year given in Q6 and S6 as specified in Appendix 10-1. Following the rule specified in Section 11.2 of this chapter the allocation for the first year is calculated in U6 and given by:

=.25+If(3.2*(Q6 –.032)<1.9*(S6 –.013),Min(.50,-5.4*(3.2*(Q6–.032)–1.9*(S6–.013))),0)

where If [x, y, z] is the logical function that is equal to y when x is true and z otherwise. The allocations for the following years are obtained by copying this relation to lower rows in column U to U50.

The relation for E6 in Table 5-8 is then rewritten as follows:

=U6*NormInv(Rand(),T6,.056)+(1–U6)*NormInv(Rand(),R6,.176)

and copied to lower rows in column E to E50. In this last relation T6 and R6 are specified in Appendix 10-1.

12

Variation in Normally Expected Returns and Volatility

The last chapter investigated the effect of cyclical variation in expected returns. This chapter looks at the effect of structural changes in expected returns and random variation in the volatility of annual returns. A structural change in the expected returns occurs when there is a change in the annual real return expected for a normal valuation.

Structural changes in the economy or financial markets could change the normal valuation of an investment and its corresponding expected annual return. This chapter considers a more limited possibility. Suppose the assumed normal valuation of the S&P 500 is correct, but there is a significant error in the expected annual real return assumed for that normal valuation.

Making use of the historical averages discussed in Chapter 3 it has been assumed that the normal expected annual real return of the S&P 500 is .07. This is the expected return when the dividend yield of the S&P 500 is at its normal value at the beginning of a year. But given the high volatility of the annual returns on the S&P 500 any average of these returns is an unreliable estimate of their true expected annual return.

Moreover, an average annual return would be an unreliable estimate even for a long series of observations under ideal conditions. And the actual conditions are far from ideal. This is because the available observations are not independent drawings from the same distribution each year.

Thus, when the dividend yield of the S&P 500 at the beginning of a year is at a normal level the true expected return for that year could well be .05 or .09 instead of the .07 that has been assumed. This chapter considers the effect of such a change on earlier results. The last chapter argued that cyclical changes in the expected annual real return have little effect on the choice of an RDR and the retrenchment decision. This chapter shows that structural changes in the expected annual real return do affect the choice of the RDR and the retrenchment decision.

It is shown for moderate changes in the normal expected annual real return for stocks that the RDR changes in the same direction and by the same number of percentage points. Suppose retirees choose an RDR of .08 in Chapter 4 when assuming a normal expected return of .07. If instead they assume that the normal expected return is .05 they will choose an RDR of .06. Their annual withdrawals early in retirement to avoid painful retrenchment will then be limited to about 6 percent instead of 7.5 percent.

If .07 is their conservative best guess for the normal expected return, however, retirees and their advisors should choose the RDR on the basis of this estimate. They should not choose a lower RDR as a precaution because of the possibility that the true normal expected return may be lower than .07. Even if the normal expected return is .05 an RDR of .08 will still provide reasonably good results. The possibility that the true normal expected return may be .05, however, is reason not to choose an RDR much higher than .08.

The other change whose effect is investigated in this chapter is random variation in the standard deviation of the annual real returns of the S&P 500. In Chapter 4 it was assumed that the standard deviation of these returns each year is constant and equal to .18. But there is reason to believe that significant random variation may occur from year to year in this standard deviation. One piece of evidence is the substantial variation that occurs over time in the volatility implied by the options traded on the S&P 500. Another is that the returns on the S&P 500 have more extreme values than implied by a normal distribution, which might be explained by random variation in the standard deviation.

This chapter assumes that the standard deviation of the annual return of the S&P 500 each year is itself a drawing from a probability distribution. The probability distribution of the standard deviations for the drawings is the same each year and such that the standard deviation of returns before the drawing each year is the same as in Chapter 4. The standard deviation from the drawing for a year is used to determine the return for that year.

The returns generated by this process have a higher chance of being very low and this increases the risk of very low withdrawals later in retirement. But this increased risk is fairly small. And a similar increase in risk occurs for the withdrawals from different discount rates.

Thus, increased chances of very low returns under these conditions reduce somewhat the sustainability of withdrawals. But there is no change in the RDR that is selected and in the retrenchment decision. This is because there is no change in the performance of one discount rate relative to another.

12.1 Variation in Normally Expected Returns

The effect of a change in the normally expected return on the streams of expected withdrawals is shown in Table 12-1. This is for a series of discount rates like those tested earlier in Chapter 4. The streams for a normally expected return of .07 in the middle panel of Table 12-1 are the same as those reported earlier in Table 4-1.

As earlier in Table 4-1 the expected return is assumed to be the same each year and equal to the expected return for a normal valuation. Suppose instead that the valuations and expected returns vary from year to year as assumed in Chapter 10. If the valuations are initially at a normal level Chapter 11 showed that the results of the simulations are very similar to those obtained earlier in Chapter 4. The results in Table 12-1 therefore also provide a test of the effect of changes in the normally expected return when valuations and expected returns vary cyclically as assumed in Chapter 10.

Chapter 4 argued based on the streams of expected withdrawals for a normally expected return of .07 that all retirees will prefer a discount rate of .08 to a lower discount rate under these conditions. This is because the streams of expected withdrawals for the lower discount rates also decline steadily over retirement, but the expected withdrawals at every age are higher for a discount rate of .08. Also, .08 is the highest discount rate in the table for which this dominance property holds with respect to lower discount rates. Note that the expected withdrawals for .10 are less than those for .08 starting at age 90.

Now look at the top panel of Table 12-1 where the normal expected return is assumed to be .05 instead .07. For the normal expected return of .05 the discount rate of .06 has the same dominance property relative to lower discount rates as .08 does in the middle panel. Moreover, In the top panel a discount rate of .06 is the highest discount rate that has this dominance property relative to lower discount rates. In the top panel the expected withdrawals for .08 are lower than those for .06 starting at age 95.

Table 12-1

Effect of Normally Expected Stock Returns on Expected Withdrawals
Normal Valuation Each Year with Selected Expected Returns

Normally Expected Return	Discount Rate	Expected Withdrawals*							
		65	70	75	80	85	90	95	100
.05	.04	4.6	3.8	3.4	3.2	3.0	2.9	2.8	2.8
	.06	6.1	4.7	4.1	3.7	3.4	3.2	3.0	2.9
	.08	7.6	5.7	4.7	4.0	3.5	3.2	2.9	2.7
	.10	9.2	6.5	5.0	4.1	3.4	2.9	2.5	2.2
.07	.04	4.6	3.9	3.7	3.5	3.5	3.4	3.4	3.3
	.06	5.4	5.0	4.5	4.3	4.1	4.0	3.9	3.8
	.08	6.1	6.0	5.2	4.8	4.4	4.2	4.0	3.9
	.10	6.9	6.9	5.8	5.0	4.5	4.1	3.8	3.5
.09	.04	4.6	4.1	3.9	3.8	3.8	3.8	3.8	3.7
	.06	6.1	5.2	4.9	4.7	4.6	4.6	4.5	4.5
	.08	7.6	6.3	5.7	5.4	5.2	5.1	5.0	4.9
	.10	9.2	7.3	6.4	5.8	5.5	5.2	5.0	4.9

*Expected withdrawals are in real terms as a percentage of the initial value of the investment.

Thus, in the top panel retirees have the same reason to choose a discount rate of .06 for their RDR as they do to choose .08 in the middle panel. In response to a 2 percentage point decrease in the normal expected return from .07 to .05 the RDR also decreases by 2 percentage points.

This shift is based just on the streams of expected withdrawals in Table 12-1. Chapter 4 showed that a discount rate of .06 does reduce the risk of low withdrawals somewhat later in retirement compared to a discount rate of .08. But this reduced risk appeared to be nowhere near enough to compensate for the lower stream of expected withdrawals for .06. Similar results are obtained for discount rates of .06 and .04 with respect to the risk of low withdrawals when the normal expected return is .05. Thus, as in Chapter 4, considering the risk of low withdrawals gives no reason to change the results based on the streams of expected withdrawals.

All retirees will choose a discount rate equal to at least .08 in the middle panel of Table 12-1. Chapter 4 noted, however, that some retirees might prefer a discount rate of .10 to .08. A discount rate of .10 has lower expected withdrawals at age 90 and thereafter. But to compensate .10 offers significantly higher expected withdrawals earlier in retirement than .08. Some retirees might reasonably decide that the higher expected withdrawals for .10 earlier in retirement more than compensate for the lower expected withdrawals it provides later in retirement.

Similarly, in the upper panel for a normal expected return of .05 all retirees will prefer a discount rate of .06 to .04, but some might prefer .08 to .06. The reason is the same as for those choosing .10 in the middle panel. These retirees feel that the higher expected withdrawals for .08 earlier in retirement more than compensate for the lower expected withdrawals late in retirement.

Few if any, however, will choose the discount rate of .10 over .08 in the upper panel. In this latter case the lower expected withdrawals start at age 85 and have a steeper discount. Few, if any, seem likely to think that the higher expected withdrawals for .10 earlier in retirement are sufficient to compensate for expected withdrawals later in retirement that are this much lower.

12.2 Considering Downside Risk

When choosing the RDR based on the middle panel there is a downside risk that the normal expected return may actually be .05 and not the assumed .07. For this downside risk it is the streams in the top panel that are relevant. This downside risk, however, seems tolerable. If the normal expected return is actually .05 those choosing .08 in the middle panel are accepting more risk later in retirement than they prefer. But they are at least being reasonably compensated for doing so.

On the other hand, if .10 is chosen in the middle panel and the actual normal expected return is .05 there is significantly more risk later in retirement than these retirees think they are accepting. And the compensation for doing so appears far from adequate. Thus, the downside risk that the normal expected return may be .05 instead of .07 provides reason not to choose an RDR of .10 in the middle panel. But this downside risk should not keep retirees from choosing an RDR of .08.

Suppose the withdrawal at the beginning of retirement is near the largest allowed by the Retrenchment Rule to avoid painful retrenchment, and therefore has poor sustainability. In this case Chapter 5 advised investing a large portion of the investment in a lifetime annuity and seeking part-time work. If the normal expected return is actually .05 instead of .07 the sustainability is further reduced and the argument strengthens for reducing risk using this strategy. To see that this is true consider the following.

In Chapter 4 with a normal expected return each year of .07 the chances that the withdrawals are less than 3 percent at ages 85 and 95 are respectively .30 and .39. But Chapter 5 showed that these chances can be reduced to .04 and .12 by investing half of the portfolio in a lifetime annuity and achieving significant part-time earnings. If the expected normal return is .05 instead of .07 these chances increase to .46 and .60. In this latter case the same strategy reduces the risk respectively to .09 and .25. The reduced risk is higher, but the reduction is even more significant than when the normal expected return is .07.

12.3 Higher Normal Expected Returns

Now look at the streams of expected withdrawals in the bottom panel of Table 12-1 where the normal expected return is .09. In this case the stream for a discount rate of .10 dominates that for lower discount rates. The dominance is not quite as strong as before because the expected withdrawals for a discount rate of .10 are the same as for a discount rate of .08 at ages 95 and 100. Nevertheless, based on the streams of expected withdrawals all retirees will prefer a discount rate of .10 to .08 in the lower panel. Thus, in the lower panel the increase in the normal expected return of 2 percentage points results in an increase in the RDR of 2 percentage points. This is when the RDR is chosen on the basis of the same dominance as before. Increases or decreases in the normal expected return result in an equal percentage point change in the RDR.

The reason why a change in the normally expected return changes the RDR is the following. Higher discount rates provide higher withdrawals early in retirement. But as these higher withdrawals deplete the investment more rapidly the higher discount rates also tend to require more retrenchment over retirement than lower discount rates. Changes in the normally expected return affect the amount of retrenchment that will be required over retirement. But this affects higher discount rates more than lower discount rates because they require more retrenchment.

For a lower expected return the withdrawals for a higher discount rate therefore decline relative to those for a lower discount rate over time. And the higher discount rate becomes relatively less attractive later in retirement. For a higher expected return the situation is reversed and the higher discount rate becomes more attractive later in retirement relative to a lower one.

On the other hand, cyclical changes in expected return tend to have a similar effect on the withdrawals for different discount rates as a temporary change in the size of the investment. Thus, the withdrawals are affected in the same way for different discount rates, and only in the short run. Cyclical changes in the expected return therefore have little effect on the choice of the RDR as shown in the last chapter.

12.4 Random Variation in Volatility

In Chapter 4 it was assumed that the standard deviation of the real return on the S&P 500 each year was constant and equal to .18. But there is good reason to believe that there is significant random variation in the standard deviation of the annual returns on the S&P 500 over time. One reason for believing that such variation exists is the significant variation over time of the VIX.

The VIX is the Chicago Board Option Exchange's index that measures the volatility implied by the value of the options traded on the S&P 500. This volatility is not strictly comparable to the standard deviation of the annual real returns on the S&P 500 assumed in the earlier simulations. Nevertheless, the observed variation in the VIX is sufficient to indicate that significant variation in the standard deviation of the annual returns on the S&P 500 is also likely.

Additional evidence for variation in volatility is the larger number of extreme values for returns on the S&P 500 than implied by a normal distribution. That stock price changes have more extreme values than implied by a normal distribution was pointed out by academic researchers over 50 years ago.[1] It has also been pointed out that one possible explanation for this observation is that stock returns are normally distributed, but with volatility that varies over time.

As an illustration of the higher number of extreme values consider the real returns on large capitalization stocks reported by the *SBBI Yearbook* for calendar years starting in 1926. The three worst calendar years for the returns in this series are negative returns of about .37 in 1931, 1937, and 2008. In the simulations of Chapter 4 it was assumed that stock returns are independently and normally distributed each year with a mean of .07 and a standard deviation of .18. Consider how many extremely low returns should be observed under this assumption.

Under this assumption a return of -.37 is 2.44 standard deviations below the mean of .07. And the chances of drawing a value this low or worse from a normal distribution are .0073.

On the basis of this low chance only one return this low or worse would be expected over 137 years. But over the 84 years from 1926 through 2009, 3 such returns were observed.

The probability of 3 returns or more that low in 84 drawings can be calculated using the binomial distribution. The chances of this happening are only .024. Thus, over this period there have been more very low returns than implied by the distribution of these returns assumed in the simulations of Chapter 4.

There are a number of possible explanations for the larger number of very low returns. One possible explanation is that the returns are being generated by a process like the one discussed in Chapter 10. More very low returns would be expected in this process because of the possibility of long runs of much lower than normal expected returns.

But a larger number of very low returns can also be obtained by a process in which the expected return each year is .07. In this process the return each year is a drawing from a normal distribution with an expected return of .07. But the standard deviation of this distribution each year varies in a random manner. This random variation is such that beforehand the standard deviation each year continues to be .18.

Suppose, for instance, each year that the chances are .25 that the standard deviation is .32, and the chances are .75 that the standard deviation is .095. Beforehand, the standard deviation of the returns each year is .18 as in Chapter 4. This is because $(.75(.095)^2+.25(.32)^2)^{.5}=.18$. But now the chances of low returns have increased.

Suppose the drawing for a year is from the distribution when the standard deviation is .32. A return of -.37 is now only 1.375 standard deviations below the expected return of .07. And the chances of a drawing being that low or lower are .0845.

There is virtually no chance of the return being as low as -.37 when the standard deviation turns out to be .095. And there is only a .25 chance of the standard deviation being .32. Nevertheless, there is now a chance of the return being -.37 or worse each year of .0211, since .25(.0845) = .0211.

Instead of being expected only once every 137 years a return of -.37 is now expected once every 47 years. And a calculation using the binomial distribution shows that the chances of 3 or more such low returns over 84 years is now equal to .26 instead of only .02. Although still not more likely than not, observing 3 such very low returns over 1926 to 2009 has become much more reasonable.

Suppose that the simulations in Chapter 4 are rerun using this process. Modifying the spreadsheet to do so is discussed in Appendix 12-1. In these new simulations the chances of very low returns has significantly increased. But this change has only a small effect on the simulated withdrawals.

In particular, there is very little change in the streams of expected withdrawals. These are just about the same as those shown earlier in Table 4-1. The only difference is that some of the expected withdrawals are now lower by 0.1.

Table 12-2

Effect of Variable Volatility on Withdrawal Probability
Expected Return Each Year of .07 with Selected Volatility*

Age	Variable Volatility	Discount Rate	Withdrawal Probability**				
			8	6	4	2	0
75	No	.08	.23	.32	.32	.13	0
		.06	0	.43	.41	.16	0
		.04	0	0	.76	.24	0
	Yes	.08	.25	.35	.26	.13	.01
		.06	0	.50	.34	.14	.02
		.04	0	0	.78	.20	.02
85	No	.08	.17	.23	.30	.27	.03
		.06	0	.35	.36	.27	.02
		.04	0	0	.67	.31	.02
	Yes	.08	.18	.24	.27	.26	.05
		.06	0	.39	.32	.24	.05
		.04	0	0	.69	.27	.04
95	No	.08	.15	.19	.27	.31	.08
		.06	0	.32	.33	.30	.05
		.04	0	0	.64	.33	.03
	Yes	.08	.16	.20	.23	.30	.11
		.06	0	.36	.29	.27	.08
		.04	0	0	.65	.29	.06

*Variable volatility assumes there is a .75 chance each year that the standard deviation is .095 and a .25 chance that it is .32. Before the random choice the standard deviation is .18 each year. Constant volatility assumes the standard deviation is .18 each year without any random variation.

**Probability that withdrawal is in a range from one above to one below 8, 6, 4, or 2, or from 0 to 1.

The effect of the increased chances of very low returns on the withdrawal probabilities is shown in Table 12-2. At each age the withdrawal probabilities are shown for the three discount rates with and without the increased chances of very low returns. When No appears in the second column from the left the withdrawal probabilities are the same as reported in Table 4-2. When Yes appears in the second column the volatility of annual returns each year is given by the process just specified.

As expected, the variable volatility increases the chances of very low withdrawals later in retirement. But the increase is fairly modest. In particular, the chances that the withdrawals will be in the zero range increase by 2 or 3 percentage points. Note that these are the chances before taking the actions advised in Chapter 5 to significantly reduce this risk.

Note also that the increase in risk for the withdrawals in the zero range is just about the same for each of the discount rates. Thus, the variable volatility has no effect on the performance of one discount rate relative to another, and on the choice of an RDR. Such increases in the probability of very low withdrawals reduce somewhat the sustainability of withdrawals, but have no effect on the retrenchment decision.

12.5 Conclusions

Cyclical changes in the expected annual real return on stocks have little effect on the choice of an RDR. Structural changes in the expected annual real return on stocks, however, cause equal percentage point changes in the choice of an RDR. Structural changes are changes in the expected annual real return for the normal valuation for the stocks.

The normally expected return for stocks cannot be reliably estimated. Nevertheless, a conservative choice for the RDR based on a reasonable estimate should not be further reduced as a precaution that the actual normally expected return may be less than estimated. The possibility that the normally expected return may be less than estimated, however, strengthens the need for taking the measures to reduce the risk of low withdrawals discussed in Chapter 5.

The volatility of returns on the S&P 500 implied by options shows significant variation over time. This provides evidence that the standard deviation of the annual returns on the S&P 500 also varies over time even though these two volatilities are not strictly comparable. Stock returns were simulated in which the standard deviation of the returns each year is obtained from a random drawing and subject to significant variation. Otherwise, the simulated returns each year were specified to be the same as those in Chapter 4, including the standard deviation of the returns before the drawings.

The streams of expected withdrawals obtained from these simulated returns were almost the same as those obtained in Chapter 4, except very slightly lower. As expected, the risk of very low withdrawals late in retirement was somewhat higher with the random variation in volatility. The increase was the same for different discount rates, however, so that the random variation in volatility caused no change in the choice of an RDR and the retrenchment decision.

Note

1. A recent discussion of this literature is given in Mark Rubenstein's *A History of the Theory of Investments: My Annotated Bibliography* published by John Wiley & Sons in 2006. See in particular his discussion of the work of Barr Rosenberg.

Appendix 12-1

Modifying the Spreadsheet to Include Variable Volatility

To modify the spreadsheet in Table 3-1 to incorporate variable standard deviations a new column is introduced to calculate the standard deviation each year. And the relations in column E to calculate the return each year are rewritten to use this standard deviation.

The standard deviation for year 1 is calculated in cell V6 by:

=If (Rand()≤ .25,.32,.095)

and copied to lower rows to V50. If (x, y, z) is a logical function in Excel with the value y when x is true and z when x is false. As Rand() is equally likely to be any value between 0 and 1, V6 has the value .32 with probability .25 and .095 with probability.75 as specified. The entry in E6 in Table 3-1 is replaced by:

=NormInv(Rand(),.07,V6)

and copied to lower rows to E50. Entries in the other cells remain the same in Table 3-1 with the possible exception of the discount rate and initial withdrawal.

13

After Tax Withdrawals

Some taxes can be viewed as simply adding to the cost of various goods and services. Sales tax, for instance, increases the cost of the goods and services to which it is applied. Real estate tax adds to the cost of owning a home. In this chapter it is assumed that these direct taxes are included in the cost of the living expenses to which they are applied.

The focus in this chapter is on the federal income tax. This tax reduces the funds available to cover living expenses in general. In this chapter it is assumed that a withdrawal is made each year to cover any federal income tax payment that may be required. These withdrawals to cover income taxes are deducted from the investment portfolio, but they are not included in the withdrawals determined by the Retrenchment Rule.

In this chapter the Retrenchment Rule is applied to the withdrawals that directly affect the standard of living. These are the withdrawals that cover living expenses other than the federal income tax. These latter withdrawals will be referred to as after tax withdrawals.

A portion of the total assets available to make future withdrawals will have to be used to pay federal income taxes. This portion is estimated and deducted from the total value of the assets each year. The Retrenchment Rule uses the remaining value of the assets to determine the largest after tax withdrawal that can be made to avoid painful retrenchment in the standard of living.

The federal income tax payment in the simulations each year in this chapter is calculated using a simplified version of the tax that existed in the U. S. in 2009. Future tax rates are assumed to be the same as in 2009. And the brackets to which these rates apply are indexed for inflation as they were in 2009. Other dollar amounts used to calculate the tax are indexed or not for inflation as was the case in 2009.

Tax rates in the future may, of course, increase even for middle income retirees. To test for this possibility simulations are also run in which the 2009 tax rates are increased by 5 percentage points after 5 years. The effect of higher tax rates at the beginning of retirement is tested by the effect of the higher rates for 2009 on the higher incomes from a larger portfolio. The basic assumptions for calculating the tax are discussed further in the next section of this chapter.

Many middle income retirees have a high proportion of their portfolio in a traditional IRA, or other retirement account treated in the same way for tax purposes. This is because much of their savings accumulated from pension plans in which tax free contributions were made to such an account for their benefit. The major result of this chapter is that the adequacy of the savings for retirement is highly dependent on the portion in a traditional IRA.

Suppose, for instance, individuals expect to have $20,000 a year from Social Security, but want to be able to cover an additional $40,000 a year of living expenses from their savings. To do this on a reasonably sustainable basis the conventional prescription is that they will need enough to provide the $40,000 initially with a 4 percent withdrawal. On this basis they will need to accumulate $1,000,000.

Suppose the additional $40,000 that is desired for living expenses is on an after tax basis. If none of the investment is in an IRA this chapter shows that about 10 percent more will have to be accumulated to pay the federal income tax and keep the sustainability the same. On the other hand, if all of the investment is in a traditional IRA 30 percent more will have to be accumulated. When all of the investment is in an IRA a reasonably sustainable after tax withdrawal for middle income retirees in this case is about 3 percent, not 4 percent.

The prescription of adequate savings for retirement typically ignores the portion of the savings in an IRA. But the portion in an IRA is clearly important, and this importance is not surprising. All of the withdrawals from a traditional IRA are fully taxable income. And most of these funds will have to be disbursed over a long retirement. This is because of the Required Minimum Distributions (RMD) after age 70½.

On the other hand, the federal income tax is of much less importance for savings outside of a traditional IRA. A significant portion of the withdrawals from these funds represents a return of cost and is not taxed. Moreover, withdrawals that represent either dividends or realized capital gains on stocks are taxed at favorable rates under the 2009 rules. And these tax rates are especially favorable for those at or below the median income range.

Note also that gains on stocks need not be realized and the tax paid until the funds are needed to cover expenses. Due to the RMD the tax on a large portion of the funds in a traditional IRA may have to be paid before the funds are needed to cover expenses. Only the interest on fixed income issues outside an IRA is fully taxable income each year. And when the principal of these fixed income issues is used to cover expenses it is a return of cost, and not taxable.

Despite the taxes that must eventually be paid, the opportunity of putting untaxed earnings from employment in an IRA is a valuable option. In an IRA investment returns are being earned on funds that otherwise would be paid as tax both initially and as the returns compound over time. This advantage easily outweighs paying the tax when income is earned and investing the remainder in stocks even though the stocks have favorable tax treatment. Putting funds in an IRA is clearly desirable. The problem is that the tax that will eventually have to be paid on these funds needs to be recognized when assessing savings needs for retirement.

It might appear possible to mitigate some of the adverse effects of the RMD for a traditional IRA by converting a portion of it into a Roth IRA. In a Roth there are no taxes or RMD, but tax must be paid on any funds that are converted. Suppose that a limited amount is converted early in retirement so that the marginal tax rate on the conversions is less than that on the subsequent RMD.

Even with this favorable differential in tax rates, however, simulations show that such conversions cause some deterioration in the after tax withdrawals. The problem is that the conversions increase taxes before the RMD begin, reducing the value of the investment. Taxes are lower after the RMD begin, but in the simulations the median value of the investment remains lower than it would have been otherwise. This shortfall gradually declines due to the lower taxes, but some shortfall remains even at age 95. Thus, the deterioration in the after tax withdrawals is not surprising.

Some other issues are also covered in this chapter. One is showing that the income tax assumed in this chapter has little, if any, effect on the choice of an RDR. In some cases, this means that this income tax affects the retrenchment decision only by adding to living expenses an additional expense to allow for the tax.

In particular, suppose that the current annual tax payment is a reasonably good estimate of the future stream of annual income tax payments. This current payment can then be considered as simply an extra expense that must be covered by the withdrawal allowed by the Retrenchment Rule when taxes are ignored.

In other cases, however, the current annual tax payment is not a reasonable estimate of the future stream of annual tax payments. For instance, suppose retirees have about half of their portfolio in a traditional IRA and have not yet reached an age of 70½. In this case, their current annual tax payment is much less than their annual tax will be after age 70½. A much larger allowance for income taxes needs to be deducted from the withdrawal allowed by the Retrenchment Rule when taxes are ignored. This is to get the largest allowed after tax withdrawal to cover living expenses before age 70½.

This chapter also shows that income taxes cause little, if any, lessening in the effectiveness of part-time earnings and annuitizing in reducing the risk of low withdrawals. On the other hand, taxes do reduce the improvement these measures provide in increasing the chances of higher withdrawals. The reason for this difference appears to be the progressivity of the tax schedule. When withdrawals are low, income and tax rates are also low. On the other hand, when withdrawals are high, so are incomes and tax rates. Thus, taxes have more of an effect on higher than on lower withdrawals.

13.1 Tax Assumptions

The federal income tax is taken into account in this chapter by calculating the tax that is owed each year. This tax is based on the taxable transactions at the beginning of that year and any dividends or interest paid over the prior year on investments outside of an IRA. The tax owed for a given year becomes the estimated tax paid for the following year. And each year there is also an additional payment or a rebate to correct for any error in the estimated tax paid for the prior year.

The tax owed each year is based on a simplified version of the U. S. federal income tax that existed for 2009. In doing so, the dollar amounts used to calculate the tax each year are indexed or not for inflation as was the case in the tax law applicable for 2009. Amounts indexed for inflation include tax brackets, the standard deduction, and the personal exemption. Amounts not indexed for inflation include the cost basis for calculating capital gain or loss, and the thresholds for calculating taxable Social Security.

In using the Retrenchment Rule to determine the limit on after tax withdrawals each year expected future tax payments must be taken into account. The present value of the expected stream of future tax payments using the RDR as the rate of interest is deducted from the present value of the retirement assets for that year. The remainder of the assets is used to determine the largest allowable after tax withdrawal for that year.

Usually, the estimated tax paid for a year is also used to forecast at that time the stream of future expected tax payments to be made. An exception occurs before age 70½, however, in cases where a significant portion of the portfolio is in a traditional IRA. In these cases a significant increase in tax payments occurs after age 70½ due to the RMD from the IRA. An addition is therefore made to the estimated tax prior to age 70½ in these cases when forecasting the stream of future expected tax payments.

It is assumed that all taxable transactions for a year occur at the beginning of that year. These transactions include any realized gain or loss on sales of stocks outside an IRA that may be necessary to raise cash for withdrawals or adjust the allocation of the portfolio at the beginning of that year. These transactions also include any disbursements from a traditional IRA for that year either because they are required after age 70½ or because they are necessary to raise additional cash for withdrawals.

It is assumed that stocks outside an IRA are sold only when necessary to raise cash to cover expenses and taxes, or to achieve a desired allocation with respect to fixed income issues. It is assumed that the cost basis of any stocks sold is the same proportion of their total cost basis at that time as the proportion of stocks sold is to their total value. It is assumed that the dividends on stocks each year are qualified dividends under the 2009 tax rules and given by the dividend yield specified in Chapter 10.

It is assumed that a retiree is using the standard deduction for those 65 and over. It is also assumed that the personal exemption applies without any limitation. To simplify, and since deductions are limited to the standard deduction, it is assumed that the tax calculated using the Alternative Minimum Tax (AMT) is not higher than the regular tax.

As a base case it is assumed that any IRA is a traditional IRA without a cost basis. Any distribution from this IRA is therefore fully taxable income. The model for calculating taxes, however, also includes the possibility of a Roth IRA. For a Roth any disbursements are tax free, and there is not any RMD. It is possible to convert all or a portion of a traditional IRA into a Roth if the tax is paid on the funds converted. The advisability of such a conversion is considered later.

As IRAs provide the opportunity to earn returns on funds that would otherwise have to be paid in tax it is desirable to avoid disbursements from IRAs except when required by a RMD. It is assumed therefore that voluntary disbursements are made from an IRA only when necessary to obtain cash for making withdrawals. If such disbursements become necessary it is assumed they are made first from a traditional IRA as any Roth that may exist is a better shelter and should be preserved when possible.

The advantage of an IRA is that it allows investment returns to be earned on funds that would otherwise have to be paid as tax. Suppose there is a choice as to which investment to put in an IRA. And one of these investments requires higher tax payments relative to its value than the other. The advantage of the IRA will be maximized if the investment that requires the higher tax payments relative to value is put in the IRA.

Such a choice occurs in this chapter when a portion of the total portfolio at the beginning of each year is allocated to intermediate term issues and the remainder to the S&P 500. It is assumed that the tax payable on the intermediate terms is typically higher relative to value than that on the S&P 500. It is therefore assumed that as much as possible of the intermediates is put in an IRA.

Suppose at times when interest rates are low it appears that the taxes paid on the intermediates may be less relative to value than the taxes paid on the S&P 500. In such cases it is assumed that the intermediates are nevertheless kept in the IRA. The reason is that converting stocks into intermediates outside the IRA will likely require the realization of extra capital gains. Taxes on these gains will likely offset any advantage that would otherwise accrue to having stocks in the IRA for a short time. Also, it may be difficult to identify when the taxes on the intermediates are temporarily less relative to value than those on the stocks.

Suppose there is a choice between putting the intermediates in a traditional IRA or a Roth. In this case the intermediates will be put in the traditional IRA.

The reason is that the Roth is the better shelter and having stocks in the Roth instead of intermediates will favor increasing its size.

Suppose it is necessary to put some of the desired overall allocation to intermediate governments outside an IRA. In this event no attempt will be made to identify a portion of the return on these intermediate term issues as capital gain or loss. Their annual return is estimated on a nominal basis and treated as taxable interest. Detailed specifications of the relations used to calculate the tax each year in the simulations and further justification for the assumptions are provided in the appendix to this chapter.

13.2 Taxes and Required Savings

Chapter 7 showed the size of the investments required at age 65 to cover a given withdrawal with increasing degrees of sustainability. These results ignored the fact that a portion of the withdrawals will have to be used to pay federal income tax. This omission would not be a serious problem if either the tax is very small or can easily be allowed for because it is a constant proportion of the withdrawals each year. Often, however, these assumptions are not reasonable.

For retirees in the middle income range income tax payments may be large and also vary significantly over retirement. Consider again those individuals in the introduction to this chapter who have annual Social Security of $20,000 and want savings to cover an additional $40,000 of after tax expenses. Suppose half of these savings are in a traditional IRA and they have just about enough to cover their after tax expenses on a reasonably sustainable basis. The simulations in this section show that they will pay little if any tax before they are age 70½. Afterwards, however, when the RMD are applicable, their median tax becomes equal to $10,000 or more.

In such a case, stable before tax withdrawals clearly do not imply a stable standard of living. Income tax will have to be paid each year and what remains to cover living expenses will vary significantly. This chapter assumes retirees are concerned with the sustainability of their after tax withdrawals. Taxes have to be paid, but variation in tax payments from year to year does not affect satisfaction. What affects satisfaction is the size and sustainability of the after tax withdrawals that provide the standard of living. For this reason the Retrenchment Rule in this chapter is applied to after tax withdrawals.

Table 13-1

Investment for Sustainable Withdrawals Before and After Taxes

Base Case Investment Returns and Inflation

Stocks/IntGovts 75/25 RDR .08

Age	Investment* Total / IRA $K@Age 65	After Tax Withdrawal $K@65	After Tax Withdrawal %	Tax Rates	After Tax Withdrawal / Initial Value** Expect	1.0	.8	.6	.4	.2	0
75	1,000	40	4.0	None	.98	.94	.04	.02	0	0	0
	1,000/500	40	4.0	2009	.97	.90	.06	.04	0	0	0
	1,100/0	40	3.6	2009	.98	.94	.04	.02	0	0	0
	1,150/575	40	3.5		.99	.95	.04	.01	0	0	0
	2,400/1,200	80	3.3		.99	.95	.03	.02	0	0	0
	1,300/1,300	40	3.1		.98	.94	.04	.02	0	0	0
85	1,000	40	4.0	None	.94	.84	.06	.06	.03	.01	0
	1,000/500	40	4.0	2009	.90	.74	.10	.09	.06	.01	0
	1,100/0	40	3.6	2009	.94	.83	.08	.06	.02	.01	0
	1,150/575	40	3.5		.94	.84	.06	.06	.03	.01	0
	2,400/1,200	80	3.3		.94	.84	.06	.06	.03	.01	0
	1,300/1,300	40	3.1		.93	.84	.07	.06	.02	.01	0
95	1,000	40	4.0	None	.90	.78	.06	.07	.06	.03	0
	1,000/500	40	4.0	2009	.84	.66	.08	.10	.11	.05	0
	1,100/0	40	3.6	2009	.90	.77	.07	.08	.05	.03	0
	1,150/575	40	3.5		.89	.77	.06	.07	.07	.03	0
	2,400/1,200	80	3.3		.89	.77	.06	.07	.07	.03	0
	1,300/1,300	40	3.1		.90	.78	.06	.08	.05	.03	0

*Assumes U.S. federal income tax for 2009 as specified in Appendix 13-1. Includes any applicable tax on $20,000 of Social Security each year. Assumes a traditional IRA with no cost basis. Assumes initial cost basis of 50% for stocks outside IRA.

**Probability that withdrawals in real terms as a proportion of their initial value are from .1 below to .1 above .8, .6, .4, or .2, or from 1.0 to .9 or 0 to .1.

When considering taxes it is no longer possible to ignore the size of the portfolio. Income taxes critically depend on the level of income and on the size of the portfolio. Table 13-1 looks at cases where retirees have annual Social Security of $20,000 and investment portfolios of varying amounts to cover living expenses and pay federal income tax.

Two cases are considered with respect to the desired coverage of living expenses. In one case retirees want to be able to cover $60,000 of living expenses each year. Taking account of the Social Security they therefore need to withdraw $40,000 from the portfolio to cover living expenses. They also need enough to be able to cover any income tax that they owe. The other case tests the effect on the results of the higher tax rates on higher incomes. In this case, the retirees want to cover $100,000 of living expenses. They therefore need $80,000 from the portfolio and enough to also pay income tax each year.

Table 13-1 assumes that these retirees want to achieve comparable sustainability for their after tax withdrawals to the tax free 4 percent withdrawal in Table 7-1. As in Table 7-1 it is assumed that a quarter of the portfolio at the beginning of each year is allocated to intermediate government issues and the remainder to stocks. As in Table 7-1 it is assumed that the retirees are using an RDR of .08. A later section of this chapter shows that taxes have little effect on selecting an RDR.

Table 13-1 considers cases in which none, half, or the entire initial portfolio is in a traditional IRA. As discussed earlier to minimize taxes as much as possible of the desired allocation to fixed incomes is put in the IRA. Stocks outside the IRA are assumed to have an initial cost basis equal to half of their value. In the event that the stocks have been held for a very long time, or that there has been a strong bull market, the possibility is also tested that the initial cost basis is equal to 20 percent of the value of the stocks.

For ease of comparison the top row for each age in Table 13-1 reports the sustainability of the tax free 4 percent withdrawal given in Table 7-1. In Table 13-1 that is a $40,000 initial withdrawal from a $1,000,000 portfolio. The second row at each age shows the sustainability of the same withdrawal from the same portfolio on an after tax basis. This is assuming that an additional withdrawal must be made each year to pay the 2009 taxes assumed in this chapter. For this test it is assumed that half of the initial portfolio is in a traditional IRA.

As expected, this test shows that the extra withdrawals to pay the tax reduce sustainability. The question is how much must the initial investment be increased to achieve approximately the same sustainability as the tax free 4 percent withdrawal in the top row at each age? The answer is obtained by increasing the size of the initial investment for each of the conditions assumed until the sustainability is about the same as shown for the top row at each age.

When none of the initial portfolio is in an IRA an increase of about 10 percent is required to get the same sustainability for the after tax withdrawal. In this case, the after tax withdrawal of $40,000 must therefore equal about 3.6 percent of the value of the initial investment to provide the same sustainability. When half of the initial portfolio is in an IRA the investment must increase by 15 percent to provide the same sustainability. And when the entire initial investment is in a traditional IRA the investment must increase by 30 percent. In this latter case, the after tax withdrawal is about 3.1 percent of the initial investment.

There are significant variations in the tax payments for these three cases. In the first case, when there is not an IRA, the initial tax is about $5,500. The median tax then rises over time becoming about $7,000 at age 75, $7,500 at age 85, and $8,500 at age 95. The gradual rise in the median tax is due to the declining real value of the cost basis for the stocks, and the increasing median value of the investment. The cost basis is declining because additional stocks are not being purchased and because the real value of the initial cost basis is declining due to inflation. Taxes are also rising gradually because the rise in the median value of the investment is increasing taxable interest income.

When half of the initial investment is in an IRA there is no tax initially. Unlike the first case, interest on the intermediate term issues is not generating any taxable income because these issues are in the IRA. Also, fewer stocks are outside the IRA generating dividends. More of the cash for withdrawals is coming from stock sales. And only about half of these sales are realized gains since the cost basis of the stocks is about half of their value. Also, due to the lower taxable income from other sources only about half of the Social Security is taxable income initially in this case.

Under the 2009 tax rules the tax depends on taxable income and taxable income less the sum of qualified dividends and gains. In this case, taxable Social Security is the only source of taxable income other than gains and dividends. And the taxable Social Security is more than offset by the standard deduction and personal exemption. When taxable income less dividends and gains is negative as it is in this case there is no tax under the 2009 rules unless taxable income is over $33,950. In this case the dividends and gains are not sufficient to put taxable income over $33,950.

Thus, surprisingly, in the second case there is no tax initially even though enough funds are being provided to cover $60,000 of living expenses. When the RMD begin after age 70½, however, large tax payments are required. The median tax is about $8,500 at age 75, $13,000 at age 85, and $18,000 at age 95.

When all of the investment is in a traditional IRA in the third case a tax of about $10,000 is paid initially. When the RMD become effective after age, 70½ further increases occur in the tax. The median tax is about $13,000 at age 75, $22,000 at age 85, and $28,000 at age 95. The latter increases are due to the rising median value of the investment and the continuing and rising proportion of the RMD. Comparing the results of these three cases clearly shows the significance of the portion of funds in a traditional IRA.

Note that a significant increase in the proportion of the investment in an IRA also has a larger effect on taxes than the higher tax rates that are applicable with a significant increase in the size of the portfolio. Consider the case in Table 13-1 in which an $80,000 investment withdrawal is required to cover living expenses. In this case achieving the sustainability of a 4 percent withdrawal in a tax free case requires a $2,000,000 portfolio.

Suppose half of the initial portfolio is in an IRA. The simulations show that a 20 percent increase in the investment is required. This is to provide the same sustainability for the $80,000 withdrawal after taxes as on a tax free basis. This compares with a 15 percent increase for a $40,000 withdrawal when half of the initial portfolio is in an IRA. And it compares with a 30 percent increase for a $40,000 withdrawal when the entire initial portfolio is in an IRA.

Doubling the size of the after tax withdrawal reduces the percentage of the after tax withdrawal required for the same sustainability. But this percentage declines only from 3.5 to 3.3 percent. This compares to a decline from 3.5 to 3.1 percent for a $40,000 withdrawal when the initial portion in an IRA increases from a half to the entire portfolio.

Another issue is the sensitivity of the results to the initial cost basis that is assumed for stocks held outside of an IRA. Table 13-1 assumes that this initial cost basis is equal to half the value of these stocks. If the stocks have been held for a very long time, however, or there has been a strong bull market, the cost basis could be less.

Suppose instead of being 50 percent that the initial cost basis is 20 percent. The maximum effect of this change occurs for the case in which none of the initial portfolio is in an IRA. Suppose the simulations are rerun for the $40,000 after tax withdrawal without an IRA. The investment must be increased by about half as much as when half of the initial portfolio in an IRA. This is to obtain the same sustainability in either case.

Finally, suppose a significant increase in tax rates occurs in the future. In particular suppose after 5 years that all the tax rates in 2009 increase by 5 percentage points, but the brackets remain the same. Thus, when taxable income is less than $33,950 the tax on qualified dividends and gains is now 5 percent instead of zero, and when taxable income is over $33,950 the tax is now 20 instead of 15 percent.

Suppose that half of the initial portfolio is in the IRA. Compare the effect on sustainability of the higher future tax rates to including the second half of the portfolio in the IRA. Simulations show that the portfolio must be increased by only about half as much to get the same sustainability with the higher tax rates. Higher tax rates in the future, in this case, increase savings requirements, but not as much as having the entire portfolio in the IRA.

13.3 Conversion to a Roth IRA

Retirees with a traditional IRA have the option of converting all or part of it into a Roth IRA if they pay the tax on the converted funds. With a Roth there is not any tax on the disbursements and there is not any RMD. The RMD in Table 13-1 can require disbursements from an IRA in excess of the cash needed to cover expenses. Also, limited conversions can be made at lower marginal tax rates each year before the RMD begin. Conversions in such a case therefore appear worth considering.

When such conversions are simulated, however, they show some deterioration in the withdrawals. The conversions are made at favorable marginal tax rates. Nevertheless, the conversions generate significant additional tax early in retirement reducing the value of the investment. As expected, taxes are less after the RMD begin. But the taxes are not reduced enough to increase the investment to what it would have been otherwise. The shortfall is gradually reduced over time, but even at age 95 some shortfall remains in the median value of the investment. Due to the lower investment values the performance of the after tax withdrawals deteriorates.

In particular, consider the effect of Roth conversions in the following case. Suppose as in Table 13-1 that a $40,000 initial withdrawal is made from a $1,150,000 investment half of which is in a traditional IRA. Suppose for this case that $15,000 of Roth conversions are made each year for five years starting at age 65.

Without the conversions there is little if any tax over the first five years. After the RMD begin, however, there is significant tax. For instance, at age 75 the median annual tax payment is about $8,500.

With the conversion there is an annual median tax for the first five years of from $5,500 to $6,000. After the RMD begin the tax increases, but remains less than it would be without the conversions. At age 75 the median annual tax is about $7,500, which compares with $8,500 without the conversions.

The annual tax with the conversions is less than that with the RMD. Since the tax schedule is progressive, the marginal tax rate on the RMD can therefore not be less than the tax rate paid on the conversions. And in general the marginal tax rate on the RMD will be higher.

The annual tax savings provided by the conversions, however, are small relative to the extra taxes of almost $30,000 paid earlier to make the conversions. As a result, the conversions have reduced the median investment at age 75 by over $30,000. Over time the annual tax savings due to the conversions increase. Nevertheless, at age 95 the simulations show that the median investment is still less with the conversions than without them.

Thus, the simulations show that the higher taxes due to the conversions early in retirement reduce the median value of the investment over retirement despite the later tax savings. It is therefore not surprising that the conversions cause deterioration in the performance of the after tax withdrawals. The effect is small, but the conversions are relatively small. The negative effect, however, is clear.

With the conversions, both the expected value of the future after tax withdrawals and their sustainability is reduced by a very small amount. As noted earlier, it is not advantageous to pay the tax and convert an IRA into stocks outside an IRA even though stocks outside an IRA have appreciable tax advantages. A Roth IRA has even more of a tax advantage than stocks as there is no tax at all on investments in a Roth. Nevertheless, the simulations show that even limited conversions into a Roth at favorable tax rates in this case are not attractive.

13.3 Effect of Taxes on the RDR

The last chapter showed that a lower investment return over all of retirement tends to reduce the RDR. Income taxes reduce the investment return available for after tax withdrawals over all of retirement. It therefore seems reasonable to expect that an income tax reduces the RDR for after tax withdrawals. This is when the distribution of before tax investment returns is the same with or without the tax.

The progressivity of the tax schedule, however, reduces taxes when there have been unfavorable investment returns. Lower taxes in these unfavorable cases should tend to reduce the adverse effects of the tax. Also, it is not clear how the size of the wedge caused by the tax assumed in this chapter compares with the lower expected returns for a normal valuation considered in the last chapter.

To evaluate the effect of the tax on the after tax withdrawals it is necessary to run some simulations. These tests include the tax in the simulations run earlier in Chapter 4 to select the RDR. Since the effect of the tax is sensitive to the size of the portfolio and the portion in an IRA these tests should consider variation in these factors. Such tests show that the tax assumed in this chapter has surprisingly little effect on the RDR.

In the scenario in Chapter 1 Louise Logan had annual Social Security of $20,000 and a $600,000 portfolio at age 65. To evaluate the effect of an IRA consider cases in which none, half, or all of her initial portfolio is in a traditional IRA. To evaluate the effect of a much larger portfolio consider also a case in which the size of the initial portfolio is increased to $2,000,000.

The top panel in Table 13-2 shows the results for the $600,000 portfolio when none of it is in an IRA. It turns out for a portfolio of this size without an IRA that little tax is payable. Consequently, the after tax withdrawals are reduced at most by 0.1 or 0.2 from the tax free values given earlier in Table 4-1. And the streams of expected after tax withdrawals look just about the same as the earlier tax free streams. Thus, the tax in this case does not affect the RDR.

For a discount rate of .08 in the top panel of Table 13-2 the median annual tax never exceeds about $600. When the initial portfolio is increased to $2,000,000, however, there is appreciable tax. For a discount rate of .08 the initial annual tax is now over $12,000, and the median annual tax later in the period is about $8,000.

The results for the $2,000,000 initial portfolio are shown in the bottom panel of Table 13-2. The tax in this case results in a readily visible decline in the streams of expected withdrawals for each of the discount rates. Relative to each other, however, these streams still look just about the same as in the top panel of Table 13-2, or in Table 4-1. Thus, even when there is an appreciable tax there is little or no effect on choosing the RDR, when there is not an IRA.

Table 13-1 showed, however, that the effect of the tax can increase appreciably when a significant portion of the investment is in an IRA. The second panel from the top in Table 13-2 shows the results when half of the initial $600,000 portfolio is in a traditional IRA. In this case there are not any tax payments for any of the discount rates before the RMD begin. After the RMD begin, however, there are appreciable tax payments and these tend to increase in the future except for the largest discount rate. For a discount rate of .08 the median annual tax payment is about $3,000 after the RMD begin. This rises to about $6,000 later in the period.

Table 13-2

Expected After Tax Withdrawals for Selected Discount Rates
Base Case Stock Returns and Inflation Selected Portfolio and IRA Sizes

Investment* Total/IRA $K@Age65	Discount Rate	Expected After Tax Withdrawals** 65	70	75	80	85	90	95	100
600/0	.04	4.6	3.9	3.7	3.5	3.5	3.4	3.4	3.3
	.06	6.1	5.0	4.5	4.2	4.0	3.9	3.8	3.7
	.08	7.6	5.9	5.2	4.7	4.3	4.1	3.9	3.7
	.10	9.0	6.7	5.6	4.9	4.3	3.9	3.6	3.4
600/300***	.04	4.3	3.7	3.5	3.3	3.2	3.2	3.1	3.1
	.06	5.8	4.7	4.3	4.0	3.8	3.6	3.5	3.5
	.08	7.3	5.7	5.0	4.4	4.0	3.8	3.6	3.4
	.10	8.6	6.4	5.4	4.5	4.0	3.6	3.3	3.1
600/600	.04	4.1	3.5	3.2	3.1	3.0	2.9	2.9	2.9
	.06	5.0	4.1	3.8	3.6	3.4	3.3	3.2	3.1
	.08	6.1	4.8	4.2	3.9	3.7	3.5	3.3	3.2
	.10	7.3	5.5	4.7	4.1	3.7	3.4	3.1	3.0
2000/0	.04	4.2	3.6	3.3	3.2	3.1	3.1	3.1	3.1
	.06	5.6	4.5	4.1	3.9	3.7	3.6	3.5	3.5
	.08	7.0	5.5	4.8	4.3	4.0	3.8	3.6	3.5
	.10	8.5	6.3	5.2	4.6	4.1	3.7	3.4	3.2

*Same as Table 13-1.

**In real terms as a percentage of the value of the investment at age 65.

***Before age 70½ increases estimated future annual tax to reflect the RMD after age 70½ in determining limit on after tax withdrawals. As discussed in the text these increases are percentages of the IRA each year equal to 0.6, 0.6, 0.7, and 1.2 respectively for the discount rates of .04, .06, .08, and .10.

These rising tax payments create increasing risk for the after tax withdrawals later in retirement. And an increase in the risk of low withdrawals later in retirement can make a lower RDR advisable. The simulations show little reason, however for reducing the RDR below .08 in this case.

The stream of expected withdrawals for .08 continues to dominate that for .06 up till age 95. At age 100 the expected withdrawal for .08 is only 0.1 less than that for .06. Thus, there continues to be little reason for retirees to choose a discount rate less than .08 for their RDR. The argument for choosing .08, however, is not as strong as in the top panel of Table 13-2 or in Table 4-1. Similar results are obtained when the initial portfolio is increased to $2,000,000 with half in an IRA.

To determine the limit on the after tax withdrawal each year a forecast is required of the stream of future tax payments. As discussed earlier, usually this future stream of tax payments is forecast by assuming that the current estimated tax payment is the tax payment that will be made each year in the future. When half of the initial portfolio is in an IRA however, this is not a reasonable assumption because large increases are expected in the tax payments after the RMD begin. In such a case the forecast for future tax payments needs to take into account the expected tax increases after age 70½.

To do so, the forecast future tax payment each year before age 70½ in this case was set equal to a percentage of the then current value of the IRA. This percentage was set approximately equal to the percentage reflected by the median values of the tax and the IRA at age 75. These percentages in general vary with the discount rate. They can be determined with sufficient accuracy by a very brief trial and error process.

The percentages obtained and used for discount rates of .04, .06, .08, and .10 were respectively 0.6, 0.6, 0.7, and 1.2. These percentages were also used to calculate the initial after tax withdrawals reported in the table for the different discount rates. For instance, the before tax limit on the initial withdrawal for a discount rate of .04 is 4.6 percent. The forecast annual expected future tax payment must be deducted from 4.6 percent to get the limit on the initial after tax withdrawal for a discount rate of .04.

The forecast tax payment is 0.6 percent of the value of the IRA at that time. As the IRA initially is half of the total portfolio the forecast tax payment is 0.3

percent of the total value of the portfolio. Deducting 0.3 from 4.6 percent gives the 4.3 percent reported on the table as the initial value of the after tax withdrawal for a discount rate of .04. The initial after tax withdrawals for the other discount rates are obtained similarly.

Suppose the entire initial portfolio is in an IRA. The results for this case are shown in the third panel from the top in Table 13-2. Increasing the portion in the IRA, as expected, further reduces the streams of expected withdrawals for each discount rate. There is no change, however, in how the stream for each discount rate looks relative to the others.

Retirees will continue to find a discount rate of .08 attractive relative to lower discount rates. Moreover, for this case, the expected withdrawal at age 100 for .08 is slightly above that for .06. Similar results are obtained when the initial portfolio is increased from $600,000 to $2,000,000. Irrespective of the portion in an IRA, or the size of the portfolio, taxes appear to have little effect on the selection of the RDR.

When the entire initial portfolio is in an IRA, however, there is a significant change in the pattern of tax payments over retirement. Now, large tax payments are required initially as voluntary IRA disbursements are necessary to obtain cash for the withdrawals. For the discount rate of .08 with the $600,000 portfolio the initial tax payment is over $9,000. This makes the initial amount available for the after tax withdrawal equal to 6.1 percent as reported in the table. In this case the payments do not increase when the RMD begin as large IRA disbursements are necessary beforehand. Late in the period for a discount rate of .08 the median annual tax payments are about $7,000.

13.5 Effect on Annuitizing and Part-Time Earnings

Table 13-2 shows that taxes have very little effect on the choice of an RDR. If retirees choose an RDR of .08 on the basis of their tax free withdrawals they will very likely choose an RDR of .08 on the basis of their after tax withdrawals. When using an RDR of .08 in either case, however, withdrawals are allowed for which there is substantial risk of very low withdrawals later in retirement. In the tax free case Chapter 5 showed that much of this risk can be eliminated for initial withdrawals with poor sustainability by annuitizing a large portion of the initial portfolio and working part-time early in retirement.

After taxes, however, the part-time earnings are fully taxable. And taxes also affect the benefits of annuitizing. If purchased with funds in a traditional IRA there is no tax when the purchase occurs, but the annuity benefits are fully taxable. If there is not an IRA a sale of stocks to buy the annuity may realize significant capital gain, but a large portion of the future annuity benefits is tax free. Thus, the question arises. Are annuitizing and part-time earnings as effective in reducing the risk of low withdrawals after taxes as on a tax free basis?

The three panels in Table 13-3 consider the same conditions as the top three panels in Table 13-2. As in the top panel of Table 13-2 the top panel of Table 13-3 assumes that none of the initial portfolio is in an IRA, and that the cost basis of the stocks is half of their value. In the second panel from the top in Table 13-3 half of the initial portfolio is in a traditional IRA. In the bottom panel the entire initial portfolio is in the IRA.

Table 13-3 assumes that retirees have selected an RDR of .08, and are making the after tax withdrawal at age 65 for that discount rate in Table 13-2 or that allowed by the rule if less. The first row for each age in each panel shows the results for the after tax withdrawals without any annuitizing or part-time earnings. The second row for each age in each panel shows the results for the maximal annuitizing and part-time earnings considered in Chapter 5.

In Chapter 5 retirees were assumed to annuitize as much as a half of their initial portfolio. The annuity paid a nominal benefit at the beginning of each year equal to 7.5 percent of its purchase cost. Retirees were also assumed to achieve part-time earnings each year for as long as 10 years equal in real terms to as much as 4 percent of their initial portfolio. The maximal cases for the annuitizing and part-time earnings are assumed in the second row at each age for each of the three panels in Table 13-3.

Compare the risk of low withdrawals in the second row to that in the first row at each age for any of the three panels in Table 13-3. The annuitizing and part-time earnings clearly provide a significant reduction in risk. Moreover, comparison with the reductions achieved in Chapter 5 shows that the reduction in the risk of low withdrawals is about the same as on a tax free basis.

Table 13-3

Effect of Annuitizing and Part-Time Earnings on After Tax Withdrawals

Base Case Stock Returns and Inflation

Portfolio $600,000 Annuity 7.5% RDR .08

Age	Investment* Total/IRA $K@Age 65	After Tax Withdwl. %Age 65	Earn/ Years	Annuity $K	After Tax Withdrawal** Expected	8	6	4	2	0	Median Portfolio
75	600/0	7.6	0/0	0	5.17	.20	.34	.33	.13	0	85
			4/10	300	5.80	.20	.52	.27	.01	0	73
85		7.6	0/0	0	4.33	.14	.25	.30	.28	.03	76
			4/10	300	5.41	.15	.45	.35	.05	0	81
95		7.6	0/0	0	3.89	.12	.21	.26	.33	.08	69
			4/10	300	4.93	.13	.37	.35	.15	0	83
75	600/300	7.1***	0/0	0	4.97	.17	.33	.37	.13	0	87
			4/10	300	5.50	.14	.51	.34	.01	0	78
85		7.1	0/0	0	4.06	.12	.21	.33	.31	.03	77
			4/10	300	5.14	.11	.43	.40	.06	0	85
95		7.1	0/0	0	3.58	.10	.17	.27	.38	.08	67
			4/10	300	4.81	.10	.37	.39	.14	0	93
75	600/600	6.1	0/0	0	4.26	0	.31	.51	.18	0	87
			4/10	300	5.37	0	.69	.30	.01	0	82
85		6.1	0/0	0	3.66	0	.23	.40	.34	.03	82
			4/10	300	4.90	0	.53	.39	.08	0	86
95		6.1	0/0	0	3.31	0	.20	.34	.38	.08	75
			4/10	300	4.51	0	.45	.36	.19	0	85

*Same as Table 13-1.

**After tax withdrawals and median portfolio values are in real terms as percent of investment value at age 65. Probability that withdrawal is in a range from 1 above to 1 below 8, 6, 4, 2, or from 0 to 1.

***Retrenchment Rule allows an initial withdrawal of only 7.1 after annuitizing and earnings.

In Chapter 5 the same annuitizing and part-time earnings reduced the chances that the withdrawals are less than 3 percent at ages 75, 85, and 95 from respectively .13, .30, and .39 to 0, .04, and .12. In the top panel of Table 13-3 there are similar reductions in the chances of low withdrawals. In the bottom panel when the entire initial portfolio is in an IRA there is more risk without the annuitizing and part-time earnings. In this case, there is a slightly larger reduction in the chances of low withdrawals, but more risk remains as there is more risk beforehand.

Thus, taxes cause little, if any, reduction in the effectiveness of annuitizing and part-time earnings in reducing the risk of low withdrawals in these cases. Taxes, however, do reduce the effectiveness of these measures in increasing the expected withdrawals, and in increasing the chances of sustaining the initial withdrawals. In Chapter 5 this level of annuitizing and part-time earnings increased the expected withdrawals at ages 75, 85, and 95 respectively from 5.2, 4.4, and 4.0 to 6.9, 6.1, and 5.7. In Table 13-3 the increases are only about two-thirds as much.

In Chapter 5 the chances that the withdrawals are over 7 percent at ages 75, 85, and 95 increased respectively from .23, .17, and .15 to .64, .46, and .40. In the top two panels of Table 13-3 there is little if any increase in the chances that the withdrawals will be more than 7 percent. In all panels there are increases in the chances that the withdrawals will be more than 5 percent. These increases, however, are not any larger than the increases that the withdrawals will be more than 7 percent for the tax free case.

Thus, the annuitizing and part-time earnings appear to be about as effective in reducing the risk of low withdrawals after taxes as on a tax free basis. Annuitizing and part-time earnings, however, are less effective in increasing the chances of high withdrawals after taxes. There is an explanation for this difference.

When incomes decline, tax rates also decline, and taxes become relatively less important. Taxes, therefore, have less effect on reducing the risk of low withdrawals because taxes are of relatively less importance when incomes decline and low withdrawals occur. Thus, taxes in general reduce the benefits of annuitizing and part-time earnings. But there is less loss of benefits in reducing the risk of low withdrawals due to the progressivity of the tax system.

Note in the bottom two panels of Table 13-3 that the IRA is large enough to accommodate annuitizing half of the portfolio. In these cases the annuitizing can be accomplished without the payment of any tax. The annuity benefits are fully taxable, but so are disbursements from the IRA. Moreover, after age 70½ taxable disbursements may be required from the IRA in excess of needs. Annuitization has an advantage in that the annuity benefits each year are more in line with needs.

In the top panel, on the other hand, $300,000 of stocks must be sold to buy the annuity. And since it is assumed that the cost basis of these stocks is half of their value these sales realize a capital gain of about $150,000. As an offset to the tax on this gain, however, a portion of the future annuity benefits is treated as a return of cost and is not taxable.

In particular, when the annuity is purchased at age 65 benefits equal to 5 percent of the purchase cost are tax free for 20 years. This is because the purchase cost is assumed to be returned in equal amounts each year over an assumed expected life of 20 years for someone at age 65. Since the assumed annuity benefit is 7.5 percent, only a third of the benefit is taxable for the first 20 years. After that the entire benefit is taxable.

Besides buying the annuity in the top panel cash is also required to make the assumed 7.6 percent after tax withdrawal of $45,600 and to pay the large estimated tax for the first year. Some of this cash is available from the first annuity benefit and the part-time earnings for the first year. This cash is far from sufficient, however, so significant stock sales are required realizing additional capital gains.

In addition to these gains the initial Adjusted Gross Income (AGI) includes the dividend portion of the initial stock portfolio, the part-time earnings for the first year, the taxable portion of the first annuity benefit, and the taxable portion of Social Security. Based on the Qualified Dividends and Capital Gain Tax Worksheet for 2009 the tax for the first year is about $31,000.

Due to the very large extra withdrawal to buy the annuity the Retrenchment Rule is not applied in the first year. It is applied in the second year, however, and in subsequent years. In the second year it is unlikely that it will be necessary to sell stocks to provide cash for withdrawals. This is because of the large amount of cash available early in retirement due to the part-time earnings. Thus, after the very large gain realized in the first year no gains are expected in the second year.

The expected tax in the second year is based on the dividends on the stocks, the part-time earnings, the taxable portion of the annuity benefit, and the taxable portion of Social Security. This estimated tax is about $7,000. This estimated tax is paid in the second year. And it is also used as the expected tax payment in future years to obtain the limit on the after tax withdrawal for the second year given by the Retrenchment Rule.

The before tax limit given by the Retrenchment Rule is based on the value of the portfolio at the beginning of the second year and the present value in the second year of the future streams of part-time earnings and annuity benefits. These present values are calculated using the RDR as the rate of interest. When the estimated future tax payment of $7,000 each year is deducted from the before tax limit the limit on the after tax withdrawal for the second year is expected to be only slightly less than the 7.6 percent after tax withdrawal for the first year. Note that despite the very large tax payment in the first year and substantial tax payments thereafter, the top panel in Table 13-3 shows significant improvement from annuitizing and part-time earnings.

In the second panel from the top there is just enough in the IRA to buy the annuity so there are not any stock sales or capital gains. Nevertheless, AGI for the initial year is substantial. The fully taxable annuity benefit is adding $22,500 and the earnings another $24,000. There is also the taxable Social Security of $17,000 and the prior year dividends of $9,600 included in the value of the stocks. The tax payment for the initial year is $10,800.

The before tax limit on the withdrawal for the initial year given by the Retrenchment Rule is $53,100. This is based on the $300,000 investment remaining after the purchase of the annuity and the present values of the anticipated streams of earnings and expected real annuity benefits. The forecast in the initial year for the future stream of tax payments is the initial tax payment of $10,800. Deducting this from the before tax limit on the initial withdrawal of $53,100 gives $42,300 as the limit on the initial after tax withdrawal.

This limit is 7.1 percent of the initial investment of $600,000. The initial withdrawal for this case in Table 13-2 is 7.3 percent. As the limit of 7.1 percent given by the rule after the annuitizing and earnings is lower, it was used for the tests in Table 13-3.

In the bottom panel of Table 13-3 the stocks that remain after the purchase of the annuity are in the IRA. Thus, in this case there are not any dividends in AGI and the initial tax is reduced from $10,800 to $9,400. Otherwise, the calculations for the limit on the initial after tax withdrawal are the same, and it rises slightly to 7.3 percent. This limit easily covers the initial withdrawal of 6.1 percent for this case in Table 13-2, and a 6.1 percent after tax withdrawal is used for the tests in Table 13-3.

Thus, in the bottom two panels of Table 13-3 there are sufficient funds in an IRA to buy the annuity and avoid realizing any capital gain. Large initial tax payments are required in these cases, however, because of the large taxable annuity benefit and taxable earnings. Despite the large increase in tax payments in these cases, however, the simulations show significant improvement in the after tax withdrawals.

13.6 Conclusions

Some taxes such as a sales tax can be viewed as increasing the cost of the goods and services to which they apply. The federal income tax, on the other hand, reduces in general the funds available to cover living expenses. As the federal income tax can be significant, and vary over time, in this chapter income taxes are deducted as an expense, and the Retrenchment Rule is applied to the after tax withdrawals that affect the standard of living.

Simulations have been made in which the tax is a simplified version of the federal income tax in the U. S. in 2009. The possibility of higher tax rates in the future has also been tested. The most important effect of the tax is to increase the savings requirements for retirement.

The increase in the savings requirement is especially sensitive to the initial portion of the investment in a traditional IRA. For those in the middle income range an increase in the portion in an IRA can increase savings requirements by as much as 20 percent. This sensitivity arises because the withdrawals from the IRA are fully taxable, and because the RMD after age 70½ require that almost all of the IRA be disbursed over a long retirement.

Limited conversions to a Roth IRA each year prior to age 70½ can be made at favorable marginal tax rates. Simulations do not show any improvement in the after tax withdrawal after these conversions, however. This is due to the higher taxes and lower investment values the conversions cause early in retirement.

The income tax considered in this chapter has little effect on the choice of an RDR. The largest withdrawal allowed by the Retrenchment Rule when the tax is ignored can therefore be used as a starting point. This is to determine the largest allowed after tax withdrawal to cover living expenses.

Suppose the current annual tax payment is a reasonable estimate of the future stream of annual payments. This current payment is then deducted to get the largest allowed after tax withdrawal. In other cases, major adjustments may be required to reflect the expected future stream of taxes.

Taxes have little effect on the reduction in the risk of low withdrawals provided by part-time earnings and annuitizing. Taxes, however, do reduce the increased chances of higher withdrawals that these measures provide. This difference can be explained by the progressivity of the tax schedule.

Appendix 13-1

Modifying the Spreadsheet to Include an Income Tax

Suppose that the rules for calculating the federal income tax in the U. S. in 2009 were to continue in the future. Some of the dollar amounts used to calculate the tax in 2009 would be indexed each year for inflation and others would not. Tax brackets, the standard deduction and the personal exemption would be indexed for inflation. The cost basis for calculating capital gain or loss and the dollar thresholds for calculating the taxable portion of Social Security would not be indexed. Using the 2009 rules the nominal value of the tax owed each year could be calculated using the nominal value of taxable income each year. The real value of the tax would be obtained by adjusting the nominal tax for inflation.

An equivalent alternative for calculating the real value of the tax each year is to calculate the tax based on real taxable income and to leave the indexed dollar amounts in the rules unchanged. In this alternative dollar amounts that are not indexed for inflation in the 2009 rules must be adjusted for inflation to keep them on the same real basis each year. This includes the cost basis for calculating capital gain or loss, and the dollar amounts for calculating taxable Social Security. This alternative is used for calculating the real value of the tax each year in the simulations.

In the simulations decisions are made and transactions occur at the beginning of each year. These decisions and transactions could in general affect the tax owed for the year. For instance, it may be necessary to realize capital gain or loss by selling stocks to obtain cash for making withdrawals. This gain or loss affects the tax owed for the year. The size of the tax in turn affects the size of the withdrawal necessary to pay that tax.

In simulating taxes it is convenient to avoid this simultaneity by determining the size of the tax payment each year using a similar procedure to that in the tax rules. Each year an estimated tax is paid that is independent of the transactions at the beginning of that year and any tax owed for that year. In addition to this estimated tax each year there is another tax payment or rebate to allow for the difference between the tax owed for the prior year and the estimated tax paid for the prior year.

Generally, the estimated tax paid each year is assumed to equal the tax owed for the prior year. If a sharp drop has occurred in the value of the portfolio over the prior year, however, the tax owed for the prior year may be unduly high as an estimate of the tax for the current year. The estimated tax is therefore limited to be no higher than a portion of the before tax limit on the withdrawal for the current year given by the Retrenchment Rule. Note that this before tax limit depends on the value of the investment before transactions for the current year, and is independent of the transactions. In particular, for middle income retirees, the estimated tax for a year is limited to be no higher than a quarter of the before tax limit on the withdrawal for that year.

Usually in the simulations it is assumed that the estimated tax for a year is also the expected tax payment that will be made each year for the remainder of the retirement period. This is to assess the allowance to deduct from the current value of the assets to determine the current limit on the after tax withdrawal to cover living expenses. The allowance to deduct from the value of the assets is the present value of the stream of future expected annual tax payments using the RDR as the rate of interest.

When the stream of expected tax payments is constant and equal to the current estimated tax, however, this present value provides an annuity equal to the current estimated tax when the present value earns a return equal to the RDR. Thus, the limit on the after tax withdrawal given by the Retrenchment Rule in this case is the following. Take the annuity that would be provided over the remainder of retirement when the current value of the assets is invested at a return equal to the RDR and deduct from the value of this annuity the current estimated tax.

There is an exception to this procedure for getting the limit on the after tax withdrawal, however, when a large portion of the portfolio is in a traditional IRA and a retiree is less than age 70½. In this case, the current estimated tax significantly underestimates the tax payments after age 70½ due to the subsequent RMD from the IRA. In this case, as discussed in the text of this chapter, a significant addition is made to the current estimated tax prior to age 70½ to obtain the future stream of expected tax payments.

The first step in calculating the tax owed each year is to determine the after tax withdrawal and the total tax payment for that year. These calculations can be made based on values that are known at the beginning of the year before any other decisions or transactions occur. Given the after tax withdrawal and the tax payment the total value of the investment after transactions can be calculated. It is equal to the total investment value before transactions less the after tax withdrawal and tax payment plus any part-time earnings or annuity benefit for the year.

The next step is to determine whether a voluntary disbursement will be necessary from an IRA. A voluntary IRA disbursement will be necessary only if there are not sufficient funds available outside an IRA to make the withdrawals that have been determined as necessary to cover the after tax withdrawal and the tax payment. This is after any RMD that may be required for the year has been made from a traditional IRA. If an additional IRA disbursement is required it is made first from a traditional IRA and then from a Roth as the Roth is the better tax shelter and should be preserved to the extent possible. Any such disbursements are made from the respective values of the IRAs at the beginning of the year before transactions to get their values after transactions.

The total value of the investment after transactions and the value of any IRAs after transactions have now been calculated. The next step is to determine the allocation of the portfolio after transactions as between the intermediate term issues and stocks. The total allocation to intermediate term issues after transactions is a given proportion of the total investment after transactions. This allocation to intermediate terms is put first in any traditional IRA to the extent possible and then in any Roth.

The reason for putting the intermediate terms in the IRAs if possible was discussed in the text of this chapter. It is assumed that the intermediate terms usually have a higher amount of taxable income each year relative to their value than stocks. It is therefore beneficial to have the intermediates in IRAs to the extent possible so as to earn returns on the largest amounts that otherwise would have to be paid as tax. It is better to have the intermediates in a traditional IRA than a Roth because having stocks in a Roth will tend to further increase the size of this more favorable tax shelter.

If some of the allocation to intermediates cannot be put in an IRA it must be put in the portion of the investment that is outside of an IRA after transactions. The difference between the amount of stocks outside of IRAs after transactions and the amount of stocks outside of IRAs before transactions (less any dividends included in that amount) gives the stocks to sell or buy outside of IRAs for that year. With the size and allocation of the investment inside and outside of IRAs after transactions determined, the amounts inside and outside of IRAs at the beginning of the next year before transactions can be obtained. This is accomplished by applying the returns for the year from the random drawings to the values after transactions for the prior year.

If stocks are to be purchased outside of IRAs for the year this purchase adds to the cost basis of the stocks outside of IRAs. If stocks are to be sold the realized capital gain or loss for this transaction is calculated using the real value of the cost basis of the stocks outside of IRAs before transactions for that year. The cost basis applied to the sale is the same proportion of the total cost basis as the stocks sold is to their total value before the sale.

Whether there is a net capital gain or loss for the tax year, however, depends on the real value of the carryover loss, if any, for that year before transactions. If there is a net gain after considering any carryover loss it is included in Adjusted Gross Income (AGI) for that year and treated as a long term capital gain in the tax calculation. If there is a net loss, up to $3,000 in real terms of this loss is deducted from AGI. The remainder of the loss, if any, becomes a carryover loss for the following year.

Any qualified dividends for the year are obtained by applying the yield given by the dividend yield relation in Chapter 10 for the beginning of that year to the value of the stocks outside of IRAs before transactions. These dividends are included in AGI and treated as qualified dividends in the tax calculation. Other items included in AGI are the following: Any interest earned on fixed income issues outside of IRAs over the prior year, Any part-time earnings, The taxable portion of any annuity benefit, The taxable portion of Social Security based on a calculation that depends on the other components of AGI, Any required or voluntary disbursements from any traditional IRA for the year.

Taxable income is obtained by deducting the standard deduction for someone 65 and over and the personal exemption from AGI. The tax is calculated using the Qualified Dividends and Capital Gain Tax Worksheet for 2009 based on the taxable income and any qualified dividends or net capital gains for the year that have been obtained. If there are neither qualified dividends nor net capital gains the regular tax schedule is applied to taxable income to obtain the tax.

The relations in the spread sheet to implement these calculations are provided below. Some of these relations are the same as those used earlier in the appendices to Chapters 3 and 5 for the tax free simulations. A few of the relations are formally the same as those used earlier, but have a different interpretation when taxes are included. Other relations are similar but require some modification.

Many new relations are required to calculate the tax each year based on the procedure just presented. These new relations are put in new columns identified by double letters. Some of the new relations have given values for the first year in row 6, or for the year prior to the first year in row 5. In some cases a special procedure is required to obtain appropriate values for these initial conditions. All of the relations provided below are copied to lower rows through year 45, which is in row 50.

B: The relation in B6 is the same as in Chapter 3 and given by: =Min(B5,D6). Now, however, the values in B are those of the after tax withdrawals, and the values in D, which are specified below, are the upper limits on the after tax withdrawals.

C: As in Chapter 3, C gives the value of the investment each year before transactions used to determine the limit on the after tax withdrawals calculated in D. Now, however, this investment value is the sum of the values before transactions outside any IRA given in AD, inside any traditional IRA given in AF, and inside any Roth IRA given in CF, where AD, AF, and CF are further specified below. The value for the first year in C6 is given by: =AD6+AF6 +CF6.

D: Gives the limit on the after tax withdrawal each year. This is based on the same annuity calculation as in Chapters 3 and 5. As earlier, the value of the assets providing the annuity is given by the sum of the value of the investment in C, the present value of any part-time earnings in H, and the real present value of any annuity benefits in I. All of the value of these assets, however, is not available to provide a stream of after tax withdrawals. A deduction from their value must be made to allow for the present value of the stream of future expected annual tax payments that will be necessary. As discussed earlier in this appendix, doing so is usually equivalent to deducting the estimated tax payment specified below in AB from the value of PMT used for D in Chapter 5. Thus, D6 is given by: =PMT($B$2,$D$2-A6+1,-C6-H6-J6*I6,0,1)-AB6.

An exception, however, applies to retirees who have a significant traditional IRA over the period before they reach age 70½. For these retirees their tax is expected to increase significantly when their RMD begin. As discussed in the text of this chapter regarding Table 13-2 an extra deduction is made for the estimated tax in these cases to reflect the expected increase in the tax when the RMD begin. This extra deduction is a percentage of the value of the traditional IRA that approximates the increase in the tax that is expected to occur.

E: Gives the real return on stocks each year as specified in Chapter 3.

H: Gives each year the present value of the stream of any current or future real part-time earnings using the RDR as the rate of interest. This is the same as the values for H in Chapter 5.

I: Gives each year the present value of the expected real stream of any current or future annuity benefits using the RDR as the rate of interest. This is the same as the values for I in Chapter 5.

J: Gives the cumulative adjustment factor for inflation that puts future nominal values on a real basis, which is the same price level as that at the beginning of the simulations. This is the same as the values for J in Chapter 5.

K: Gives the value of inflation each year obtained by a random drawing as in Chapter 5. K5 is a given value of inflation prior to the first year, which generally is assumed to be .025 in the simulations.

L: Gives the unexpected change in inflation each year obtained by a random drawing as in Chapter 5.

M: Gives the real return on intermediate term government issues each year obtained from a random drawing and used in the simulations to represent the returns on fixed income issues. This is the same as the values for M in Chapter 5.

Q: Gives the dividend yield on stocks at the beginning of each year as specified in Chapter 10. For the tax simulations it is assumed that this yield gives the proportion of the value of the stocks outside of IRAs provided by qualified dividends paid on those stocks over the prior year. Q6 is a given initial value, which for the tax simulations is generally the assumed normal value in Chapter 10 of .032. Q7 is given by: =.12*.032+.88*Q6+NormInv(Rand(),0,.0055).

AA: Tax owed for a year based on the transactions at the beginning of that year and dividends and interest on investments outside of IRAs received over the prior year. There are 10 possible schedules for calculating this tax depending on the value of taxable income for the year and the value of any capital gains or qualified dividends outside of IRAs. The value of the tax for each of these conditions is calculated in a separate column. The value of the tax in these columns is zero if the conditions for the tax calculation in that column are not satisfied. The value of AA for a year is obtained by summing the values for that year over those in these 10 columns. The relations for calculating the tax in these columns are specified at the end of this appendix. The value of the tax owed for the first year in AA6 is obtained by a brief trial and error process discussed below in the specification for the tax payment each year in AC.

AB: Gives the estimated tax paid for a year. In general as discussed earlier in this appendix AB7 is given by: =Min(AA6,.25*PMT) where PMT is the value of the annuity for year 2 as specified above for calculating D7. AB6 is a value determined by a brief trial and error process described below in the specification of AC.

AC: Gives the total tax payment for a year, which is composed of an estimated tax payment for the year and an adjustment for the error made in paying the estimated tax for the prior year. Thus, AC7 is given by: =AB7+AA6-AB6. AC6 is obtained by a brief trial and error process. To do so assume a value for AB6 and assume also that this is the value of AC6. The spreadsheet then calculates a value for AA6 based on this assumed value for AC6. If AA6 is reasonably close to AC6 the assumed estimated tax in AB6 is sufficient. This is because any difference between the estimated tax paid in AB6 and the tax owed for the first year in AA6 is covered in the tax payment for the second year in AC7. If there is a substantial error between AA6 and AB6 a new assumption for AB6 is made and the process repeated.

Note that the assumed estimated tax in AB6 may limit the value of the after tax withdrawal in B6 through the limit on B6 in D6. If the value of B6 is less than the desired value in B5 extra care should be taken in arriving at an appropriate initial value of the estimated tax in AB6. This is to make sure that any desired after tax withdrawal in B5 is not feasible after considering the tax that must be paid.

AD: Value of investment outside of IRAs at the beginning of a year before transactions. In general, may include both stocks and fixed income issues and includes any dividends or interest paid on these investments over the prior year. AD6 is a given value, and AD7 is given by: =AE7+AJ6*(1+M6). In this relation AE is the value of the stocks in AD specified next below. AJ6 is the value of the fixed income issues outside IRAs after transactions at the beginning of the first year. AJ is further specified below.

AE: Value of stocks outside of IRAs at the beginning of a year before transactions. AE includes any dividends paid on these stocks over the prior year. AE6 is equal to the given value of AD6 less any given initial allocation to fixed incomes that cannot be accommodated by the given initial value of IRAs. AE7 is given by: =(AK6-AJ6)*(1+E6). In this relation AK6 is the total value of the investment outside of IRAs after transactions at the beginning of the first year. AJ6 is the amount of AK6 in fixed income issues. AJ and AK are specified further below.

AF: Value of the investment in a traditional IRA before transactions at the beginning of a year. AF6 is a given value. AF7 is given by: =AI6*(1+M6)+(AF6-AG6-AH6-CA6-AI6)*(1+E6). In this relation AI6 is the amount of fixed income issues in the IRA after transactions at the beginning of the first year. AH6 is the value of any voluntary disbursement that may be necessary from the IRA at the beginning of the first year to provide cash for withdrawals. AG6 is any RMD from the IRA for the first year and is equal to zero for a retiree less than age 70½. CA6 is any amount in the IRA converted into a Roth IRA at the beginning of the first year. AG, AH, AI, and CA are specified further below.

AG: Value of any RMD from a traditional IRA at the beginning of a year. Before age 70½, AG=0. After age 70½, it is assumed that AG is equal to AF-AG at the beginning of the prior year divided by a factor given by the tax rules that depends on the age of the retiree at the beginning of the current year. Suppose a retiree is age 65 for year 1 in row 6. That retiree will then be age 71 for the transactions in year 7 in row 12. In this case AG12 is given by: =If((AF11-AG11)/AZ12<AF12,(AF11-AG11)/AZ12,AF12). The values in AZ are the factors given in the tax rules that depend on the age of the retiree. As AZ12 is assumed to be the factor for age 71 it is equal to 26.5. The factors for AZ13, AZ14, and AZ15 are then respectively 25.6, 24.7, and 23.8. The conditional expression for AG says that the required disbursement cannot exceed the current value of the IRA. Note that AG11=0 when it applies to age 70 as assumed above.

AH: Value of a voluntary disbursement from a traditional IRA at the beginning of a year when necessary to provide cash for making withdrawals. It is assumed that such a disbursement will be made only if funds are not available outside the IRAs to cover the after tax withdrawal and tax payment. Also, the disbursement from the traditional IRA cannot exceed the funds available in the IRA. Assuming there are not any part-time earnings or annuity benefits AH6 is given by: =If(B6+AC6>AD6+AG6,If(B6+AC6-AD6-AG6<AF6-AG6-CA6,B6+AC6-AD6-AG6,AF6-AG6-CA6),0). Note that AG6=0 if the first year is for a retiree prior to age 70½.

CA: Value of the amount in a traditional IRA converted into a Roth IRA in the transactions at the beginning of a year. These are given values, CA*, except that they cannot exceed the amount in the IRA at the beginning of the year before transactions. CA6 is given by: =If(CA6*<=AF6,CA6*,AF6).

CF: Value of the investment in a Roth IRA before transactions at the beginning of a year. CF6 is a given value. CF7 is given by: =CI6*(1+M6)+(CF6+CA6-CH6-CI6)*(1+E6). In this relation CI6 is the amount of fixed income issues in the Roth after transactions at the beginning of the first year. CH6 is the value of any voluntary disbursement that may be necessary from the Roth at the beginning of the first year to provide cash for withdrawals. CA6 is any amount from the traditional IRA converted into a Roth at the beginning of the first year as specified above.

CH: Value of a disbursement from a Roth IRA at the beginning of a year when necessary to provide cash for making withdrawals. Such a disbursement is made only if no other funds are available to cover all of the withdrawals. Assuming there are not any part-time earnings or annuity benefit CH6 is given by: =If(B6+AC6>=AD6+AF6-CA6,B6+AC6-AD6-AF6+CA6,0).

AI: Value of fixed income issues in a traditional IRA at the beginning of a year after transactions. To determine this value it is assumed that a fixed proportion of the total investment at the beginning of each year after transactions is allocated to fixed incomes. As discussed earlier it is also assumed that all of these fixed incomes are put in a traditional IRA to the extent possible.

The total investment at the beginning of a year after transactions is the total investment before transactions given by AD+AF+CF plus any part-time earnings or annuity benefit for that year less the after tax withdrawal, B, and tax payment, AC, for that year. The value of any traditional IRA after transactions is its value before transactions, AF, less any required disbursement, AG, less any voluntary disbursement, AH, and less any Roth conversion, CA6. Suppose that there are neither part-time earnings nor an annuity benefit and that the desired allocation to fixed incomes is .25. AI6 is then given by: =If(.25*(AD6+AF6+CF6-B6-AC6)<AF6-AG6-AH6-CA6,.25*(AD6+AF6+CF6-B6-AC6),AF6-AG6-AH6-CA6).

CI: Value of fixed income issues in the Roth IRA at the beginning of a year after transactions. As discussed earlier any of the allocation to fixed incomes that cannot be put in the traditional IRA is put in the Roth to the extent possible. Suppose there are neither part-time earnings nor an annuity benefit and that the desired allocation to fixed incomes is .25. CI6 is then given by: =If(.25*(AD6+AF6+CF6-B6-AC6)>=AF6-AG6-AH6-CA6,If(.25*(AD6+AF6+CF6-B6-AC6)-(AF6-AG6-AH6-CA6)<CF6+CA6-CH6,.25*(AD6+AF6+CF6-B6-AC6)-(AF6-AG6-AH6-CA6),CF6+CA6-CH6),0).

AJ: Value of the fixed income issues outside of IRAs at the beginning of a year after transactions. Any of the desired allocation to fixed incomes that cannot be put in IRAs must be put outside the IRAs. Under the same conditions as for AI6 and CI6 above, AJ6 is given by: =If(.25*(AD6+AF6+CF6-B6-AC6)-(AF6-AG6-AH6-CA6)>=CF6+CA6-CH6,.25*(AD6+AF6-B6-AC6)-(AF6-AG6-AH6-CA6)-(CF6+CA6-CH6),0).

AK: Total value of the investment outside of IRAs after transactions. If there are neither part-time earnings nor an annuity benefit AK6 is given by: =AD6+AG6+AH6+CH6-B6-AC6.

AL: Value of the stocks to be sold at the beginning of the year outside of IRAs, if any, to achieve the desired allocation to stocks after transactions. This value is equal to the value of the stocks outside of the IRAs before transactions less the desired value of the stocks outside of the IRAs after transactions if this difference is nonnegative. Thus, AL6 is given by: =If(AE6*(1-Q6)>=AK6-AJ6,AE6*(1-Q6)-(AK6-AJ6),0).

AM: Value of stocks to be purchased to achieve the desired allocation to stocks at the beginning of the year after transactions. AM6 is given by: =If(AE6*(1-Q6)<AK6-AJ6,AK6-AJ6-AE6*(1-Q6),0).

AN: Cost basis in real terms of the stocks outside of IRAs at the beginning of a year before transactions. AN6 is a given value. If stocks are sold it is assumed that the cost basis for calculating realized gain or loss on the sale for tax purposes is the same proportion of the total cost basis before the sale as the proportion of the value of stocks sold is to the total value of the stocks before the sale. It follows that AN7 is given by: =If(AL6>0,If(AE6>0,AN6*(1−AL6/(1−Q6)*AE6),0),AN6+AM6)/(1+K6). Note that the cost basis must be adjusted for inflation so that it is on the same real basis at the beginning of the following year. The conditional relation for AE6>0 assures that AE6≠0 in case AL6 is very slightly positive due to rounding.

AO: Realized gain or loss for tax purposes of any stocks sold at the beginning of a year. AO6 is given by: =If(AL6>0,If(AE6>0,AL6-AN6*AL6/(1-Q6)*AE6,0),0). Note that AO has a negative value if there is a loss.

AP: Carryover loss in real terms at the beginning of a year before transactions. If there is a carryover loss it is deducted from AO to get the net gain or loss for tax purposes for the year. If there is a net loss after taking the carryover loss into account up to $3,000 of it in real terms is a deduction from AGI for the year. The remaining loss, if any, becomes a carryover loss for the next year after adjustment for the inflation over the year. If there is a net gain it is an addition to AGI and treated as a long term gain in the tax calculation. The initial carryover loss, AP6, is a given value usually set equal to zero. AP7 is given by: =If(-(AO6-AP6)>3000*J6,-(AO6-AP6)-3000*J6,0)/(1+K6).

AQ: Net long term capital gain that is an addition to AGI for the year. AQ6 is given by: If(AO6-AP6>=0,AO6-AP6,0).

AR: Net long term capital loss for the year that is a deduction from AGI. AR6 is given by: =If(AO6-AP6<0,Min(-(AO6-AP6),3000*J6),0).

AS: Real value of the interest income on which tax is payable at the beginning of a year due to any intermediate term government issues held outside an IRA over the prior year. For simplicity no attempt is made to differentiate the return on these intermediate term issues each year as between taxable interest income and capital gain or loss. The real return given in M each year is adjusted by the inflation rate in K for that year to get a nominal return that is assumed to be taxable interest income.

This taxable interest income over the year is put on a real basis as of the beginning of the year after it is earned by adjusting the interest income for the inflation rate in K for the year in which it is earned. Based on these assumptions AS7 is given by: AJ6*((1+M6)*(1+K6)-1)/(1+K6). In some years a significant portion of the real return in M will actually represent capital gain or loss, and not interest. And even if the real return in M does reflect interest, adjusting it for the actual inflation for the year in K may sometimes be a very poor approximation for the nominal interest rate earned over the year on which tax is payable. Nevertheless, over long periods much of such error should be offsetting so that these assumptions give a tolerable approximation for the effect of the intermediate term government issues on taxes. Note also that the effect of these assumptions will be moot over the early years of retirement when there is a significant IRA because these intermediates will be in the IRA.

Before transactions at the beginning of the first year the taxable interest earned over the prior year is assumed to be .055 of the value of the intermediates that are outside of an IRA. It is assumed that none of the intermediates are outside of an IRA if .25 of the total investment value, C6, is less than the combined value of the IRAs, AF6+CF6. If .25*C6>AF6+CF6 the difference is assumed to be the value of the intermediates outside of the IRAs. In this case, AD6-AE6=.25*C6-AF6-CF6. Thus, AS6 is given by: =.055*(AD6-AE6), and AD6-AE6 by: =If(.25*C6>AF6+CF6,.25*C6-AF6-CF6,0).

AT: Adjusted Gross Income (AGI) for calculating the tax for a year except that it excludes taxable Social Security. AT is specified in this way because it is required to calculate taxable Social Security in the tax rules as shown below for AU. AT includes the qualified dividends and taxable interest income on the investment outside an IRA over the prior year, any required or voluntary disbursements from a traditional IRA, any conversion of an amount in a traditional IRA into a Roth, any net capital gain, any allowed deduction for a net capital loss, any applicable part-time earnings, and any taxable annuity benefit. Thus, AT6 is given by: =Q6*AE6+AS6+AG6+AH6+CA6+AQ6-AR6 plus any applicable part-time earnings or taxable annuity benefit. Note that when purchased by funds in the traditional IRA that all of any annuity benefit is taxable each year. When purchased by funds outside of an IRA the taxable annuity benefit is obtained as discussed in the text of this chapter.

AU: Real value of taxable Social Security for the year based on the calculation specified in the tax rules for 2009. This calculation is based on the value of AT plus half of Social Security. The threshold dollar amounts for this calculation were not being indexed for inflation in 2009. In the simulations they are therefore adjusted each year for inflation to keep them on the same real basis each year. For the $20,000 of Social Security assumed each year by the simulations, and using the 2009 calculation, AU6 is given by: =If(AT6+.5*20000<=25000*J6,0,If(AT6+.5*20000<=34000*J6,.5*(AT6+.5*20000-25000*J6),Min(4500*J6+.85*(AT6+.5*20000-34000*J6),.85*20000))).

AV: Real value of taxable income for the year, which is equal to AGI less deductions and less the personal exemption. AGI is equal to the value in AT plus the value of taxable Social Security in AU. For the simulations the deductions are assumed to be the standard deduction for someone 65 or over. For 2009 this is equal to $7,100 and indexed for inflation. The personal exemption is equal to$3,650 and also indexed for inflation. In 2009 for those with an AGI over $166,800 up to a third of the exemption is subject to a limitation. This limitation, however, will be ignored as its effect is small and AGI in the simulations for middle income retirees is not large enough to be affected. AV6 is therefore given by: =AT6+AU6-7100-3650.

AW: Sum of the value of the qualified dividends paid over the prior year and any taxable net capital gain for the year. AW6 is given by: =Q6*AE6+AQ6.

AX: Taxable income for the year less the dividends and gains in AW. AX6 is given by: AV6-AW6. The values in AV, AW, and AX are all required to calculate the tax for the year in the Qualified Dividends and Capital Gain Tax Worksheet for 2009.

In general, there was not a tax on dividends and long term capital gains for 2009 unless taxable income exceeded $33,950. When taxable income exceeded $33,950 and taxable income less the dividends and the gains was less than $33,950 the excess of taxable income above $33,950 was taxed at 15 percent. When taxable income less dividends and gains exceeded $33,950 any dividends and gains were taxed at 15 percent. Any taxable income less dividends and gains was taxed at a schedule starting with a marginal tax rate of 10 percent up to $8,350, 15 percent up to $33,950, and rising eventually to a rate of 35 percent for amounts above $372,950.

With these schedules there are 10 possible combinations of ranges for calculating the tax based on the amount of taxable income and the amount of dividends and gains. The general approach is to specify each of these 10 possible sets of conditions as the first argument of a conditional logical function, If(x,y,z). The tax is calculated for each of these sets of conditions in the second argument of the function. The third argument of this function is 0. Each of these conditional functions is put in a separate column in the spreadsheet designated by a double letter starting with B. The tax owed for a year in AA is the sum of the values in the same row in these columns starting with B. Thus, AA6 is given by: =BA6+BB6+BC6+BD6+BE6+BF6+BG6+ BH6+BI6+BJ6. The relations for calculating the tax for the first year for each of these sets of conditions is given below.

```
BA: =If(And(AV6<=33950,AX6<0),0,0)
BB: =If(And(AV6>33950,AX6<0),.15*(AV6-33950),0)
BC: =If(And(AV6<=33950,AX6<=8350,AX6>=0),.1*AX6,0)
BD: =If(And(AV6>33950,AX6<=8350,AX6>=0),.1*AX6+.15*(AV6-33950),0)
BE: =If(And(AV6<=33950,AX6>8350),835+.15*(AX6-8350),0)
BF: =If(And(AV6>33950,AX6<=33950,AX6>8350),835+.15*(AX6-8350)+.15*(AV6-33950),0)
BG: =If(And(AX6>33950,AX6<=82250),4675+.25*(AX6-33950)+.15*AW6,0)
BH: =If(And(AX6>82250,AX6<=171550),16750+.28*(AX6-82250)+.15*AW6,0)
BI: =If(And(AX6>171550,AX6<=372950),41754+.33*(AX6-171,550)+.15*AW6,0)
BJ: =If(AX6>372950,108216+.35*(AX6-372950)+.15*AW6,0)
```

14

Utility Optimization Under Certainty

The Retrenchment Rule appears to be a reasonable way to make withdrawals from an investment. But is it the best way? This chapter shows that it is the best way under some very special conditions. Although these conditions are highly artificial they do represent some of the key features of the problem. The optimality of the rule under these conditions enhances its credibility under more realistic conditions.

To find the optimal way to make withdrawals from an investment economists maximize a utility function for the withdrawals. This utility function assigns a value to any stream of withdrawals depending on the size and timing of each withdrawal. The maximization of this utility function is constrained by a requirement that the withdrawals satisfy a budget constraint. This budget requirement depends on the initial value of the investment and the returns it will earn in the future.

To simplify in this chapter it is assumed that the real returns each year on the investment are known in advance and are the same. Suppose this return is denoted by r. It will also be assumed that the length of life is known. Under these conditions the budget relation is easily stated. It says that the present value of the withdrawals using r as the rate of interest must be equal to the initial value of the investment.

For the retirees considered in this book there is also another constraint on their withdrawals. It is assumed that these retirees have a strong desire to sustain their existing standard of living. But the withdrawal each year required to do so gives a stream that violates their budget relation. In particular, the present value of the withdrawals required to sustain their existing standard of living exceeds the value of their initial investment.

Thus, these retirees will have to retrench. They will have to select a stream in which one or more of the withdrawals is smaller than would be necessary to sustain their existing standard of living. Because they will have to retrench and because they have a strong desire to sustain their existing standard of living there is a further constraint on their withdrawals.

This constraint is that they cannot select a stream in which there is a withdrawal that is larger than the one necessary each year to sustain their existing standard of living. Suppose they do select a larger withdrawal. This larger withdrawal will increase their utility. But due to the budget relation it will also reduce one or more other withdrawals below the level required to sustain their existing standard of living. Due to their strong interest in sustaining their existing standard of living it is assumed that the loss in utility due to these reductions exceeds the gain in utility provided by the larger withdrawal. The withdrawals each year are therefore constrained not to exceed the withdrawal each year that is necessary to sustain their existing standard of living.

Thus, the optimal withdrawals in this chapter are those that maximize a utility function and also satisfy two constraints. One constraint is a budget relation that requires the present value of the withdrawals to equal the initial value of the investment. The other constraint is that any withdrawal cannot exceed the withdrawal each year that would sustain the existing standard of living each year over retirement.

The next step is to specify a simple utility function for the withdrawals. The stream of withdrawals will then be found that maximizes the value of this utility function while satisfying the two constraints. It is then shown that this optimal stream is the same as the one obtained by following the Retrenchment Rule under the same conditions.

14.1 A Simple Utility Function

Retirees have a strong aversion to having a low standard of living in any year over their retirement. As a simple way of reflecting this aversion suppose that they focus on the smallest withdrawal in any stream of withdrawals. In particular, suppose that the utility of any stream of withdrawals for these retirees is measured by the value of the smallest withdrawal in that stream.

Maximizing this utility function subject to the constraints is straight forward. The optimal stream must have withdrawals that are all the same. Otherwise, the value of this utility function could be increased by increasing a lower withdrawal and decreasing a higher withdrawal in such a way as to not violate the constraints.

Thus, the optimal stream is found by making the value of all of the withdrawals the same as the initial withdrawal. The value of the initial withdrawal under this condition is then found that satisfies the budget relation. The value of the initial withdrawal that does so is the fixed annuity that can be obtained each year over retirement from the initial investment when it earns the given return of r.

A stream of withdrawals equal to the value of this annuity maximizes the utility function and satisfies the two constraints. It satisfies the budget relation because its value has been determined so that it does. It also satisfies the other constraint because all of the withdrawals are equal and less than the value of the withdrawal each year necessary to sustain the existing standard of living.

14.2 Time Equivalence

The utility function just presented represents a key objective of retirees. This objective is to avoid low withdrawals at any time over their retirement. But retirees are likely to be more averse to low withdrawals early in retirement than later on. For instance, many individuals have pent-up plans for activities such as travel in the early years of their retirement. They would be willing to spend less later in retirement if necessary to carry out those plans. Moreover, later in retirement they envision a slowing in their lifestyle making it easier to accommodate some cuts in spending.

If retirees are less averse to low withdrawals later in retirement this difference should be reflected in the utility function. To do so later withdrawals can be multiplied by an equivalence factor to make their effect on utility comparable to that of earlier withdrawals. But what equivalence factor should be used to give later withdrawals the same effect on utility as earlier withdrawals?

It is difficult to evaluate an appropriate size for the equivalence factor without seeing how it actually affects the withdrawals. A reasonable approach is therefore to assume various sizes for the time equivalence factor. The stream of optimal withdrawals given by each of these factors is determined. The best of these streams is then chosen. The time equivalence factor for that stream is the one that should be used.

Presumably the time equivalence factor should gradually increase as withdrawals are made successively further in the future. Suppose a withdrawal in the next year is multiplied by a factor slightly larger than 1 to make its effect on utility the same as a withdrawal in the current year. In particular, suppose this factor is denoted by 1+b, where b is a non negative number that is very small. For instance, b might be equal to .01, .02, or .03.

The value of the factor for withdrawals further in the future is obtained by compounding 1+b. This is for each year in the future until the withdrawal occurs. For instance, the time equivalence factor for a withdrawal after 10 years has elapsed is equal to $(1+b)^{10}$.

14.3 Maximizing Time Adjusted Utility

Before utility was maximized by making the value of each withdrawal equal to that of the initial withdrawal. Utility given by the time adjusted utility function is maximized by making the utility of each time adjusted withdrawal the same as the value of the initial withdrawal. This means that future withdrawals are optimal when their value multiplied by the time equivalence factor for the year in which they occur is equal to the initial withdrawal.

It is convenient to change the form of this relation by dividing both sides of the relation by the time equivalence factor. This changes the relation to say that each optimal withdrawal in the future is equal to the initial withdrawal divided by the time equivalence factor for the future year in which that withdrawal occurs. For instance, the optimal withdrawal after 10 years has elapsed is equal to the initial withdrawal divided by $(1+b)^{10}$.

To determine the initial withdrawal these optimal future withdrawals are substituted for their values in the budget relation. In the budget relation a future withdrawal is divided by 1+r compounded for each year in the future until it occurs. When the future withdrawal is replaced by its optimal value this becomes the initial withdrawal divided by both 1+r and 1+b each compounded for each year in the future before the withdrawal occurs. For instance, the present value for the withdrawal after 10 years becomes equal to the initial withdrawal divided by both $(1+r)^{10}$ and $(1+b)^{10}$.

This divisor can be rewritten as $((1+r)(1+b))^{10}$. And this term can be interpreted as the present value of the initial withdrawal in 10 years calculated using as an interest rate r+b+rb, as (1+r)(1+b)=1+(r+b+rb). If r and b are small this rate of interest is approximately equal to the sum of r and b.

The initial withdrawal that satisfies the budget relation is again a fixed annuity. Now, however, it is the fixed annuity that can be obtained each year over retirement from the initial investment when it earns a return equal to r+b+rb. The other withdrawals are equal to the value of this fixed annuity discounted at the rate b for each year in the future before they occur. For instance, the withdrawal after 10 years has elapsed is the value of the fixed annuity divided by $(1+b)^{10}$.

These withdrawals maximize the utility function while satisfying the budget relation. These withdrawals, however, may not satisfy the second constraint. The second constraint requires all of the withdrawals to be less than the withdrawal each year that would provide the existing standard of living. And if b is large enough the initial withdrawal may exceed this value.

Thus, the optimal withdrawals have been found only if a special condition is satisfied. This condition is that the value of the fixed annuity cannot exceed the withdrawal required each year to provide the existing standard of living. If this condition is satisfied all of the withdrawals satisfy the second constraint because none can exceed the initial withdrawal. This is because they are equal to the initial withdrawal discounted at the rate b, and b≥0.

Suppose the value of the fixed annuity exceeds the required withdrawal each year to provide the existing standard of living. In this case, to satisfy the second constraint the initial withdrawal must be set equal to the required withdrawal to provide the existing standard of living. The value of the investment at the beginning of the second year is then calculated assuming this required withdrawal is made for the first year and the investment earns the assumed return of r over the first year.

The next step in this case is to calculate the value of a new fixed annuity. This is the fixed annuity that can be obtained each year over the remainder of retirement from the value of the investment at the beginning of the second year. As before this is when the investment earns a return equal to r+b+rb. Suppose the value of this fixed annuity does not exceed the required withdrawal to provide the existing standard of living. The optimal second withdrawal is then equal to the value of the fixed annuity calculated for the second year. The optimal subsequent withdrawals are equal to the value of the second withdrawal discounted at the rate b for each year in the future until they occur.

Suppose the value of the fixed annuity for the second year exceeds the required withdrawal to provide the existing standard of living each year. In this case the second withdrawal is set equal to the required withdrawal for the existing standard of living and the same process is repeated for the following year. This procedure continues until the fixed annuity calculated for a year no longer exceeds the required withdrawal to provide the existing standard of living. Such a year will occur because it has been assumed that the required withdrawal to sustain the existing standard of living cannot be sustained over all of the retirement period.

14.4 Selecting the Time Equivalence Factor

The optimal stream of withdrawals has been determined for a given value of b. This is significant progress, but the appropriate value of b is unknown. The appropriate value of b is determined by calculating the streams of withdrawals for a series of values for b. By selecting the best of these streams individuals reveal the value of b that is appropriate for their own utility function.

Those that choose the stream for b=0 prefer a constant standard of living over retirement. Those that choose a larger value of b want to spend relatively more early in retirement when they can enjoy a more active lifestyle. There are no right or wrong answers as to which is the best stream and the appropriate value of b. It is a personal decision. It is very difficult, however, to select a value for b without seeing the streams of withdrawals that various values of b provide. This is when an optimal policy is followed for making withdrawals for a given value of b.

The value of b that is chosen could depend on other factors that affect the streams of withdrawals. The choice could depend, for instance, on the return of the investment, the length of the retirement period, or the size of the initial investment. It is assumed that these factors are known when the choice is made. Testing the sensitivity of the choice to these factors indicates whether or not they are important.

To illustrate the process it will be assumed that the length of the retirement period is 30 years. It will also be assumed that the size of the initial investment does not affect the value of b that is chosen so that for choosing the value of b the withdrawals can be expressed as a percentage of the investment. This latter assumption is reasonable when Social Security as well as investment withdrawals are available to cover living expenses. The availability of the Social Security helps to reduce the negative effect of lower withdrawals later in retirement. This makes the size of the investment less important in assuring that a subsistence level of standard of living can be provided.

Table 14-1 shows the streams of withdrawals obtained under these conditions for values of b equal to 0, .01, .02, and .03. The effect on the stream of the value of r is indicated by showing streams when its value is .02 or .03. The table also shows the effect on the streams of the required withdrawal to cover the existing standard of living.

Table 14-1

Withdrawals for Selected Time Equivalence Factors
Withdrawal for Existing Standard of Living Is ≥ 6.9

b	Withdrawals for r = .03*				Withdrawals for r = .02			
	1	10	20	30	1	10	20	30
0	5.0	5.0	5.0	5.0	4.4	4.4	4.4	4.4
.01	5.6	5.1	4.6	4.2	5.0	4.5	4.1	3.7
.02	6.2	5.2	4.3	3.5	5.6	4.7	3.8	3.1
.03	6.9	5.3	3.9	2.9	6.2	4.8	3.6	2.6
Withdrawal for Existing Standard of Living Is 5.6								
.02	5.6	5.4	4.4	3.6	5.6	4.7	3.8	3.1
.03	5.6	5.6	4.3	3.2	5.6	4.9	3.6	2.7

*Withdrawals are in real terms as a percentage of initial investment value.

Looking at the streams in the table those who want a steady standard of living over retirement can achieve this objective by choosing the streams with b=0. Those who want to provide more for an active lifestyle early in retirement can do so by choosing an appropriate stream with a larger value of b. It is important to emphasize again, however, that all of these streams are optimal. The one to choose and the appropriate value of b is a personal decision.

Suppose retirees require a withdrawal larger than 6.9 percent to carry out their planned activities early in retirement. The table assumes that they will nevertheless choose a b no higher than .03 and limit their initial spending to an initial withdrawal of 6.9 percent. The reason is that higher values of b unduly depress the standard of living late in retirement. It is assumed that these later withdrawals are sufficiently low that retirees will not choose a b higher than .03.

Suppose r declines and the value of b remains the same. With the same b the optimal stream of withdrawals continues to decline at the same rate, or to be flat if b=0. To make this possible and still satisfy the budget relation the initial withdrawal must decline. The decline in r has effectively reduced the initial value of the investment.

Retirees could choose a different value of b with a lower r. But it seems unlikely that they will do so. Their choice of b will largely depend on the rate of decline in their withdrawals over retirement that they are willing to accept so as to increase their withdrawals early in retirement. And this tradeoff remains the same with the lower r.

Suppose retirees need to withdraw only 5.6 percent to carry out their plans early in retirement. In this case the optimal streams are the same when b is equal to 0 or .01. When b is equal to .02 or .03, however, the initial withdrawal is limited to 5.6 percent as shown in the bottom panel of the table. In this case when r=.03 the withdrawal does not decline below 5.6 percent until the 9th withdrawal for b=.02. Subsequently, the withdrawals decline at the same rate as before for b=.02 in the upper panel. When b=.03 the withdrawals do not decline below 5.6 percent until the 12th withdrawal. Subsequently they decline at the same rate as for b=.03 in the upper panel.

In this case for r=.03, choosing .02 instead of .01, or .03 instead of .02, defers the time until retrenchment first becomes necessary. Choosing a higher b in this case provides higher withdrawals in the middle of retirement at the cost of lower withdrawals later on. Retirees could choose a different b in this case, but they seem unlikely to do so. The tradeoff of higher earlier withdrawals for lower withdrawals later on appears similar to the case with a higher initial requirement.

Choosing a stream with a b larger than .03 seems unreasonable, and choosing .03 instead of .02 may be questionable. Whether to choose a b of 0, .01, or .02, however, appears to be a personal preference as to how standard of living should be distributed over retirement. There appears to be nothing irrational about choosing withdrawals that decline moderately over time in real terms instead of being flat. Declining withdrawals are suboptimal and presumably irrational only if it is assumed that b=0. The value of b, however, is a personal choice that can properly be made only by looking at the streams of withdrawals.

14.5 Equivalence to Retrenchment Rule

Suppose retirees are using the Retrenchment Rule in the case just considered. If they have the assumed utility function and the same value of b in either case they will make the same withdrawals. When using the Retrenchment Rule they will choose as their RDR the discount rate that gives the same stream of withdrawals as the value of b that they choose in Table 14-1.

When using the Retrenchment Rule retirees determine the streams of withdrawals provided by different given values of a discount rate. They then select the best stream of withdrawals from among those given by the different discount rates. The stream selected determines the discount rate they should use and the stream of withdrawals that they should make.

Given a discount rate and using the rule the first step in determining the initial withdrawal is to calculate the value of a fixed annuity. This is the fixed annuity that can be obtained each year over the retirement period from the initial investment when it earns an annual real return equal to the discount rate. Suppose the value of this annuity exceeds the withdrawal required to provide the existing standard of living. Then retirees continue doing what they have been doing. They make the withdrawal necessary to cover their existing standard of living. If the value of the fixed annuity is less than what is necessary to cover their existing standard of living retrenchment is necessary. In this case the withdrawal is equal to the value of the fixed annuity.

The value of the investment at the beginning of the second year is obtained by deducting the withdrawal for the first year from the initial value of the investment and increasing the remainder by the return r over the first year. The Retrenchment Rule then calculates the value of a new fixed annuity based on this new investment value. This is the annuity that can be obtained each year over the remainder of retirement when starting in the second year. This is when the investment earns a real return each year equal to the discount rate. The withdrawal for the second year is determined as for the first year. It depends on whether or not the new value of the fixed annuity exceeds the withdrawal needed to sustain the existing standard of living. The process continues as before in the future with the calculation of new fixed annuities each year based on the value of the investment at the beginning of each year.

Suppose that the discount rate used for the Retrenchment Rule is equal to r+b+rb. The withdrawals obtained by the rule are then the same as before as long as the value of the fixed annuity obtained each year exceeds the value of the withdrawal required to cover the existing standard of living. Suppose, however, that the value of the fixed annuity does not exceed the required withdrawal for the existing standard of living.

Before, the future optimal withdrawals were obtained as follows from the value of the fixed annuity in such a case. To get the optimal withdrawal in a future year the value of the fixed annuity is discounted at the rate b for each year in the future until it occurs. For instance, the optimal withdrawal 10 years in the future is the value of the fixed annuity divided by $(1+b)^{10}$.

Using the Retrenchment Rule, however, the future optimal withdrawals in future years are the values of fixed annuities calculated in those years. These are the fixed annuities that can be obtained from the remaining value of the investment at that time over the remainder of retirement when the investment earns a return equal to the discount rate. It can be shown, however, that the values of these fixed annuities are the same as the optimal withdrawals obtained before.[1] Thus, when the discount rate is equal to r+b+rb the withdrawals obtained using the Retrenchment Rule are the same as the optimal withdrawals obtained before.

Suppose the value of rb is ignored as an approximation as it is small when r and b are small. The withdrawals on the left side of Table 14-1 are then those obtained for discount rates when the value of r of .03 is added to the stated value of b. Suppose, for instance, that retirees choose the stream for b=.01. They will then choose the stream for a discount rate of .04 and make the same withdrawals when using the Retrenchment Rule as they did before for b=.01.

On the right side of the table the streams for discount rates are obtained by adding an r of .02 to the value of b. Suppose, for instance, that retirees again choose the stream for b=.01. After adding r=.02 to b=.01 they are now choosing a discount rate of .03. They are choosing the same b as before, but the discount rate has declined to reflect the lower value of r.

In general, using the Retrenchment Rule under these conditions is equivalent to maximizing the utility function that was specified earlier. This is assuming that the appropriate value for the time equivalence factor for that utility function is also determined as specified earlier. The appendix to this chapter shows that the Retrenchment Rule is also equivalent to maximizing under certainty a linear utility function that is frequently used in economics.

14.6 Conclusions

The Retrenchment Rule appears to be a reasonable way of making withdrawals from an investment, but is it the best way? In economics the best withdrawals from an investment are determined by maximizing a utility function for the withdrawals. This is subject to the withdrawals satisfying a budget relation and possibly other constraints.

Suppose that the returns on an investment and the length of life are known with certainty. Suppose under these conditions that retirees seek to maximize the smallest time adjusted value of any withdrawal that they make over retirement. And suppose they determine the appropriate time adjustment by choosing among the optimal streams for different adjustments.

It has been shown that the Retrenchment Rule provides the same stream of withdrawals in such a case. These conditions are highly artificial. Nevertheless, the optimality of the rule under these conditions enhances its credibility for use under more realistic conditions.

Note

1. This can be demonstrated by a simple inductive argument. Suppose it is true for up through t years in the future. It can be shown as follows that it is then true for the next year. The investment in the next year is equal to $(1+r)(V_t-C_t)$ where V_t and C_t are the values of the investment and withdrawal in year t respectively. Set this expression equal to a sum in which C_{t+1} each year is divided by 1+r and 1+b compounded for each year in the future until the withdrawal occurs. Dividing by 1+r and moving C_t to the other side gives a relation for C_{t+1} that is satisfied by $C_{t+1}=C_t/(1+b)$. This is because it is the same relation that C_t satisfied in year t. Since C_1 is the same in either case it follows by induction that the withdrawals given by the fixed annuities calculated each year by the Retrenchment Rule are the optimal values of the C_t. These are the C_t equal to C_1 divided by 1+b compounded for each year in the future until the withdrawal occurs.

Appendix 14-1

Maximizing a Linear Utility Function

A utility function frequently used in economics adds together discounted values of the utility of the withdrawals each year. Before the discounting, the utility of the withdrawal each year is a power function of the withdrawal. Suppose that the value of the withdrawal is denoted by C. Its utility before discounting is then given by $C^{1-g}/(1-g)$ where g is a positive number not equal to 1. It will also be assumed that the withdrawals are discounted at the rate d for each year in the future until they occur. For instance, the utility for the withdrawal for the coming year after 10 years has elapsed is given by $C^{1-g}/(1-g)(1+d)^{10}$.

The maximum utility for this utility function is obtained by equating marginal rates of exchange. These are the marginal rates of exchange for the withdrawals in consecutive years that leave both the utility of the withdrawals and their effect on the budget unchanged. The marginal rate of exchange between C_t and C_{t-1} that keeps the utility of the withdrawals the same is given by: $-U'(C_{t-1})/U'(C_t)$, where $U(C_t)=C_t^{1-g}/(1-g)(1+d)^{t-1}$. This equals $-(1+d)(C_{t-1}/C_t)^{-g}$. The marginal rate of exchange between C_t and C_{t-1} that keeps the budget for the withdrawals the same is given by: $-(1+r)$. Equating these two marginal rates of exchange and rearranging terms shows that the optimal C_t and C_{t-1} must satisfy: $C_t/C_{t-1} = ((1+r)/(1+d))^{1/g}$. This compares with the earlier ratio for consecutive optimal withdrawals of 1/(1+b) for the earlier utility function.

Suppose, for instance, that the discounting for future utility each year is the same as the real return on the investment so that d=r. The relation $((1+r)/(1+d))^{1/g}$ is then equal to 1 for any g. In this case, the optimal withdrawal each year is the same as the initial withdrawal. Thus, the optimal withdrawals are the same as for the earlier utility function when b=0.

Suppose that r=.02, d=.03, and g=.5. In this case the value of the relation is about .98. The optimal withdrawals now decline in the future at about the same rate as when b=.02 for the earlier utility function.

Before, the optimal future withdrawals were obtained by multiplying the initial withdrawal by 1/(1+b) compounded for each year in the future before the withdrawal occurs. Now the same is true except $((1+r)/(1+d))^{1/g}$ replaces 1/(1+b). The optimal initial withdrawal is obtained as before by substituting these optimal future withdrawals into the budget relation and solving for the value of the initial withdrawal.

Consequently, the optimal initial withdrawal is the fixed annuity that can be obtained each year over retirement when the initial investment earns a return equal to the rate i determined as follows. For the earlier utility function it is the value of i that satisfies the relation:

$$1/(1+i) = 1/(1+b)(1+r).$$

For the linear utility function i is the value that satisfies the relation:

$$1/(1+i) = ((1+r)/(1+d))^{1/g}/(1+r).$$

In the earlier case i was therefore equal to r+b+rb. Now i has a more complex relation to r, d, and g. Given these values, however, the value of i is easily calculated. For instance, suppose r=.02, d=.03, and g=.5. In this case i is about equal to .04, or about the same as when r=.02 and b=.02 for the earlier utility function.

Suppose that the withdrawals are obtained using the Retrenchment Rule. Suppose the discount rate used for the rule is the i for given values of r and b. It was shown earlier that the stream of withdrawals obtained when using the rule is the same as the optimal stream obtained for those same values of r and b when maximizing the earlier utility function. The appropriate value of b to use for a given r can therefore be obtained by selecting the best stream provided by the rule when using a series of possible discount rates and that value of r.

For the linear utility function suppose that the Retrenchment Rule is used with a discount rate equal to the i obtained for given values of r, d, and g. It follows similarly that the stream of withdrawals obtained using the rule is also an optimal stream. This is the optimal stream obtained when maximizing the linear utility function with those same values of r, d, and g.

Appropriate values of d and g to use for a given r can be obtained by selecting the best stream provided by the rule when using a series of possible discount rates and that value of r. Before, the choice of the stream with the best discount rate determined the appropriate value for b. For this linear utility function the choice of the stream with the best discount rate determines an appropriate value of d or g given the value of the other. The key point, however, is that the Retrenchment Rule gives an optimal stream for the linear utility function with appropriate values of d and g. This is just as the rule gives an optimal stream for the earlier utility function with an appropriate value of b.

For a given value of b the relative rate of decline in the optimal withdrawals for the earlier utility function is unaffected by a change in r. In theory, however, a decline in r could cause a faster decline in the optimal withdrawals. The reason is the following.

When the withdrawals early in retirement are reduced the savings are invested to increase the withdrawals later in retirement. Thus, when the return on investment declines, there is a smaller increase in the future withdrawals. Increasing the early withdrawals has become cheaper in terms of its effect on the later withdrawals. A decrease in r might therefore cause retirees to accept a faster rate of decline in their withdrawals in exchange for higher early withdrawals because the early withdrawals have become cheaper in terms of the later withdrawals.

The earlier utility function, however, ignores this possible substitution effect. Changes in r affect the withdrawals only through an income effect. The initial withdrawal changes as if there had only been a change in the initial value of the investment.

When r decreases, however, retirees could choose a larger value of b. Thus, if they wanted to incorporate a substitution effect in their optimal withdrawals they could do so by choosing a higher value of b when r declines. It appears unlikely, however, that they will want to do so to any significant extent.

By choosing the same value of b when r declines they are accommodating the loss by reducing their withdrawals comparably over all of retirement. They could well feel that any further increase in the early withdrawals and decline in the later withdrawals is not desirable. In fact, it is possible that they might now want to increase the later withdrawals relative to the earlier ones due to their new lower value. In any case, the stream given by the same value of b appears to be a good compromise.

The key difference between the linear utility function and the one used earlier is that the linear function includes a substitution effect. With the linear function when r declines the optimal withdrawals decline at at faster relative rate for given values of d and g. Unless they choose different values of d and g when r declines a faster rate of decline in the withdrawals is automatic in exchange for higher early withdrawals.

Typically in economic studies values of g are used in a range of from 2 to 5. This is based on the implications for risk aversion of these values when outcomes are uncertain. It is of interest, however, to also consider the implications of these same values for the streams of optimal withdrawals under certainty.

If d=r as sometimes assumed the streams are, of course, flat. Suppose that r=.03, d=.04, and g=2. In this case, the relative decline in the stream each year is .995 or about the same as when b=.005. Suppose r declines from .03 to .02. The relative decline in the stream each year then increases to .990 or about the same as when b=.01. When r=.03 the withdrawals decline from 5.3 percent at the beginning of retirement to 4.6 percent after 30 years. When r=.02 the withdrawals decline from 5.0 to 3.7 percent. A faster rate of decline has been traded for higher early withdrawals.

Such a choice cannot be called unreasonable. But it is certainly questionable as to whether it is a choice that most retirees would make. It seems more likely that their response to a decline in r would be to keep the rate of decline in their withdrawals about the same as is true of the earlier utility function for a given value of b.

In fact, it is a peculiarity of the linear utility function that there exists no fixed values of d and g that will allow retirees to keep the rate of decline of their withdrawals exactly the same in response to a change in r. This follows because $((1+r)/(1+d))^{1/g}$ cannot have the same value for two different values of r. To have the same rate of decline in their withdrawals a change will have to be made in the value of d or g.

As the value of g increases the rate of decline in the withdrawals decreases and there is less of an increase in the rate of decline of the withdrawals when r decreases. For instance, for g=5 the rate of decline is .998 for r=.03, and .996 for r=.02. Thus, as g increases retirees are tending towards choosing the same streams of withdrawals as when b=0 with the earlier utility function. Also, as g increases the effect of d on the withdrawals is suppressed.

These results, however, are implications of a linear utility function, not a requirement of rational choice. There seems to be nothing unreasonable about selecting the streams for b=.01 for both r=.03 and r=.02 in Table 14-1. But these choices are ruled out of bounds by the linear utility function. This is unless a change occurs in d or g when going from r=.03 to r=.02.

The earlier utility function suppresses the substitution effect and reflects only the income effects of changes in r. But income effects are likely to dominate the choices of most retirees about their withdrawals. They may also prefer larger withdrawals early in retirement when they are better able to pursue a more active lifestyle. The earlier utility function allows them to make such a choice or not as they prefer.

For the linear utility function the income effects of changes in r are dominant only for large values of g. But large values of g suppress the effects of time discounting on utility and necessarily make streams of withdrawals relatively flat. Retirees, however, are likely to have dominant income effects and may in some cases also prefer some downward slope in their withdrawals. The earlier utility function allows such choices whereas the linear function does not, unless its parameters are allowed to change with r.

Index

Made in the USA
Monee, IL
04 November 2026

67382742R10174